J. Kuik

CHURCH HISTORY

CHURCH HISTORY

P.K. Keizer

Translated by T.M.P. VanderVen

A TEXTBOOK FOR HIGH SCHOOLS AND COLLEGES

INHERITANCE PUBLICATIONS
NEERLANDIA, ALBERTA, CANADA

Canadian Cataloguing in Publication Data

Keizer, P. K. (1906-1985)
    Church history (A textbook for high schools
and colleges)

  Includes Index.

  Translation of: Kerkgeschiedenis 1 en 2

  ISBN 0-921100-02-7

  1. Church history. 2. Reformed Churches - Europe
- History. I. Title.
BR145.2.K4513 1990   270   C90-091295-2

Translated with permission from De Vuurbaak, Barneveld, The
Netherlands. Original title: *KERKGESCHIEDENIS 1 en 2 (Leerboek voor
middelbaar en voorbereidend hoger onderwijs).* Groningen: De Vuurbaak,
1975

Translated by T.M.P. VanderVen

The Scripture quotations in this publication are from *The Holy Bible, New King James
Version*, copyright 1982, and are used with permission from Thomas Nelson Inc.,
Publishers.

Quotations from the rhymed versions of the psalms, the Belgic Confession, the Heidelberg
Catechism, the Canons of Dort, and the liturgical forms of the Church Order in use by
the Canadian Reformed Churches have been taken with permission of the Standing
Committee for the *Book of Praise* of the Canadian Reformed Churches, c/o Theological
College, 110 West 27th Street, Hamilton, ON, L9C 5A1.

Cover illustration
"Willibrord, Missionary to the Frisians" by J.H. Isings
Used with permission from WOLTERS-NOORDHOFF B.V.
Groningen, The Netherlands

All rights reserved, 1990
by Inheritance Publications
Box 154, Neerlandia, Alberta
Canada, TOG 1RO

ISBN 0-921100-02-7
Printed in Canada by
Premier Printing Ltd. Winnipeg, MB

CONTENTS

FOURTH PERIOD: 590 - 1520:
THE CHURCH UNDER THE YOKE OF PAPAL HIERARCHY

FIFTH PERIOD: 1520 - 1648:
REFORMATION AND COUNTER-REFORMATION

SIXTH PERIOD: 1648 - 1795:
THE CHURCH IN CONFLICT WITH RATIONALISM AND ENLIGHTENMENT

SEVENTH PERIOD: 1795 - PRESENT:
THE STRUGGLE TO BE AND TO REMAIN TRUE CHURCH

The Synod of Dort (1618-1619)

1. Deputies of the Dutch government.
2. Deputy Secretary, Daniel Heinsius.
3. English theologians.
4, 5, 7, 9. German theologians.
6. Swiss theologians.
8. Genevan theologians.
10. Professors: Johannes Polyander, & Franciscus Gomarus, and others.
11. Ministers and elders from Gelderland.
12. Ministers and elders from South Holland: Festus Hommius, Gysbertus Voetius, and others.
13. Ministers and elders from North Holland: Jacobus Trigland, and others.
14. Ministers and elders from Zeeland.
15. Ministers and elders from Utrecht.
16. Ministers and elders from Friesland.
17. Ministers and elders from Overysel.
18. Ministers and elders from Groningen.
19. Ministers from Drenthe.
20. Ministers and elders from the French refugee churches.
21. number not on this picture.
22. The president of the Synod: Johannes Bogerman with the clerks.
23. Professors and ministers of the Remonstrants.

PREFACE

This book is designed as a textbook and not as a reader. I have found that features that might be irritating in a reader are well suited for a textbook since they facilitate learning by using such devices as sub-headings, points, and overviews.

The book assumes that students have been exposed to basic church history education at the elementary and junior high school. Obviously, one lecturer will find some sections too lengthy while another might find certain things missing. It was necessary to leave out much while other points received only minimal attention, for instance, Islam, pagan relig- ions, and the sects. A choice had to be made because the time available on a school's schedule is limited.

I offer some background information in an attempt to prevent church history from becoming a dry summation of dates and facts or perhaps merely an illustration of the history of dogmatics.

According to Revelation 12, the history of mankind revolves around the history of Christ's church. This is the justification for the political and social excursions which are made every now and then to retain as much as possible a sense of the true unity of history.

This book itself is not of primary importance; more important is the *viva vox* of the lecturer who with thanksgiving and amazement relates the *magnalia dei*, the acts of God's faithfulness and lovingkindness in founding and maintaining the covenant of grace and reconciliation, a covenant that remains valid despite man's disdainful disregard.

It is my prayer that this book may help students keep safe the greatest treasures they have in their lives, and especially so in a time when the evil one is working hard to take those treasures away from them.

P.K. Keizer
Groningen
March 1975

Translator's Note

Where appropriate the text has been adapted to increase clarity. In most cases the New King James Version has been used with permission in the translation of parts of Scripture. When other Bible translations have been used, this has been indicated in the text.

Quotations from the rhymed versions of the Psalms, the Belgic Confession, Heidelberg Catechism, and the Canons of Dort as well as from the liturgical forms and the Church Order in use by the Canadian Reformed Churches are taken with permission from *Book of Praise: Anglo-Genevan Psalter* (revised edition), 1984.

The help of a number of competent people who scrutinized earlier drafts of this translation has been invaluable and is gratefully acknowledged.

T.M.P. VanderVen.
Hamilton, ON,
July 1990.

THE APOSTOLIC PERIOD: THE FOUNDATION LAID

1. PAUL'S STRUGGLE AGAINST THE JUDAIZERS

1.1   On the Jewish feast of Pentecost, the Holy Spirit stormed into Jerusalem with a mighty display of power, making this day a Christian feast day. The apostles became the witnesses of the great deeds of God. In this way God fulfilled His age-old plan of salvation for the world through His Son, our Lord Jesus Christ (Acts 2).

1.2   At that moment, the first free Christian church was instituted under the leadership of the apostles. The foundation charter of this "holy catholic Christian Church" as it is described in the Apostles' Creed reads: "And it shall come to pass, that whoever calls on the name of the LORD shall be saved" (Acts 2:21).

1.3   The Pentecost congregation in Jerusalem consisted of converted Jews, among them many Pharisees. These Jews did believe in Jesus as the Messiah, but they were not completely free from the pharisaical leaven: the teachings of the Pharisees and Sadducees (Matt. 16:12). They were more Jewish than Christian, forcing heathen converts to be as Jews (Gal. 2:14). Therefore they became known as Judaizers. They did not repent from their pharisaical self-exultation, claiming to be God's chosen people, and proudly claimed Abraham as their ancestor. They did not understand that after Pentecost the uncircumcised also belonged to the church through faith alone.

1.4   The Judaizers demanded, besides faith in Christ, a strict observance of the Jewish law: circumcision, abstinence from unclean foods, and observance of the Jewish religious calendar (Acts 15:1, 5). They were zealous for the law (Acts 21:20). They did not completely trust the sufficiency of Christ's sacrifice on the cross and searched for additional certainty in their own piety and strict legalistic observance of the law, trying to establish their own righteousness before God (Rom. 10:3). They did not recognize themselves as the saved possession of Christ (as slaves) but lived as true Pharisees, fully convinced that they were able to earn their own salvation by their good works.

1.5   The Apostle Paul attacked them strongly because they did not trust in Christ alone for their salvation but rather in Christ *plus* their own good works. In opposition to the Judaist (Jewish) observance of the law (salvation through works), Paul taught Christian observance of the law (obedience out of love for God in thankfulness). Over against the Judaist zeal for the law and the temple (forcing Gentiles to become Jews first), Paul taught both Jew and Greek to become Christians. The Judaizers wanted to retain the wall of enmity between Jew and Gentile, but on the cross Christ broke down that wall of separation. He made these two worlds into one and united them into one (church) body: neither Jew nor Greek, but *Christian* (Eph. 2:14-16).

Before Pentecost, only Israel was God's chosen people, but after Pentecost, Christ gathered His church from many nations ("the manifold wisdom of God," Eph. 3:10).

1.6   The hard struggle put forth by Paul and his helpers against Judaism was a means in the hands of the Lord Jesus Christ to save the church from becoming a Jewish sect. In this way Christ maintained the true ecumenical, that is, catholic, character of the church in which Jew and Greek were saved through faith alone.

1.7   How did this struggle against the Judaizers develop? By means of a special vision at Joppa, the Holy Spirit had dramatically shown Peter that nothing separated Jew from Gentile. The apostle was forced to baptize the Roman officer Cornelius and his people. To the amazement of the circumcised Jewish Christians, the Holy Spirit descended upon them. But Peter was called to account by his fellow Christians of Jerusalem, who demanded an explanation. He defended himself by pointing to the work of God, "'Who was I to withstand God?' And when they had heard this, they quieted down" (Acts 11: 17,18). However, the Jewish Christians continued to find the mystery that in Abraham not only Jews but all nations would be blessed difficult to understand. Not Jerusalem but Antioch was deemed worthy to become the first missionary church. Here the disciples became known as Christians; the Gentiles had noticed the difference between those who believed in Christ and those who belonged to the Jewish synagogue (Acts 11:26). Earlier they had been known by various names, such as disciples, brethren, saints, sect of the Nazarene. The church of the Lord has always been ill-prepared when God has begun a new work of reformation as He did on Pentecost (see Stephen's speech in Acts 7).

With Antioch as a base, Paul commenced his missionary journeys by preaching the gospel in Asia Minor and Europe. "Japheth's children" were allowed to live in the tents of Shem (Gen. 9:27) and were blessed in Christ, the seed of Abraham (Gen. 22:13).

After returning from their first missionary journey, Paul and Barnabas were troubled by the Judaizers in Antioch (Acts 15:2). During the apostolic convention at Jerusalem (A.D. 49), freedom in Christ for the Gentiles was maintained (Acts 15). No Jewish sect, but a Christian church! At Antioch, Paul publicly admonished Peter for considering converted Gentiles to be second-rank Christians. Out of fear for the Judaist zealots, Peter jeopardized the existence of the Christian church (Gal. 2:11-14).

Paul struggled against the Judaizers especially in his letter to the Galatians. They spied on him with increasing fanaticism, causing great confusion within the church. In fact, they brought a different gospel (Gal. 2:12).

It was the Apostle James, perhaps influenced too much by the Judaizers, who was partially responsible for Paul's arrest (Acts 21:18ff; Gal. 2:12).

Even before his arrival in Rome, Paul had already written to the congregation there that he was not ashamed of maintaining the gospel of faith alone over against the Judaizers (Rom. 1:16). It was because of the urging of false prophets (2 Cor. 11:13) and jealousy and betrayal within the congregation that both Paul and Peter were executed at Rome. One of Nero's concubines, a proselyte, was instrumental in this.

The battle against Judaism was finally decided after the destruction of Jerusalem (ca. A.D. 70). The centre of the Old Testament service was gone. Throughout history, Judaism, as the continuation of Pharisaism, has done great damage in the church through its self-exultation, zealotry, and party spirit. The true ecumenical character of Christ's church (by faith alone) was threatened many times by the Judaist heresy.

The Roman Catholic church has accepted the teachings of Judaism as part of its doctrine of good works, thereby denying the ecumenical character of Christ's church.

NOTES: ANTINOMIANISM

a.   Over against Judaism stands *antinomianism* (derived from the Greek *anti* = against, and *nomos* = law). Antinomians rejected the law totally. Although they did not form a movement like the Judaizers, the early Christians had to be constantly on guard against this heresy.

b.   Antinomians not only reject the Judaist observance of the law but also the Christian law observance.

c.   A Judaizer forgets the superscription of the Ten Words. He changes God's glorious Torah from a rule of thankfulness into a rigid set of commands that gain salvation for him. The antinomian, on the other hand, hears only the introductory words but loathes all preaching of the law, including the words of Christ, "For My yoke is easy, and My burden is light" (Matt. 11:30).

d. A Judaizer is uncharitable, strict, legalistic. An antinomian is liberal, licentious, worldly, living according to his own lusts. Antinomians claim that everything is allowed; they are often godless and careless Christians (see Heidelberg Catechism, Lord's Day 24).

e. A Judaizer does not recognize the need for forgiveness of sins through the blood of Christ. An antinomian does not accept the need for redemption from sin through the Holy Spirit of Christ.

f. Judaism corrodes the true ecumenical character of the church while antinomianism is a constant threat to the holiness of the church. Judaism changes the church into a sect by preaching a "yes-but-first" gospel. Antinomianism removes the distinction between Christ's precious church and the world. "For you were bought at a price: therefore glorify God in your body, and in your spirit, which are God's" (1 Cor. 6:20).

g. Among the Anabaptists of the sixteenth century were many anti-nomians, the so-called *freethinkers*. The word of the Apostle John applies to them: "If we say that we have no sin, we deceive ourselves, and the truth is not in us" (1 John 1:8).

h. The church is always threatened by these dangers:
1. A legalistic life style: trusting personal piety and living a grim and fearful life instead of a cheerful and careful life in love.
2. A worldly life style: rejoicing in the cross of Christ but mean-while following the evil lusts of the heart (see Gal. 5:13-26).
Jesus rejects both life styles at the same time: the leaven of the legalistic Pharisees and the leaven of the worldly Herod (Mark 8:15).

2. THE JEWISH WAR (A.D. 66 - 70)

2.1 The destruction of Jerusalem was foretold by the Lord Himself (Luke 21:6). These were days of vengeance because of the Jewish rejection of the Lord Jesus.

The Jewish officer Flavius Josephus was an eyewitness. The Roman generals were Vespasian and Titus, the latter during the final stages of the war (the Titus Arch in Rome was named after him). The Jews resisted the Roman onslaught with unparalleled fanaticism. They chose death rather than surrender in the mistaken belief that God would come to their rescue. They firmly expected that at the most critical moment the long-awaited Messiah would appear. But because they did not recognize the time of their visitations, the things which make for peace were hidden from their eyes (see Luke 19:41-44). Some 1,100,000 died; 97,000 were taken prisoner; and thousands were used as slaves in Roman building projects such as the Colosseum. This was the end of Israel as a nation.

2.2   The Christians fled to Pella, going against the stream of refugees who were seeking protection within Jerusalem's walls (Luke 21:11). "But not a hair of your head shall be lost" (Luke 21:18). Just like Lot was saved during the destruction of Sodom, so Christ protected His church from the covenant wrath which poured out over the old city of God.

2.3   After Pentecost, Jerusalem lost its special importance as the place where God dwelled: "our mother" is not Jerusalem's Pentecost congregation but the Jerusalem above (Gal. 4:26). The Pentecost congregation was the first free, local, Christian congregation, but this congregation was of no greater importance than the congregations of Antioch, Ephesus, or Rome. Soon it needed Christian charity from the Gentile Christian congregations.

NOTES

a.   Are the promises that God made to Abraham and Israel directed, after the coming of Christ, toward the Christian church? Or are they also for the Jewish nation as it still exists?

b.   Jesus foretold, "And Jerusalem will be trampled by Gentiles until the times of the Gentiles are fulfilled" (Luke 21:24). Paul wrote about his brothers, his kinsmen according to the flesh, "But it is not that the word of God has taken no effect. For they are not all Israel who are of Israel" (Rom. 9:3, 6). Paul did not want the Christians at Rome to be unaware of the mystery that a partial hardening had happened to Israel until the fullness of the Gentiles comes in, and in this manner (in the course of world history) all Israel (as a people) would be saved (Rom. 11:25, 26). First the Jew and then, in the fullness of time, the Greek. But in the fullness of time, Israel will be remembered. What else could be the content of this mystery? Because of their attitude to the gospel they are still enemies, yet they remain God's beloved for the sake of the fathers. For God knows no repentance over His gifts of grace, neither over His calling (Rom. 11:28, 29). But remember: when Jesus redeemed us through His sacrifice on the cross in the Middle East, our forebears lived as pagans in Northern Europe.

c.   Attempts to assimilate with the nations among which the Jews lived often ended in tragedy. God prevented assimilation; there were the ghettos, pogroms, Auschwitz.
    What you have in your mind shall never be, when you say, "We will be like the Gentiles, like the families in other countries, serving wood and stone". As I live, says the LORD God, surely with a mighty hand, with an outstretched arm, and with fury poured out, I will rule over you. I will bring you out from the peoples and gather you out of the countries where you are scattered, with a mighty hand, with an outstretched arm, and with fury

poured out (Ezek. 20:32-34). . . . but later you will surely listen to me . . . (Ezek. 20:39 NASB).

d.   The Jewish nation, the modern nation of Israel, does not merely present a political problem nor is it a racial question; it is a biblical and church-historical mystery.

e.   The political nation in the Middle East must not be identified with God's covenant people. More Jews live in the diaspora outside present day Israel than within.

3. THE STRUGGLE OF THE APOSTLE JOHN AGAINST ANTI-CHRISTIANITY

3.1   Toward the end of the apostolic age, only the Apostle John remained. He lived at Ephesus where he undoubtedly had seen the great temple of Artemis. In his days, a most dangerous heresy surfaced: the false gospel of an anti-Christianity.

At that time, John was allowed to lay the last of the foundation stones (Matt. 16:18; Rev. 21:14) on which the Christian church was to be built, namely the teaching of the apostles. These last foundation stones were the Gospel of John, the three general epistles of John, and the Revelation of Jesus Christ. In these writings, John strongly attacked this anti-Christianity.

3.2   An antichrist is someone who places himself over against, or even instead of, Christ. Paul says that it is someone who takes his seat in the temple of God (the church), displaying himself as God (2 Thess. 2:4). An antichristian claims to be god because he considers himself above the law. Therefore he is the man of lawlessness (2 Thess. 2:3).

These antichristians were apostate (1 John 2:19). They denied the Father of our Lord Jesus Christ and the Son who came in the flesh (1 John 1:22; 4:2). They denied that the Son of God was incarnate of the virgin Mary, that He had died on the cross, and that He will return as true man to judge and reform this world. They denied that the Word became flesh (John 1:14) and that God was revealed in the flesh (1 Tim. 3:16). Therefore they denied the redemption of creation which God so loved "that He gave His only begotten Son . . ." (John 3:16).

As a consequence, antichristians despised all that God had created. They viewed the creation (our daily, ordinary life) as the domain of the devil. They believed that God does not concern Himself with that. They claimed that a true Christian is aloof, removed from this ordinary life. They felt themselves free from daily life because they did not accept that they were called by God to any earthly task whatever. Many of these people lived in lawlessness, sin, and licentiousness (Rev. 2:14, 20). They hated the faithful people who kept the covenant with God in loving fear of the LORD.

3.3   Anti-Christianity does not expect the return of the Lord Jesus in the clouds to judge. It does not expect the resurrection of the dead and the redemption of the body in eternal life on the new earth.

This heresy attacked the church furiously during the second century. It became known as *Gnosticism*, rearing its ugly head time and again, also in our time. Christianity of the twentieth-century Western World leans more and more toward this anti-Christianity because of its conscious rejection of the biblical facts of the history of redemption (for example, the return of Christ) and the acts of God's covenant wrath (for example, the flood).

Now that Christ has completed His work here on earth and has ascended into heaven, the devilish spirit of the antichrist (1 John 4:3) wants to take His place and wants to negate Christ's redemptive work by making Him an unknown (Ex. 32:1: ". . . as for this Moses, the man who brought us up out of the land of Egypt, we do not know what has become of him.").

3.4   The apostolic age is a brief summary of the whole of church history. It starts with the day of Pentecost and ends with the day of judgement which John was allowed to experience on the Isle of Patmos. During this age, the foundations of the world church (Rev. 21:14) were laid. The gospel of Christ had been preached to the ends of the then-known world, the borders of the Roman Empire.

John, the last apostle, had indeed remained till Christ's return according to His Word (John 21:22, 23). In a series of majestic visions, John saw Christ's return on the Isle of Patmos. He was allowed to see the prophetic-historic completion of what had been started on Pentecost: the heavenly Jerusalem descended upon the earth in the spirit, the Father's house with many dwelling places (John 14:2).

During the following ages, the Christian church returned repeatedly to the apostolic teaching (the Word of God) and continued to look forward to the future that had been revealed to the last apostle.

THE CHURCH UNDER THE CROSS

1. PERSECUTION AND BEARING THE CROSS

1.1   From the very beginning, the church of Christ has been under attack from false doctrine and slander, and this will always continue to happen. As it became clear that the Christian church was certainly not a Jewish sect, the Roman authorities began to persecute the believers, especially because they confessed that the LORD God is the only true God and that Jesus Christ is the only Saviour of the world. All other gods are idols (non-gods). At first, these persecutions occurred only sporadically and often locally, for instance, in the city of Rome, or were restricted to a province, such as Asia Minor or Northern Africa.

Simeon was the son of Cleopas, a relative of Jesus, and lived to be about 120 years old. He was scourged and crucified by the Jews in Jerusalem.

Ignatius was a student of the Apostle John at Antioch. After an earthquake struck the city, people cried, "This is the wrath of the gods over the apostate Christians!" During a state visit, Emperor Trajan personally condemned Ignatius to die in Rome's arena. While travelling to Rome, Ignatius wrote seven letters of comfort to various congregations.

Polycarp of Smyrna was also a student of the Apostle John. At the time of his death, he was almost a hundred years old. During his trial, he willingly shouted, "Away with the atheists!" but then he addressed the crowd by saying, "For eighty-six years I have served Him and never has He harmed me. How could I curse my King who redeemed me?" He was burnt to death, with eager Jews supplying the firewood.

Justin Martyr was a scholar. While walking along the beach, he met an old man who drew his attention to the prophets of the Old Testament. In this way he became a Christian at the age of thirty. In Rome, he often defended the Christian doctrine in a scholarly manner but unfortunately not always correctly. He was arrested during one of those disputations and beheaded.

Blandina came from Vienne near Lyons (France). As a result of the silk trade with Asia Minor, Christian congregations were founded in southern France. Blandina was a slave girl. Blessed with a very strong faith, she died in the arena, encouraging to the end the fifteen-year-old Ponticus who died at her side.

Vivia Perpetua was a young mother of noble birth. Together with the slave girl Felicitas, she was killed in the arena of Carthage during the reign of Emperor Septimus Severus. Although this emperor, a Moor from Africa, had been healed by a Christian slave, he became a feared persecutor. Since he was interested in architecture, he was angered by the deterioration and neglect of so many of the beautiful pagan temples.

Finally, the persecutions spread throughout the Roman Empire by order of various emperors. Emperor Decius (249-251) was the first to order such nationwide persecutions. The last general persecutions took place during the reign of Diocletian (284-305), whose wife and daughter were Christians as were many of his courtiers. By that time there were so many Christians in the empire that the emperor's orders could not be executed.

1.2 There were several motives for these persecutions. The Christians were accused of atheism because they had no altars, no temples, nor any idols. This made it easy to believe the Jewish slander that in the (obviously) secret meetings of the Christians all sorts of outrageous things were happening, such as child sacrifices (the cry of just-born babies had been heard in their meetings), consumption of human flesh ("those who eat of My flesh and drink of My blood"), incest (communion of saints, brothers and sisters).

The Christians did not join with the godless and immoral public activities. Therefore they were regarded as enemies of the human race.

The Christians rejected the worship of the emperor. They honoured him but refused to regard him as divine. However, the emperor was the embodiment of the eternal glory of the Roman empire: *divus* = the emperor is god; *advent* = the coming of the emperor; *soter* = the emperor is saviour. Compare this with Daniel 3. Nebuchadnezzar threw three men into the fiery oven as criminals against the Babylonian state religion. But after their God had proven to be more powerful than any other god, all people were ordered to worship him!

1.3 How was it possible that the martyrs were able to withstand such terrible tortures, and how did a mighty Redeemer in heaven benefit them? From heaven Christ poured forth His heavenly gifts over His members through the Holy Spirit, and when they needed it, He gave them such wonderful strength that they could indeed withstand everything cheerfully (see Heidelberg Catechism Lord's, Day 19). It is said that on the eve of an important battle, Emperor Maximinian demanded the so-called emperor's sacrifice from his troops. The legion from Thebias (Egypt), consisting mainly of Christian soldiers, refused to bring this sacrifice. Despite warnings, they remained steadfast and were, therefore, massacred as traitors. Legend has it that this happened at St. Moritz, Switzerland

(Sanctus Mauritius). In this way the Saviour was also glorified and became known to the whole world.

1.4 God's Word teaches that often the true believers are severely troubled by their own unfaithful brothers. These persecutions are often motivated by hatred between brothers. The very first murder was not committed for gain but for religious reasons. Cain killed Abel because God loved Abel rather than Cain. We find the same in the stories of Saul and David as well as in the stories of the false prophets against Jeremiah, the Sanhedrin against Jesus and his disciples, the Jews against Paul, the Roman church against Luther and Calvin, the false church against the true church (1 John 3:11-17). Jesus warned His disciples against these persecutions by the church: "They will put you out of the synagogues; yes, the time is coming that whoever kills you will think that he offers God service" (John 16:2).

The persecution of the church by the world (Nero and other Roman emperors) stems from different motives.

As time went by, Christians came to revere those who had died during the persecutions of the Roman emperors. They became known as martyrs, and often the day of their death was commemorated as a holy day. The stories of martyrs who had been thrown to the lions (such as Ignatius) were much more impressive than the stories of those who had been thrown out of the synagogue such as Paul. But God's Word mentions neither Nero nor the deaths of Paul and Peter in Rome. It speaks of Stephen's death in Jerusalem and of Paul's sufferings at the hands of the Jews for Christ's sake. The most severe form of persecution of the faithful witnesses of Jesus Christ came from their own brothers, whose hatred was fuelled by the mistaken belief that their actions were pleasing to God. "But, as he who was born according to the flesh (Ishmael) then persecuted him who was born according to the Spirit (Isaac), even so it is now" (Gal. 4:29).

Throughout the ages, the unfaithful church has also been persecuted. For instance, the Jewish people were persecuted during the destruction of Jerusalem by the Romans. After the Russian Revolution (1917), the communists heavily persecuted the Russian state church. However, these are not examples of true persecution. Rather, it was God's judgement over an unfaithful Russian church which had killed or banished to Siberia many faithful members of the *Stundists*, of German descent. These Christians had refused to join the lifeless Orthodox state church and had organized their own devotional hours (*Bibelstunden*; *Stundists*).

1.5 Not all suffering is *bearing the cross*—sufferings we bear for Christ's sake without cause (Ps. 25:3; Ps. 44:23; Rom. 8:36; 1 Pet. 3:14). All other suffering that we may bear together with other people is a result of punishment.

". . . he who does not take his cross and follow after Me (but throws it down and denies Me) is not worthy of Me. He who finds his life (by denying Me and is then set free) will lose it (he has lost his relationship with Me), and he who loses his life for My sake (like the martyrs) will find it (in eternal life)" (Matt. 10:38, 39).

2. GNOSTICISM

2.1   Gnosticism did not originate from within the Christian church but found its origin in pagan religions from Asia. The term is derived from the Greek word *gnosis* (knowledge). This kind of knowledge is not the faith by which we accept as true all that God has revealed to us in His Word; it refers to an extraordinary, a supernatural knowing, a so-called deeper understanding of the divine mystery. Gnosticism is characterized by the belief that man is a son of the gods from a higher world who is now condemned to live as a criminal in a lower world. It is gnosis (the higher knowledge of the unknown god, the hidden one, the archetypal being who in fact wants nothing to do with this world) that enables man to look beyond the contemptible world of daily life.

2.2   According to the Gnostics, this world was not created by God the Father, the almighty Maker of heaven and earth. This world was created by an evil god, and therefore this world is of a different order—lower, unholy, and sinful.

Man is a dualistic being. With his body he belongs to this world, but with his deeper self, his essence, he belongs to a higher world, the world of the divine. Every person has within himself a spark of divinity. He is really a god, but a god imprisoned in this earthly life. Man is both beast and spirit, both criminal and angel, both a lower and a high being.

Christ is the Son of God. He came from the higher realm, from the hidden God, and appeared in the person of Jesus of Nazareth. The person Jesus was crucified as a sign that the whole world was cursed. But Christ, the Son of God, was not crucified. He left the person Jesus for the higher realm after he had shown us the way to salvation, namely to die to the world (which is *not* the same as mortifying our old, sinful nature as Scripture teaches us).

The Gnostics claimed that the resurrection happens when a person comes to this kind of higher, divine knowledge. They scorned the idea of the resurrection of the flesh. How could spiritual man who was removed from this earthly existence still be in need of a body? (2 Tim. 2:18).

The Gnostics did not institute another church as Marcion would do later. They desired to raise Christianity to the spiritually higher level of Gnosticism. To achieve this, they wrote several (false) gospel stories, for instance, the Gospel of Thomas.

2.3   The early Christians were much more afraid of Gnosticism than of persecution. The first articles of the Apostles' Creed came into being as a defence against the attacks of the Gnostics: I believe in God the Father almighty, Creator of heaven and earth. I believe in Jesus Christ . . . born of the virgin Mary.

Throughout the ages, Gnosticism has been recognized as the most dangerous enemy of Christ's church. In the many variations of Gnosticism, Satan, disguised as an angel of light, was preaching the great lie: God's creation is bad and contemptible; Christ's work of salvation is not necessary because man himself is god having an essentially divine nature which enables him to save himself from this wretched world.

2.4   The Apostle Paul already opposed the forerunners of Gnosticism in his letter to the Colossians (Col. 1:15-23). Paul reserved the longest chapter in his letters to the church at Corinth (1 Cor. 15) to explain the necessity of the resurrection from the dead and the renewal of our lives. He warned Timothy against the opposing arguments of what is falsely called "knowledge" (1 Tim. 6:20, 21; 2 Tim. 2:16-18).

The Apostle John also attacked this devilish heresy. He called its followers antichrists. In his gospel, John wrote, "For God so loved the world that He gave His only begotten Son . . ." (John 3:16), but the antichrists despised this creation.

Ignatius of Antioch, and in particular Irenaeus, bishop of Lyons, sharply attacked this seemingly pious heresy of antichristian Gnosticism. Ignatius maintained that Christ is truly God and truly man. Irenaeus refuted the Gnostic teachings in five books, *Against Heresies*.

Gnosticism returns again and again in various forms:
- During the Middle Ages with, for instance, the mystic Eckhart.
- Thomas à Kempis, in his book *The Imitation of Christ*, shows Gnostic tendencies.
- Gnosticism was again noticeable in the teachings of Sebastian Franck and Coornheert in the sixteenth century.
- During the eighteenth century it returned in the form of many pious but mystic hymns.
- The so-called new theology (new hermeneutics) is, in fact, nothing but Gnosticism revived. It wants to give a reinterpretation of Scripture. Already the apostles knew about such demonic distortions of Scripture. Paul even names the leaders: Hymenaeus, Alexander, and Philetus (1 Tim. 1:20; 2 Tim. 2:17, 18).

3. MARCION

3.1 Marcion (85-160) was the son of a God-fearing bishop of the congregation of Sinope, a Greek trading city on the south coast of the Black Sea in the Roman province of Pontus. Aquila came from this province, and the Apostle Peter wrote two epistles to the Christians in Pontus. Marcion was a rich shipowner. He was irreproachable in conduct and certainly no antinomian. He was modest, serious, gentle, and a realistic businessman. But he was a fanatic hater of Jews. Just at that time, the Jewish rebellion under their messiah Bar-Cochba (with an appeal to the Old Testament) aroused a great deal of anti-Semitic sentiment throughout the Roman Empire. More than a half million Jews perished in this rebellion.

3.2 Marcion read holy Scripture from an anti-Semitic point of view. He found that the Jews of his days were like those of the Old Testament—warring, killing, harsh, cruel. Marcion taught that this was the nature of the Old Testament god, Yahweh, who had created this miserable world. How much better was the New Testament, full of compassion and kindness!

Marcion claimed that there were two gods: the god of the Old Testament, the Jewish god, strict and righteous; and the god of the New Testament, the unknown god, the strange god, merciful and compassionate.

The creator-god of the Old Testament had revealed himself in the harsh Jewish laws. The unknown god of the New Testament revealed himself in the gospel of lovingkindness.

Marcion basically taught irreconcilable contrasts (antitheses) between:

- the creator-god and the unknown god who is the completely different one
- the Old Testament and the New Testament
- law and gospel
- what is material and earthly and what is spiritual and heavenly
- body and soul

3.3 As a true antichrist, Marcion denied that the Word had come into the flesh. He taught that Jesus had no true human body. His appearance was like that of the angels who visited Abraham. He also rejected the return of Christ and the resurrection of the body. Marcion claimed that these ideas came from the Jewish god. He maintained that resurrection is something of a higher order, of a spiritual nature, and certainly not a matter of the lowly physical body.

Marcion's Bible studies were true conspiracies conceived against God's Word (Heidelberg Catechism, Lord's Day 48). His main work was *Antitheses*. He rejected the Old Testament and cleaned up the New Testament by retaining only his version of the Gospel of Luke and the epistles of Paul. However, he deleted the words *of heaven and earth* from Luke 10:21 ("In that hour Jesus rejoiced in the Spirit and said, 'I praise Thee, Father, Lord of heaven and earth . . .') because he denied that the Father of the Lord Jesus is also the creator of the earth. He changed the fourth petition of the Lord's Prayer to read, "Give us Thy bread", referring to his version of the (unreal) Jesus, "thy Son".

He was excommunicated by his own father (Matt. 10:37). He sailed for Smyrna in one of his own ships and met Polycarp, who called him "the firstborn of Satan". He was not accepted anywhere. Finally he arrived in Rome, where he donated a huge sum of money to the poor. However, after he was banished from the church at Rome, this money was returned to him.

He instituted rival churches in many locations. These became known as the Marcionite churches with their own bishops, elders, beautiful buildings, and Bible. Their worship included no psalms (full of violence) but hymns (full of piety). Among the martyrs were also followers of Marcion!

3.4   During the second century, the whole of the catholic Christian church from the Euphrates to the Rhone (France) was in severe crisis because of Marcion's teachings; much damage was done. It is certainly wrong to assume that during the first centuries there was only one undivided Christian church. Writings of those days clearly show that it was necessary to search carefully for the true church since it was possible to arrive unawares in one of Marcion's churches where "the new gospel" was preached.

Marcion was excommunicated as a heretic. His name is mentioned in the Belgic Confession, Article 9. He is the father of Bible criticism because he rejected the Old Testament, which was the Bible of the Lord Jesus and his disciples.

3.5   Marcion claimed to be a follower of Paul because he also rejected Judaism. However, there are major differences between the teachings of Marcion and Paul:

Marcion: -   Man's misery = sorrow, distress which asks
                         for "understanding"
                -        God's love = lovingkindness, compassion
                -        Our earthly existence = fate, beyond our
                         responsibility
                -        Jesus = Mediator only
                -        Anti-semitic

Paul: -   Man's misery = debt, transgression, sin
                                  which must be paid for and reconciled
                                  through Jesus' blood
                         -        God's love = forgiveness of sin and guilt in
                                  grace
                         -        Our earthly existence = wilful disobedience
                                  caused by turning away from God (Heidel-
                                  berg Catechism, Lord's Day 4)
                         -        Jesus has made peace through the blood of
                                  His cross (Col. 1:20)
                         -        Anti-Judaist

The teachings of Marcion were revived by the modern anti-Semitic pseudo-Christians in Hitler's Germany. The Old Testament was regarded as the book of the Jewish god. Modern theology also places the New Testament far above the Old Testament.

3.6   It is remarkable that Peter, in his epistle to the faithful in Pontus, often quotes from the Old Testament. We may assume that Marcion's father would have quoted the words of David in Ps. 34:9 more than once and spoken of God's goodness as Peter did in 1 Pet. 2:3. Undoubtedly, Marcion would have been offended by his father's preaching and by Peter's teaching: ". . . the God of the Jews a god of lovingkindness and grace? Certainly not!" Marcion did not acknowledge man's guilt of rebellion against God, neither did he accept the covenant of grace and reconciliation. Little did he realize the seriousness of the covenant wrath.

The apostles were not aware of any inconsistencies between the Old Testament and their gospel. They were not forced to rely on a few carefully selected messianic passages nor on a few Old Testament types or indications of the Christ. The complete Old Testament speaks of God's lovingkindness in Christ, who is the fulfilment of the Old Testament. Reconciliation came from God, who had given the promise of His Son for their salvation immediately after Adam and Eve rebelled. The Old Testament is full of this promise. If the Old Testament is rejected, the New Testament cannot be understood.

Through his Greek-pagan construction of a series of contrasts, Marcion broke the unity of the Bible (John 10:35), and the destructive effects of these satanic teachings (1 Tim. 4:1) are clearly noticeable in modern Christendom. The Roman Catholic church emphasizes celibacy for the clergy (in Marcion's churches only unmarried persons were baptized), asceticism and chastisement of the body in monasteries (subjection of the body to spiritual exercises since the body is of a lower order than the soul), and gives instructions for fasting, especially in the so-called holy weeks.

3.7 Paul's emotional and timely warning against opposing arguments of the so-called gnosis is certainly pertinent today (1 Tim. 6:20). "For every creature of God is good, and nothing is to be refused if it is received with thanksgiving" (1 Tim. 4:4). God "alone has immortality, dwelling in unapproachable light, whom no man has seen or can see, to whom be honour and everlasting power. Amen" (1 Tim. 6:16).

4. MONTANUS

4.1 Montanus (ca. 170) lived in the central region of Asia Minor known as Phrygia, in a place called Pepuza. Before his conversion to Christianity, he had been a pagan priest. In reaction to the decline of Christianity and deeply concerned with the political and social situation of his time (terrible wars, appalling pestilence), Montanus began to emphasize sobriety, ascetism, and morality. His preaching was based on his belief that Christ's return was imminent and that it would take place in Pepuza. His followers became known as the *saints of Pepuza*, or the *latter-day saints*. He was assisted by two prophetesses, Maximilla and Priscilla.

Montanus taught that the Paraclete, the promised Holy Spirit, had appeared in his own person. Through him, the Holy Spirit gave new revelation. He baptized in the name of the Father, the Son, Montanus, and Priscilla. He spoke in tongues and was often moved to ecstasy; at times he even fell unconscious. In this way he started a large revivalist movement in Pepuza.

4.2 During the second century, the church revealed its unity and catholic character more and more through:
a.   The institution of the offices - first apostles, then presbyters or episcopi. During their first missionary journey, Paul and Barnabas had already appointed elders in each congregation (Acts 14:23).
b.   The formulation of a confession.
c.   The acceptance of a canon.

4.3 Montanus fiercely opposed these things since he regarded himself as *the* prophet.
a.   He opposed the institution of the offices, emphasizing his own prophetic talents, which he claimed were far superior to the instituted offices.
b.   He opposed the development of a confession against the teachings of Gnosticism and Marcion by maintaining that his own prophecies were of greater importance than the apostolic witness.
c.   He rejected the generally recognized canon of the New Testament (the list of apostolic writings, the authority of which gained recog-

nition in the churches), claiming direct revelation from the Holy
Spirit.

4.4   The struggle of the church against Montanus was about the *canon*
of Scripture, God's Word, which was maintained by Montanus's excommunication. The time of revelation had come to an end. The foundations
of the New Jerusalem are the teachings of Christ and His apostles in
their gospels and epistles. The Christian church maintained the administration of God's Word and the sacraments through the offices, rejecting the
unspiritual zealotry of Montanus.

4.5   In his later life, Tertullian, the Christian lawyer at Carthage, was
attracted to the piety of Montanus's zealotry. Tertullian turned away from
the church. He was a spirited person with a sharp pen. He was one of
the first to use the Latin language in defence of the Christians during
times of persecution. Fearlessly he defended the civil rights and liberties
of Christ's church, demanding that Christians should not be condemned
without a trial. Recall that Paul also could claim that right, and with
good effect (Acts 25:16, 21). But Tertullian's struggle against the secularization of the church went largely unheeded. The office bearers, instead
of serving the congregations, claimed more and more power, calling
themselves metropolitans, archbishops, and even patriarchs. As a reaction
to this increasing misuse of the church's offices, Tertullian rejected the
apostolic institutions altogether. He claimed special revelation from the
Holy Spirit, and that was the end of the matter for him. The zealot of
the "church of the saints" had become a spiritualist and a man of the
experiential conventicles.

4.6   Especially in a time of neglect of the covenant such spiritualism
had its opportunities:
-          2d century: Montanism
-          5th century: Donatism (during the time of Augustine)
-          16th century: Anabaptism
-          18th century: Labadism
-          20th century: Pentecostals, sectarianism

4.7   Compare:

Gnosticism:	The divine spark within man needs to be freed from this evil creation.
Marcion:	The human soul needs to be freed from a lower-order creation.
Montanus:	Man should live in the Spirit, not bound by offices, confession, or canon.

God's Word: Man must be saved from sin and the devil.
                                 The creation is God's glorious handiwork.

5. RELIGIOUS FREEDOM

5.1   In 313, Constantine, emperor of the Western Roman Empire, and
Lucinius, lord of the Eastern Roman Empire, decreed the Edict of Milan.
The church received unlimited freedom of religion. Confiscated property
was returned or generously compensated. This edict has been of world-
historical significance. A new era began, in particular after 323, when
Constantine became sole ruler over the Roman Empire. The Christian
religion became the religion of the state; the Christian church became
state church.

5.2   Emperor Constantine came to his decision to allow the Christian
church unlimited freedom for mainly political reasons. Despite severe
persecutions, the church, with its institution of bishops and archbishops,
proved to be a much more solid foundation for the battered and divided
Roman Empire than decadent heathendom. Therefore, Constantine made
the church serve the political unity of the state.
       The Roman emperors regarded the execution of religious duties an
important part of the responsibilities of citizenship (like military service,
for instance). The favour of the gods had to be gained for the well-being
of the great Roman Empire. Therefore, every citizen was required to
bring the necessary sacrifices, irrespective of the person's beliefs. The
purpose of this sacrifice was *do ut des*, meaning "I bring a sacrifice and
therefore I expect you (the gods) to provide help". The Christians could
no longer join in with the practice of *do ut des* in the pagan temples, and
as a result, they were accused of neglecting the required citizen's duties.
It was said that therefore the gods were angry, and that was considered
dangerous to the state. For this reason, the Christians were persecuted as
enemies of the state. However, the steadfastness of the Christians made a
deep and lasting impression, and the number of Christians steadily
increased. In the meantime, heathendom deteriorated and many temples
fell into ruin. It seemed that the God of the Christians was much more
powerful than the ancient gods of the state. Therefore, that God must be
served for the greater well-being of the Roman Empire. Constantine was
the first emperor to switch to the worship of the God of the Christians.
As a result and in due time, being a Christian came to be regarded as a
duty of citizenship (*do ut des*).

5.3   The introduction of the Christian religion as state religion was a
gradual process. Constantine did not attempt to eradicate paganism by
force. He announced publicly that Christianity was the emperor's religion
because it was the true religion. Anyone wishing to gain the favour of

the emperor felt obliged to become a Christian. The emperor did not prohibit the cruel and violent gladiator contests, but he openly denounced them and did not visit the arenas. The result was obvious. Heathendom was officially banned in Europe by Emperor Theodosius the Great in 380. Laws for Sunday observance were proclaimed; pagan temples were destroyed; the last Olympic games were held in 394.

6. The Edict of Milan

6.1   Advantages:
a.   The legal position of the office-bearers of the church was secured (tax exemptions, a state income). It is questionable whether this was a real advantage.
b.   The traditional rights and privileges granted to the temples and holy places were now transferred to the churches.
c.   Gradually Sunday became the national day of rest throughout the empire.

Disadvantages:
a.   The church lost its independence and liberty to state control.
b.   In reality the emperor became the head, father, of the church (caesaropapism). He had authority to call councils and to appoint and dismiss bishops.
c.   The church became secularized. Many joined not out of conviction but for reasons of expediency.
d.   Perhaps the greatest disadvantage was the fact that the clear distinction between heathendom and Christianity disappeared. All pagan religions were religions of profit (*do ut des*) and power (ward off angry gods). Christianity is the only religion that speaks of redemption through God's love (John 3:16).

6.2   One Roman emperor, Julian the Apostate (361-363), attempted to turn the clock back by revoking the Edict of Milan. In his younger years, he had pretended to be a Christian. Although he was a reader in the Christian church of Nicomedia during the day, at night he officiated as a priest in a pagan temple. As emperor, he strongly promoted heathendom and financed the rebuilding of many ruined temples with money taken from the Christians. However, for the solemn dedication of the restored temple at Antioch, only an old man and a goose turned up. The temple of Jerusalem was rebuilt to ridicule the prophecies of the Lord Jesus, but it was destroyed first by an earthquake and later, after repeated repairs, by fire and storm. Finally, Julian gave in. He wanted a purified heathendom and a divided Christendom; therefore, he also protected the followers of the heretic Arius. After two years of persecutions, he died during a military campaign in Persia. ("Yet you have won, man of Galilee!")

6.3 Satan had in vain attempted to destroy the church with the help of the awesome power of the Roman empire which had defeated and subjected many pagan nations. During the following centuries, Satan continued his attack on the church, for instance, during the eighth century when the Mohammedan nations swept across Northern Africa (Gibraltar = Gibr-al-Tarik = Strait of Tarik). In the Battle of Poitiers (or Tours), in 732, Charles Martel defeated the Mohammedans, driving them back across the Pyrenees into Spain. In the sixteenth century, the Mohammedan Turks marched right into the heart of Europe but were defeated before the gates of Vienna.

7. REVIEW OF THE FIRST TWO PERIODS

7.1 Beginning at Jerusalem and spreading across the whole of the known world, the Saviour founded a kingdom for Himself, "'Not by might nor by power, but by My Spirit,' says the LORD of hosts" (Zech. 4:6). He gathered, protected, and maintained His church. He purified it through judgements and glorified Himself in the lives of those who were His own.

7.2 The pious life style of the true Christians was in sharp contrast with the life style of the pagans living around them.
a. They respected the holy bond of marriage and did not permit divorce. In this way, the women were restored to their honourable position.
b. They obeyed the government and were respectful to those in authority (Rom. 13:1; 1 Pet. 2:17ff) and never preached rebellion or revolution.
c. They acknowledged private ownership and did not steal. They emphasized stewardship and recognized labour as a divine calling.
d. They did not disturb the order in society, nor did they demand immediate abolition of slavery. God's Word demanded that owners treat their slaves justly and that slaves show Christian obedience out of respect for God's law (Col. 3:22).
e. Sometimes slaves were office bearers within their congregation. This was unheard of in a world where a slave was regarded as a human object and was treated as four-footed merchandise. Philemon, the lord-director, and Onesimus, the slave who ran away, sat side by side at the Lord's table as brothers in Christ. What would have been the reaction of Philemon's fellow slave owners in Colossae to this strange behaviour? What anxieties might have been caused in a world that was used to punishing runaway slaves by branding or execution in a lion's den? Paul did not demand the immediate abolition of such dehumanizing slavery. Such revolutionary demands would have totally disrupted the existing structures of

society. Christ's kingdom does provide immediate relief from distress by making slave and master brothers. The Word of the Lord works like yeast, which hidden in three measures of meal, leavens the whole loaf (society) (Matt. 13:33); by the end of the Middle Ages, the slave trade had all but disappeared in christianized Europe (except in Venice) and had been replaced by a system of guilds in which the rights and duties of master and pupil were organized even better than the modern systems advocated by the trade unions. Paul's epistle to Philemon proved to be a true foundation of the heavenly Jerusalem descending on Europe.

f.   Often prisoners of war were ransomed.

g.   The poor, strangers, and prisoners were supported.

h.   The fruit of the Spirit (Gal. 5:22) was seen in the lives of thousands of faithful Christians in all countries of the known world.

i.   No wonder the Christians were persecuted as enemies of the human race because they preached the new man in Christ. The walls of enmity between Jew and non-Jew, slave and free, poor and rich, and man and woman were removed (Gal. 6:15; Eph. 2:2; Col. 3:11). And that was shocking! The very foundations of the pagan society (in the power of Satan and the evil spirits in the air) were being undermined. Wherever the gospel was preached and the kingship of Christ was established, there the dethroning of the world forces of this darkness took place, even visibly so! (Eph. 6:12; Col. 2:15). Although the thousands who shouted for the blood of the innocent and defenceless Christians in Rome's Colosseum did not realize this at all, the devils certainly did, and they trembled.

j.   The many Christian soldiers in the Roman legions were the first to spread the gospel of Christ into Northern Europe.

7.3   Very soon the kingship of Christ over His local churches was attacked by heresies. The successors of the apostles were the elders (presbyters, episcopi) and the deacons. There were two kinds of elders (1 Tim. 5:17): elders who worked at preaching and teaching (later the ministers) and the ruling elders. It would be better not to call Ignatius and Polycarp (and others) *apostolic fathers* as is often done. It would be better to call them the successors, or the pupils, of the apostles. Tertullian and others should not be called *church fathers*. Matthew 23:9 clearly forbids that.

Already in the postapostolic age, the offices of pastor and teacher came to be regarded as of greater importance than the other offices. Soon only the pastor (teacher) was known as episcopus, or bishop. The bishops demanded obedience to their official authority on the basis of their claim that they were the direct successors of the apostles. Thus they derived their authority not from God's Word but from the line of succession (that is, directly from the apostles). In this way, the hierarchy crept into the church.

7.4   Although many would rather lose their life in cheerful and faithful obedience to their Saviour than deny Him, at times the loving fear of the LORD God was not present, and the boundary between the church and the world was often smoothed over. Judgement had to come over an increasingly apostate church.

Even though the church had received political freedom of religion and even though the civic rights of Christ's church were generally recognized, persecution of the true church by the false church continued, also after the Edict of Milan. At the instigation of his ecclesiastical enemies, Athanasius was exiled by Constantine the Great because of his faithful confession that Christ is the Son of God.

THE CHURCH SUBJECT TO THE STATE: CAESAROPAPISM

1. THE FIRST ECUMENICAL COUNCIL: NICEA 325

1.1   Arius was a presbyter of the Christian church of Alexandria in Egypt. He was a charming but serious person who was well able to captivate his audience with his sermons about Jesus. But it was noted that he never called Him the eternal, only Son of God. Arius taught that God had not always been Father; there had been a time that Christ was not the Son of God. Christ was the first, the most important, creature, a kind of in-between being between God and the evil world. Christ was God in name only.

1.2   Opposition arose against this heretic, even leading to bloody street fights in Alexandria between followers and opponents of Arius. The unrest spread throughout Egypt. Many bishops sided with Arius, and the conflict became so serious that the entire Eastern Empire was in commotion, threatening the unity of the empire. It was Constantine's view that the unity of the empire demanded one state religion. (Compare this with the story of Nebuchadnezzar: everyone was allowed to serve his own gods, but above those gods rose the golden statue of Daniel 3.) For this reason, Constantine interfered and called together a large meeting of bishops to settle this matter. The costs of this gathering were borne by the empire's treasury. From the East, 318 delegates attended while only six came from the West. Each delegate was accompanied by his own elaborate retinue of assistants and servants, turning the public transportation system into chaos. Such a large ecclesiastical meeting was a new phenomenon; it was an imperial invention (caesaropapism). It seemed as if the church had no Head in heaven who ruled His congregation by His Word and Spirit.

1.3   The Council of Nicea (325) met in the imperial summer palace at Nicea. The meetings began with bitter disagreements and all kinds of personal feuds. The emperor attended the council dressed in full regalia and seated on a golden throne of honour. He was "appointed" honourary chairman and quickly settled the personal disputes of the delegates by

ordering the petitions to be burnt by the basketful. With imperial permission, Arius was allowed to take part in the discussions, but his great
opponent, Athanasius (also from Alexandria), was not permitted to appear
before the council, even though he was present. At first, the emperor
chose the side of the Arians. Later, however, he changed his mind,
approving the condemnation and banishment of Arius.

1.4   The major thrust of the important doctrinal decisions of Nicea is
the confession that since our Saviour is truly God, we are saved by God
in Christ. God Himself came to save us in His Son. If Jesus were only a
creature, our salvation would not be sure because then it would not be
God Himself who saved us in Christ (John 1:1; 1:14; 20:28).

1.5   Despite its rejection at Nicea, Arianism gained great influence.
Under pressure from members of the imperial court, the emperor became
somewhat milder in his attitude toward Arius. He was even to be re-
admitted during a solemn ceremony in the church of Constantinople.
However, on the eve of that ceremony, Arius died suddenly at the age of
eighty.

1.6   After the council, the struggle became more clearly focused:
Arius: Christ is *homoi-ousios*—similar in essence to God.
Athanasius: Christ is *homo-ousios*—in essence equal to God.

1.7   The Nicene Creed confesses that Christ is "of one substance with
the Father". This confession was not formulated by the Council of Nicea
but was named after it.

1.8   The Arian bishop Ulfida (187 pages of his Bible translation are
still kept in Upsala, Sweden) is known as "the apostle of the Goths".
These Goths, fleeing before the terrible Huns in what is now known as
the great migration of nations, forced their way into Italy and Spain.
Western Europe came under the rule of the Arian Goths. It was not until
589 that Arianism was finally condemned by King Recared and his wife
at the Council of Toledo (Spain). Europe was finally saved from this
heresy; this was truly a church-historical miracle.
    Arianism reappears in many modern theologies, for instance, the
theology of the libertines of the nineteenth century and the theology of
all the modernist churches in the twentieth century.

2. ATHANASIUS

2.1   Athanasius was born in Alexandria (Egypt) in the year 295. He
died in the same place in the year 373. He became secretary to the
bishop of Alexandria and later succeeded him as bishop. He was a wise

and eloquent man but unfortunately also rather ambitious and imperious. With all his power, he struggled against the Arian falsification of the gospel. Exiled five times by various monarchs, he spent altogether some twenty years of his life in exile. Once he was exiled to the western borders of the empire (Trier). This, however, made it possible for him to exert good influence on the church in the West as well. The hatred against him was so strong that at one time he was even forced to defend himself against an accusation of murder. His accusers produced the hand of the "victim" to prove his guilt. Athanasius, however, was able to prove his innocence quite convincingly by bringing along the victim himself, a certain Arsenius!

2.2   One of his festival epistles (letters addressed to all the congregations within his diocese) contains the complete canon of the Bible. This shows that the Holy Spirit had quietly ensured that only those books that now make up the New Testament (and no other gospels and epistles that were circulating at the time) were accepted as having divine authority in the churches. This enabled the Christian churches to distinguish between canonical and apocryphal books. Article 5 of the Belgic Confession reads, "We receive all these books, and these only, as holy and canonical. . . ." God's Word was not compiled by persons or ecclesiastical councils. Just imagine!

2.3   The whole of the Eastern church was under the powerful influence of the emperor. Athanasius did not free himself completely from this tendency either. Although he was a fierce opponent of imperial influence in the church, at times he unintentionally even promoted it. Once, after again being condemned by an ecclesiastical council, Athanasius managed to escape by ship to Constantinople. Meeting the emperor's carriage in the street, he boldly stopped it and forced the emperor to give him a hearing so that he could plead his cause. Thus Athanasius appealed to the emperor after having been condemned by an ecclesiastical council, although he had been exiled before by the same emperor. In those days, such actions were not considered unusual nor inconsistent. Unfortunately, to this day it has become the custom of the Eastern churches to accept state supervision and state interference in church matters. This is the Byzantine tradition. In later centuries, the Western church strongly opposed such state influence, and not without success.

Even though Athanasius was forced to recognize the influence of the emperor, he clearly saw that it was against God's Word to regard church membership as one of the duties of citizenship that could be enforced by the government. People cannot be forced into believing in Christ Jesus. God has reserved for Himself the honour of converting the human heart. This happens not by might, but by His Spirit (Zech. 4:6). Athanasius strongly defended and confessed this: "God's truth defends itself, force is a sign of heresy." Athanasius in the East saw this much more clearly than Ambrose and Augustine in the West.

During the Middle Ages, the distinction between ecclesiastical and political matters disappeared in Europe. All of life became dominated by the church. This caused a great deal of bloodshed and tears and greatly hindered the true freedom that only the gospel of Christ brings.

2.4   Athanasius did not see the end of the struggle for the confession of the Godhead of our Saviour. That came during the second ecumenical council of Constantinople in 381. Although the Athanasian Creed was not written by Athanasius, it does contain his teachings, and therefore it is named after him.

2.5   The teachings of Arius:

a.   The Son existed indeed before the creation of the world. But He is not from eternity; there was a time that He did not exist.

b.   The Son is the most important creature of the Father. As creature of the Father, He is subject to the Father.

c.   Christ, as the noblest of men, opens the way to salvation; the power of (super) man turns the scales in that process.

2.6   The teachings of Athanasius:

a.   The Son is begotten of the Father before all worlds (Nicene Creed); not made, but begotten (Athanasian Creed).

b.   The Son is not subject to the Father but equal to the Father. Athanasian Creed, Article 6: "But the Godhead of the Father, of the Son, and of the Holy Spirit is all one, the glory equal, the majesty co-eternal."

c.   Athanasian Creed, Article 30, 44: "For the right faith is that we believe and confess that our Lord Jesus Christ, the Son of God, is God and man. . . . This is the catholic faith, which except a man believes faithfully, he cannot be saved."

3. ANTONY THE HERMIT

3.1   Antony was a contemporary and fellow countryman of Athanasius. One day he heard a sermon on the words of Jesus to the rich young man, "Go your way, sell whatever you have and give to the poor. . ." (Mark 10:21). However, that young man did not follow the Lord's advice. If he had only known who was standing before him and personally invited him to join His followers! But that would have cost him his career in the ecclesiastical world of his time. Antony, too, was rich. He decided to give away all his earthly possessions and went to live away from the people in the Egyptian desert in the mistaken belief that in this way he could serve the Lord even better. But neither the rich young man nor Antony himself listened to Jesus' words, ". . . and come, take up the cross, and follow Me." That was the point: follow Jesus.

3.2   Antony became the sad example for thousands of monks and nuns who thought it most meritorious to flee ordinary life (that is, a life in covenant with God) and as a result regarded themselves holier than others. They despised marriage, possessions, and money as worldly and carnal. Antony even considered his body to be a hindrance; he wore only a sheepskin and ate as little as possible because he was ashamed of the need to feed himself. He, too, forgot that although our human body is still corruptible, it is not to be despised. After the resurrection, the Lord appeared as a real, complete man with a real human body.

   During the last outbreak of persecution in Alexandria, Antony appeared on the streets, loudly calling that he was a Christian and dearly wanting to become a martyr, but without success. The authorities did not dare to arrest him out of fear for the people who greatly respected this hermit. In divine irony, God let him live in that body which he despised so much till the age of 105 years! He bequeathed his old sheepskin to Athanasius, who was greatly honoured by this gift. Athanasius wrote a biography of the much-admired Antony. Many followed his example, among others the so-called pillar saints.

3.3   During the second century, the church fought a difficult battle against pagan Gnosticism. However, the church proved to be unable to free itself completely from the temptation of the Gnostic contempt for God's glorious creation and His ordinances that govern our life here on earth (see 1 Tim. 4:1-5). We must be saved from Satan and the sins of our heart (Mark 7:21-23) and not from this earthly existence. Antony did take his own sinful heart with him into the desert; a monk takes it along into the monastery.

a.   The monastic ideal (namely contempt for the body, marriage, ordinary life, possessions, and the desire to flee from this earthly, fleeting life as a means to earn eternal bliss) has remained the ideal of the Eastern church.

b.   During the sixth century, this persuasive heresy infiltrated the Western church through the teachings of Benedict of Nursia. From the East, the monastic orders overwhelmed European Christianity.

c.   Antony was the first hermit. Pachomius founded the first monastic organization on a small island in the Nile River, Tabennisi. His sister Mary formed a similar organization for nuns.

hermit	-	inhabitant of the desert
monk	-	from *monos* (Gr.) = alone
nun	-	chaste, pure

| anchorite | - | one who lives as a hermit, refugee, one who retires |
| cloister | - | *claustrum* (Lat.) = closed-off place |

4. THE SECOND ECUMENICAL COUNCIL: CONSTANTINOPLE 381

4.1   In his youth, the Syrian bishop Apollinarius had been a friend of Athanasius. He fervently taught that our Saviour is truly God. But the question arose whether Jesus Christ was truly and completely man. This was denied by Apollinarius. He considered man in the same way as the Greek-Roman world of his days, namely according to the philosophy of the stoics.

The main tenets of the stoic philosophy were as follows:

a.   To achieve happiness, man must strive to be completely without human need. That is to say, the fewer needs a person has, the lesser the sorrow when those needs are not filled.

b.   An ideal in life is that of "passionless-ness" (*apatheia*). That is, a person must be trained in impassiveness (apathy) by controlling all human passions. Such an ideal life reflects the characteristics of the godhead, who is without needs and passions.

c.   Man consists of two parts: a higher and a lower "I". The higher "I" (man's personality, his ego) is sovereign, exalted above all feelings and passions such as friendship, love, compassion, hunger, thirst, and sorrow. It is free from all those concerns, like the godhead. The stoic must shake off all these feelings and passions much like a swan shakes off water drops. Those feelings belong to the lower part.

What a terrible disfigurement of the human life! A stoic did not know anything about a real, living human being made by God after His own image.

4.2   Apollinarius read God's Word through the eyes of a stoic. He taught that the Godhead of Christ takes the place of the stoic "I" of man and that he had only taken on the "lower part". Therefore, Jesus was not a real, living, complete man but a stoic human being without passions, ". . . so that he was only half a man" (Calvin: *Institutes* II:16:12).

But if Apollinarius was right, then our Saviour would not be a true and complete man, as we are. We should not think of the Lord Jesus according to the stoic model. He is a true, complete, real man (remember Gethsemane). He is not removed from sorrow and fear. In the garden, He longed for the comforting presence of His disciples. Yet He was without sin and always perfect in His faith in God, even when God left Him. If the Lord Jesus had been a man different from all of us, we would not have been saved completely. Then He could not have been our Paraclete, our Surety; then His work of redemption would still have required completion by the works of stoic asceticism.

4.3   Emperor Theodosius the Great called together the second ecumenical council at Constantinople in 381. The teachings of Apollinarius were condemned. At this council, the catholic church confessed the true Godhead and the true manhood of Christ.

The Christian church also came to confess the Trinity during this council: Father, Son, and Holy Spirit. This is the summary of the Christian faith. With this confession, the church of Christ is elevated above all false religions with their lifeless gods. Without this confession of the triune God, Christ's work in past, present, and future would be a closed book. We would have been left without answers to the great questions of life: from where, how, why? We would not have known of the origin, the sense and the purpose of our life, and of all that happens on earth in the history of the world and mankind.

a.   In the christological struggle, the word *person* was understood to mean "sovereign individual", that is, the stoic "I", and therefore only a part of man. This caused great confusion because God's Word does not know such a stoic division of man. In the Bible, the word *person* means simply a man, a human being, the complete man. The "I" means the total person. The person of our Saviour is God and man (Canons of Dort II, 4).

b.   Belgic Confession, Article 19 speaks of "the two natures in the one person of Christ."

5. THE THIRD ECUMENICAL COUNCIL: EPHESUS 431

5.1   Nestorius, patriarch of Constantinople, was also influenced by stoic philosophy. He rejected the heresy of Apollinarius and confessed that the Saviour is true man, but of course a stoic man with a higher and lower "I". Nestorius taught that there were in Christ two "I"s: a divine and a human-stoic "I". Two persons, two sovereigns, a divinely exalted "I", and a humanly exalted "I", but His joy, tears, sympathy, fears, suffering, and death were felt only by His human "I". In Jesus, therefore, God stood next to man. They were as two friends, closely united, as oil and water (sympathetic unity). Nestorius taught that Christ as God lived in man as a temple. In this way, Nestorius separated the two natures.

But if this were true, we cannot say that God's Son has suffered for us on the cross. Then the sufferings of Christ lose their infinite value (see Canons of Dort II:3,4).

5.2   Although the teachings of Nestorius were rejected by the third ecumenical council of Ephesus (431), he gained a great following outside the Roman Empire, especially in Persia. Today there still exist Nestorians known as Assyrian Christians. There are some 700,000 Nestorians in India. Those who did not join with Rome are now members of the World Council of Churches. The Nestorians penetrated Asia as far as China. In about the year 850, there was a large Chinese Nestorian church. These Christians had great influence as mercenaries in Mongol armies. Nestorian Christians kept watch over the Chinese Wall. Even during the period of the third ecumenical council, there were already some Christian churches in China. In 1625, an inscription was found containing a list of ministers from the Chinese churches in 781. Compare this with the situation in Europe and America at that time!

6. THE FOURTH ECUMENICAL COUNCIL: CHALCEDON 451

6.1 Despite the doctrinal struggles at previous councils, the catholic church had not yet completely shaken off the Greek-pagan philosophy of the stoics.

After Arius (325), Apollinarius (381), and Nestorius (431) came Eutyches, a prior of a monastery in Constantinople. He taught that Christ had one nature, which was a fusion of a divine and a human component. Christ's humanity was absorbed by His divinity like a drop of wine in the sea. Thus Christ was said to be one sovereign, exalted, divine human person.

But if this were true, our Saviour was not our equal in respect to His human nature.

6.2 Eutyches gained many followers in Egypt. Since Egypt (Alexandria) threatened to become the ecclesiastical leader within the Roman Empire, the emperor interfered once again (caesaropapism) by calling together another council, the Council of Ephesus (449). This council was one of utter confusion and fighting. The representatives of Pope Leo I of Rome were forced to flee while Leo himself was excommunicated. Therefore he called this council the *Robber Council*. Leo appealed to the emperor for help. The latter called together the bishops for a second time, this time at Chalcedon (451).

At the Council of Chalcedon, Eutyches was condemned. The following important decisions were made, proposed by Pope Leo I (the Great, ca. 400-461) and supported by the emperor ("Peter has spoken through Leo".):

The natures of Christ are:
- unconfused and unchangeable (against Eutyches)
- indivisible and inseparable (against Nestorius)

This has been the greatest and most important council of the Eastern churches.

6.3   The followers of Eutyches and Nestorius left the church. The beginning of the separation between Eastern and Western churches dates from this time, with the official break coming in 1054. Pagan thoughts about the "old man", strongly promoted by the "evil spirits" (1 Tim. 4:1), attempted to destroy the work of Christ. The "old leaven" (1 Cor. 5:6-8; Gal. 5:9) brings division time and again. Only the Word of God binds together. The followers of Eutyches remained in the majority in the East (Egypt and Syria). They formed the Coptic churches in the mainly Mohammedan countries of Egypt and Ethiopia. In his teachings concerning our Saviour and his ascension, Luther showed that he also was a follower of Eutyches.

NOTES

a.   Arius: Christ is a creature, not God's Son.
     Apollinarius: Christ is God and half (stoic-passionless) man.
     Nestorius: In Christ, God is next to man (sympathetic unity).
     Eutyches: In Christ, God is "fused" with man.

b.   The *Definition of Chalcedon* states that Christ is to be acknowledged in two natures, which are without confusion, change, division, or separation. The distinction between the two natures of Christ is in no way to be abolished because of the union, but rather the characteristics of each nature are to be preserved and come together to form one person and one entity. The Lord Jesus Christ is God (". . . the Word was God . . ." John 1:1) and man (". . . the Man whom He has ordained . . ." Acts 17:31). It is in this way that we may know Him, without understanding this mystery. And for this reason, the words of the man Jesus are at the same time God's own Word. He spoke those words some nineteen centuries ago and still speaks to us in the living words of the Scriptures.

c.   Under the guidance of the Holy Spirit, the ecumenical church, which had developed from a mustard seed into a tree (Matt. 13:32), was allowed to confess the truth of God's Word concerning the Saviour in its battle with the then fashionable philosophy of the stoics.

d.   Even councils and other ecclesiastical meetings can err badly. Later councils of the Eastern churches introduced images into their worship services. Many councils and synods of the Western churches have often denied and opposed God's truth. Gregory Nazianzus, chairman of the second council of Constantinople, was deeply disturbed by the attitude and behaviour of the attending bishops and patriarchs. Dejected, he remarked, "I have never seen good results from any council, but the quarrelsomeness and ambitions of the participants caused the problems to increase. . . ." Pope Leo I did not hesitate "to charge the Council of Chalcedon, which he admits to be orthodox in its doctrines, with ambition and inconsiderate rashness . . ." (Calvin, *Institutes* IV:9:11). Calvin claims that the Roman Catholics force upon us "the determination of all councils, in all matters without distinction, as the oracles of the Holy Spirit." He maintains that "though councils, otherwise pious and holy, were governed by the Holy Spirit, He yet allowed them to share the lot of humanity, lest we should confide too much in men" (Calvin, *Institutes* IV:9:11).

e.   Indeed, we should not glorify ecclesiastical councils as if they are infallible. John Hus was brought to the stake and Luther was excommunicated because they placed the authority of God's Word above the pronouncements of the councils of the church, pronouncements which the church of Rome considers to be infallible.

7. AMBROSE

7.1   Ambrose of Milan was born at Trier (340) and died at Milan (397). His father was prefect of the whole of Gaul, and this made Ambrose a member of the Roman nobility. After the death of his father, his mother educated him at Rome. Ambrose chose a military career and became governor of Milan (in northern Italy). At one time it became necessary for him to restore civil order during the election of a new bishop. Just then, a child's voice shouted, "Ambrose must be our new bishop!" Although at that time he was a believer, he was not yet baptized. As bishop, he fought energetically against the Arians. He was very eloquent, rich, and generous, and he often bought the freedom of slaves. He is said to have introduced the so-called *Ambrosian hymns* (with the congregation responding to the singing of the choir). Pope Gregory considered this kind of singing too worldly and replaced the Ambrosian hymns with the monotonous Gregorian church music.

7.2   Ambrose's dealings with Emperor Theodosius I were a major event in the history of the church. In a fit of anger, Theodosius ordered a punitive expedition against the citizens of Thessalonica who refused to pay heavy taxes. Some seven thousand citizens, adults and children alike, were massacred. Prophetically, Ambrose persuaded the emperor to confess his sins in public because even the emperor is not more than the church; he is an ordinary member of the church. In the East, Athanasius (and others) also spoke against emperors and the court (often because of their wantonness or unjust claim to authority in ecclesiastic matters). In the West, Ambrose did not turn against an emperor who defended heresies (for instance, one who favoured Arianism), but he turned against an emperor who sinned in nonchurch, political matters of state! In this way Ambrose destroyed the pagan myth of a divine emperor. Never before had this happened, and it was never to happen in the Eastern churches.

The Son of David of Bethlehem stands above the Emperor Augustus of Rome!

7.3   Ambrose was also a child of his time, a real Roman Christian. As a result of the Edict of Milan, Christianity had become a state religion (therefore the citizen's duty) to the greater glory of the Roman Empire. Christianity therefore merely replaced the worship of the Roman gods. Politically the state was intolerant and forced non-Christians such as Jews and heretics to accept current beliefs. Even a man like Ambrose defended Christians who set fire to Jewish synagogues and monks who destroyed pagan temples! In those days of religious intolerance, the Christian church and its leaders found it difficult to understand the words of Christ spoken to Pilate, the representative of the Roman emperor, "My kingdom is not of this world. If My kingdom were of this world, My servants would fight . . ." (John 18:36).

After Constantinople became the capital city and the imperial residence (located in the East), the head of the church (the pope of Rome) became recognized increasingly as the symbol of political unity in the West. During the Middle Ages, this led to the terrible tyranny of papal power over all citizens of the western empire.

8. AUGUSTINE - Part A

8.1   Augustine was born in 354 at Tagaste (northern Africa) and died in 430 in Hippo Regius (Algeria). His mother, Monica, was a believing woman, but it was his frivolous father, Patricius, who influenced him in such a way that until adulthood he was without hope and without God in the world (see Eph. 2:12). He never married, but already at the age of eighteen he had a son (Adeodatus). Many of his Christian friends did not really fear God either.

8.2   After completing his studies, he settled in Carthage as a lawyer. At that time he was a follower of *Manicheism* and believed only those parts of God's Word that he could rationally explain. But the imperial city attracted him, and he sailed for Rome. He also wanted to escape his mother, but she followed her son. A bishop, impressed by the fruits of God's Spirit noticeable in Monica's great perseverance in prayer, comforted her, "As truly as you live, it is impossible that a son of such tears will be lost." In Rome he failed to find what he was searching for. But God did not leave him. He became dissatisfied with Manicheism, and shortly afterwards he left Rome for Milan to study rhetoric with Ambrose. Ambrose had a reputation as a great orator. Again Monica followed him. While in Milan, Augustine came under the teachings of *Neoplatonism*, and unfortunately he never fully succeeded in shaking off the influence of this philosophy.

8.3   But God intervened and brought Augustine to faith and conversion. It was not Ambrose's rhetoric that fascinated him but his preaching. Augustine described his spiritual struggles during that decisive hour at length in his famous book *Confessions*: "I cried in the most bitter shattering of my heart. And behold I heard a voice from the house next door; it was of a boy or girl, I do not know, repeatedly singing, 'Take and read, take and read.'" He took the Bible and "silently read the passage which happened to be before me," Romans 13:13, 14 (*Confessions* VII, 12). At the age of thirty-three he was baptized. Just before returning to Carthage from Ostia (Rome's port), his mother Monica died in his arms.

8.4   Augustine's *Confessions* is a long prayer to God in which he confessed his sins and gave thanks for the long road along which God had led him from the slavery of sin and pagan thought to the knowledge of the Bible.

8.5   For thirty-five years Augustine was bishop of Hippo Regius. This was a most eventful period in the history of the world as well as in the history of the church. The Roman Empire collapsed, and Rome itself was ransacked. The migration of nations overwhelmed Europe, and people believed that the world had come to an end. Inspired by these events, Augustine wrote his famous *City of God*, the main work of his second period. Often he preached seated on a platform, and at times his sermons were even interrupted by applause.

8.6   Augustine was actively involved in the final discussions concerning the recognition of the canon of the Bible at the synods of Hippo Regius (393) and Carthage (397). He also recognized the work of the Holy Spirit, who had brought the churches to the recognition of the canon of the New Testament. Neither Athanasius, nor Augustine, nor synods have selected the books of the New Testament, nor did they grant divine authority to them. This, indeed, was not the work of men. The churches recognized and confessed that these books were divine writings and in grace received power to reject the apocryphal books as human writings.

8.7   After his conversion, Augustine did not marry the mother of his son; he sent her away. No one knows her name nor what happened to her. Augustine sacrificed the honour of this woman in the (mistaken) belief that his celibacy would be of service to God. Augustine died while the city of Hippo was beleaguered by the Vandals. These barbarians from northern Germany had fought their way through France, Spain, and northern Africa toward Rome, leaving behind them a trail of death and destruction. Indeed, these barbarians were God's scourge.

8.8   Unfortunately Augustine did not succeed in "bringing every thought into captivity to the obedience of Christ" (2 Cor. 10:5). Among other things, Augustine taught that the soul is by nature Christian, related to God and immortal-divine. He considered the unmarried state to be higher than the married state (this view removed sexuality from the service of God). He claimed that the government must serve the church with its sword in the struggles against heretics.

These thoughts belong to the "old leaven" that unfortunately has leavened the dough of the Christian church and has done much damage (1 Cor. 5:6, 7). Because Augustine is one of the founders of the Christian European culture, his pagan dualism, which he was never completely able to conquer, has had serious consequences, even till the present time. Even the clearest Word of God (for instance 1 Tim. 4:1ff) is ignored by the demonic doctrine that forbids marriage of the clergy.

8.9   What God has done for His church in the East through Athanasius (Alexandria) and Chrysostom (Constantinople), He has done also through Augustine (northern Africa) and Ambrose (northern Italy) for His church in the West, despite their shortcomings and heresies.

9. AUGUSTINE - Part B
THE STRUGGLE AGAINST PELAGIUS

9.1   Pelagius (ca. 400) was an Irish monk. As a strict ascetic, he denied himself all kinds of ordinary things in order to make himself more holy by means of his own good works. Arriving from his Irish monastery in the metropolis of Rome, he was disgusted (and rightly so) by those who excused their sinful life style by appealing to their old nature, which had been spoiled by the sin of Adam. However, Pelagius's annoyance was not scriptural. In reaction, he taught that there is no original sin. Sin is the result of the bad example of sinful people. Christ is only our example; man did not need grace which takes away guilt. He needed merely to follow a perfect example in order to live a life without sin. Fleeing before the West Goths, Pelagius finally arrived in northern Africa.

9.2   Augustine, who did not grow up in a monastery, opposed Pelagius. He taught the depravity of the human heart as well as original sin (Rom. 5:12: ". . . because all sinned"). He preached the grace that God shows to lost sinners in Christ. "So then it is not of him who wills, nor of him who runs, but of God who shows mercy" (Rom. 9:16). Augustine strongly confessed God's election in sovereign grace: man cannot be his own saviour. The teachings of Pelagius were condemned at the Council of Carthage (418). But in the meantime, Pelagius had already left for Jerusalem.

9.3   Belgic Confession, Article 15: "In this regard we reject the error of the Pelagians who say that this sin is only a matter of imitation."

Pelagius:	Man is healthy.
God's Word:	Man is dead before God (Eph. 2:5).
Church of Rome:	Man is sick. He needs the help of sacramental grace (semipelagianism).

9.4   The Pelagian spirit returned strongly in the teachings of the remonstrants of the seventeenth century. This spirit is characterized by its pride, which does not recognize its own depravity and gives man himself the final word in the matter of redemption. In essence, this teaching claims that man is noble and good and stands free, sovereign, and exalted over against God. The ideas of Pelagius are still alive also among us, illustrated by the example of a mother who might sigh, "A few years ago little Johnny was such a nice boy, but now his bad friends teach him all sorts of dirty words."

10. AUGUSTINE - Part C
THE STRUGGLE AGAINST THE DONATISTS

10.1   The Donatists formed a group of zealous Christians who, by the beginning of the fourth century, had separated themselves from the church under the leadership of their bishop, Donatus. They had a large and widespread following, and these churches grew to be almost equal in size to the rest of the Christian church. At times they were victims of persecution, at times they were favoured by the emperor, depending on political circumstances. Augustine opposed them strongly and brought many back to the church. The last of the Donatist churches were destroyed by the Islamic movement in the seventh century.

Enchanted by the sectarian idealism of Montanus, the Donatists wanted an absolutely holy and perfect church, made up of only those over whom sin no longer had any power. Everyone who did not fully agree with them was deemed to be a heretic. They worshipped martyrs, and despised those who had committed *traditio* (handing over or betraying the Scriptures during the great persecutions). Preachers who had committed such sins were no longer allowed to administer baptism, and those who had been baptized by such false ministers were to be rebaptized.

They regarded themselves as *milites Christi*, soldiers of Christ, guarding the purity of the church and especially of the office bearers. Their zealotry led at times to violence against those who did not share their views. They even planned an attempt on Augustine's life. He escaped their ambush because their guide lost his way!

10.2   At first Augustine fought against them with the Word of God only. He maintained that baptism is a divine institution and does not depend on the person who administers it. All sin cannot be banished from the church either. We are called to tolerate much from one another. "Let a man then mercifully correct what he can; what he cannot correct let him bear patiently, and in love bewail and lament" (Calvin, *Institutes* IV:12:11). The fanatical Donatists separated themselves from the church because they did not tolerate the wretchedness and imperfections of its members.

10.3   In the end, Augustine reluctantly called upon the help of the emperor in his struggle against the Donatists. Unfortunately, he was of the opinion that the government should force them to rejoin the church for their own good. He incorrectly appealed to Luke 14:23: ". . . compel them to come in."

Ambrose opposed state interference, which led to political intolerance (one empire, one religion: being a Christian is the duty of every citizen—*do ut des*). Augustine accepted state interference for the sake of spiritual care of the lost. Therefore he was guilty of pastoral intolerance. He confused the task of the government with the calling of the Christian church. Scripture says, "'Not by might, nor by power, but by My Spirit,' says the LORD of hosts" (Zech. 4:6).

10.4   Augustine wanted the government to serve the church with its sword. Later the church of Rome relentlessly continued along this heretical path and taught that the government is subject to the church. Much blood was shed in later centuries because of this serious error. The popes could appeal to the authority of Augustine in support of this heresy. This became even more evident after the popes decreed that the word of the church is equal to the Word of God and that papal authority is equal to spiritual authority in the church. In this way, Augustine's ideas resulting from his struggle against the Donatists became in part the unwitting cause of:

-    the bloody persecution of the Waldensians
-    the murders committed by the Inquisition
-    the death of Hus and other martyrs during the time of the Great Reformation
-    the many religious wars

This had never been Augustine's intention. He himself emphasized strongly that discipline must be exercised in moderation and love, without losing the purity of the scriptural bond of love. (See the quotations from Augustine's writings in Calvin's *Institutes* IV:12:11.)

God's Word teaches that governments may not hinder the church in its calling to proclaim the gospel. They are called upon to protect the church in the public and political sphere. God's Word, which is "the sword of the Spirit" (Eph. 6:17), teaches that the church may never call upon the sword of the government to force people to believe.

10.5 Montanism and Donatism returned in the sixteenth century in the form of Anabaptism (Munster) as well as in every unscriptural spiritualistic movement that so often caused the whole Christian church to be in an uproar because of intolerant zealotry that wants to "overthrow everything which tends to edification" (Calvin, *Institutes* IV:12:12). Those who do not live by grace alone will deal without compassion with their neighbours.

11. THE EASTERN ORTHODOX CHURCH

11.1 As time went by, the Eastern church continued to decline. Primary causes for this decline were:

a.   *Jealousies among the patriarchs, especially those of Constantinople and Alexandria.* For this reason the important doctrinal decisions of the Council of Chalcedon (451) did not bring peace to the Eastern churches as was the case in the Western churches.

b.   *Liturgical ceremonies.* Gradually the preaching of the gospel was replaced by liturgical ceremonies. In a sense, a service in an Eastern church is a dramatic enactment of part of the life of Christ on earth, performed by the priests. For hours on end, the faithful view the glitter and pomp of such a service in mystical rapture. Under the light of thousands of candles, they follow the ceremonial act of the priests, who are dressed in splendid, gold-embroidered garments and who reverently kiss the icons. During such a service, the faithful experience something of the mystical union with the divine itself. The drama of the liturgical enactment of the facts of the redemptive history in the life of Christ bridges the chasm between the eternal, the heavenly, and the temporal, the earthly. The mystical "viewing" of these liturgical dramas is the highest religious experience possible here on earth, and this experience in fact replaces faith in the promises of the gospel. But the gospel comes to the believers in the administration of God's Word, not in mystical experiences! Easter is the great feast of the Eastern churches. Resurrection means deification (becoming God). The goal and purpose is not the forgiveness of sins, but immortality. Dionysius wrote, "Lord, when we are in Thy church, only then it is as if we are in paradise. The worship service is a service of silence, and in this silence a sense of eternity is revealed."

c.   *Worship of images.* Images are seen as bearers of divine power. Therefore, sometimes paint is scraped from these images and mixed with the wine of the Lord's Supper to strengthen the divine medicine of immortality. An icon (image) has a totally different meaning from the images in the Western churches. It is the spiritual connection, the mediator, between the divine and the earthly world. The visible icon is not important; it is the invisible, the mystical, the heavenly that matters. An icon does not resemble the original very well. This does not matter, in fact, it heightens the spirituality of the image. The painter of an icon is not a Rembrandt who tries to depict life; no, he is a tool of the Spirit, depicting religious ecstasy. An icon is the personal presence of the saint it represents. By mystical viewing, touching, or kissing such an icon, a person receives heavenly, divine life, a life totally separated from the earthly life.

d.   *The filio-que* (and of the Son, John 15:26, Acts 2:33; Nicene Creed: "And I believe in the Holy Spirit . . . who proceedeth from the Father and the Son"). The Eastern church rejected the filio-que in the Nicene Creed. It teaches that the Spirit proceeds from the Father only and not from the Father and the Son. In Christ, a person can see divine life, but it is the Spirit who, independently from Word and gospel, brings the deity closer in sporadic and sudden mystical rapture. This serious heresy removes the Word of God from the life of the Eastern churches.

e.   *Form cult.* Because of its empty religiosity and asceticism, the Eastern church has removed itself from the realities of daily life, lost as it is in spiritual contemplation.

11.2 The official break with the Western church came in 1054 when representatives of the pope of Rome placed a bull of excommunication on the steps of the high altar in the Hagia Sophia in Constantinople. In the same place, the patriarchs of the East put a bull against the Roman pope. In a similar manner, this mutual excommunication was revoked by Pope Paul VI in Rome and Patriarch Athenagoras in Constantinople on December 7, 1965. This event signalled closer connections between the two churches, but as yet no full unity has come about. The doctrine of papal infallibility is a great stumbling block in efforts toward unity. It is unacceptable to the mystical Eastern church (where everyone lives according to personal mystical-spiritual insights) that the Spirit of God would work through popes only.

11.3 During the fifth century, the Western church survived the migration of nations; the Eastern church suffered the Islamic "storm" of the seventh century. However, the results of these two sets of events were totally different. The German tribes were gathered to the Christian church. God had "thoughts of peace and not of evil, to give (Europe) a future and hope" (Jer. 29:11). The Eastern churches, however, were mowed down by Mohammedanism. Rev. 3:3 warns, ". . . if you will not watch, I will come upon you as a thief, and you will not know what hour I will come upon you." It is remarkable that in just a few years, the whole of the Eastern Roman Empire was vanquished by the Islam onslaught. Christian Europe was caught in the Islamic encirclement from Gibraltar (Tours) to Constantinople.

11.4 Until the time of the Crusades, Constantinople was the greatest and richest city of Christendom, with many beautiful churches and monasteries. But papal church politics ensured that it was totally unknown in the West. Emperor Justinian (sixth century) built the imposing cathedral Hagia Sophia ("I have exceeded you, O Solomon!"). The crusaders marvelled when they reached Constantinople. The city was conquered by the Mohammedans in 1453 and its inhabitants massacred without mercy. The church in the East had lost its place in public life. And yet the promise of the future is not for Islam but for Japheth, who lives in the tents of Shem (Gen. 9:27).

11.5 Today the Eastern church calls itself the Eastern Orthodox Church or the Greek Orthodox Church. This church consists of the state churches in Russia and the Balkan states. The organization of the Eastern churches is not as elaborate as that of the Roman Catholic church. Although archbishops and patriarchs have great influence, they have no direct authority over the ordinary bishops. The highest authority in the state church is the synod of bishops.

11.6 There are also a number of other churches in the Middle East that have joined with Rome. They are known as the churches of the Eastern rites. They differ from the Roman Catholic church in their religious customs and ceremonies, while they also permit their priests to marry. In the West, orthodox means *orthodox in doctrine*. In the East, orthodox means *orthodox in liturgy*.

11.7 It was not until 1876 that a Russian Bible translation became available, although the Bible remained a forbidden book until 1917. Since every member of the church has a mystical relationship with God through mystical worship, knowledge of the Bible is not necessary. Sermons are heard on holy days only, but these often deal with the life of a saint rather than being a proclamation of God's Word. The patriarch of Moscow has ambitions toward total control of all Eastern churches.

11.8 Since the Russian revolution (1917), there is also a Russian Orthodox Church in exile. This church is strongly anticommunist and considers itself the true continuation of the Russian Orthodox Church from the time before 1917. This church has established itself in North and South America, western and central Europe, and in Australia. It did not join the World Council of Churches since it is strongly opposed to the ecumenical movement.

11.9 The Orthodox churches of Greece and Russia joined the World Council of Churches. In this council, complaints are heard that the Eastern churches do not recognize other churches but have only one demand: that all churches return to the seven ecumenical councils. The Russians are much more liberal and modernist than the Greeks. They sent representatives to the Second Vatican Council, from which the Greeks were noticeably absent. The Russians are much more active in the World Council of Churches and exercise a leftist influence under pressure from the Kremlin. The patriarch of Moscow is a willing servant of this regime. For the eyes of the world, he must appear as living proof that there is indeed freedom of religion in Russia.

FOURTH PERIOD: 590 - 1520

THE CHURCH UNDER THE YOKE OF PAPAL HIERARCHY

1. PAPAL POWER

1.1   According to the Roman Catholic church, Christ gave Peter a place above all other apostles; only Peter received authority to use the heavenly keys. Peter is said to have been the first bishop of Rome. His successors claim that they occupy his chair. The geographical location and the history of Rome—for centuries the capital of the whole world—helped establish the primacy of the bishop of Rome.

Question 152 of the old Catechism of the Dutch Bishops asks, "What is the pope?" Answer: "The pope is the bishop of Rome, the legal successor of Peter, and Jesus' deputy on earth." This means that the authority of our Lord Jesus has been transferred to a human being. The word of man has become identified with God's own Word.

1.2   Against these papal arrogations stand the following points:

a.   Jesus said to Peter, ". . . and on this rock will I build My church . . ." (Matt. 16:18; see also Isa. 28:16, 1 Cor. 3:11, and 1 Pet. 2:4, 6, 7). Not the person of Peter (Rome), but Christ Himself is that Rock.

b.   Scripture does not teach anywhere that Peter had authority over the other apostles, on the contrary:

1.   Galatians 3:9: James is mentioned first as one of the pillars of the congregation of Jerusalem while Cephas (Peter) and John are mentioned second and third.

2.   Galatians 2:11: Paul strongly opposes Peter.

3.   Ephesians 4:11: A number of office bearers are mentioned, but not a pope.

4.   1 Peter 5:1: Peter calls himself a fellow elder, and in verse 4 he refers to Christ as the Chief Shepherd.

c.   The foundation stones of the New Testament contain twelve names, not just one, Peter: Rev. 21:14.

d.   Scripture speaks of two priestly orders: the order of Levi (Aaron), which was abolished with the coming of Christ; and the order of Melchizedek, which is the order to which Christ himself belongs in eternity without successor (Hebrews 7). According to which order have the Roman Catholic popes (high priest) and priests been ordained?

e.   Why Rome, and not Jerusalem, where Christ died and rose from the dead and where he founded the first Christian church?

f.   Peter was never bishop of Rome.

1.3   Papal rule (hierarchy) is the consequence of a wrong tendency that began already in the second century.

a.   The minister of God's Word became more and more a priest, that is, the dispenser of grace enclosed in the sacraments.

b.   The priest became king over God's people because of the apostolic succession.

c.   The high priest (pope) became Christ's deputy and claimed authority over the whole world (governor).

1.4   The basic heresy of the pope's claim to authority is twofold:

a.   The rejection of Christ as the only Head of the church. He governs His church directly by means of the local office bearers (Eph. 4:11-16).

b.   The claim that the church's office bearers also have political power. Papal troops, mainly mercenaries, were often commanded by ecclesiastical, that is, papal commanders-in-chief. Luther maintained, however, that the church desires no earthly power. Rome claims that Christ continues His work of redemption in the pope, the priest, and the Roman Catholic church. In fact, Christ is, as it were, the invisible Prisoner of the church: only through the church can we attain full communion with Him.

1.5   The history of the medieval church is dominated by the papal struggle to gain authority and power over all churches and princes. This struggle has seriously harmed the truly Christian life style of Christ's congregations in Europe. The catholic church deteriorated into a papal church. Papism results in hierarchy.

1.6   590-1073:   Rise of papal power from Gregory I to Gregory VII.

1073-1294:   Flourishing of papal power from Gregory VII to Boniface VIII.

1294-1520:   Decline of papal power from Boniface VIII to Leo X.

1.7   The Vatican is increasing its political activities in our days. The pope made an appearance before the United Nations in his capacity as head of state. He is in league with the world powers in political agreements (see Rev. 17:2).

2. THE RISE OF PAPAL POWER: 590 - 1073

2.1   The migration of nations around the year 400 (the so-called wandering of the nations) was a terrible time for Europe. At the same time, it was a period of great importance for the expansion of the church. The Western Roman Empire (the iron kingdom) was destroyed (476), but in the midst of this Germanic storm, God maintained His church and increased it greatly through the christianization of many nations. After 476, the people became aware that the church was gradually replacing the state and that the bishop of Rome in fact replaced the emperor of Rome. People remembered how Pope Leo himself, dressed in a simple, white garment, had persuaded Attila (king of the Huns, "God's scourge over Europe") to spare the city for a price (452). Later, this same pope persuaded the Vandals not to massacre the people, even though the city of Rome was ransacked. Papism triumphed over caesaropapism. God's judgement was heavy: the church in the East came under judgement of Islam, and the church in the West came under the yoke of papal authority. The focal point in church history moved from the eastern to the western regions of the empire, especially with the appearance of Pope Gregory I.

2.2   Gregory I the Great, 590-604, came from a distinguished Roman senatorial family. Gregory first became an important civil servant (prefect of Rome). Later, he held the highest office in the church, the office of pope. Thus he became the founder of what eventually became the church-state (the Vatican) in 1870.

This man led the church away from God's Word toward the heresy of the Roman Catholic church (remember Jeroboam, "who made Israel sin"). Increasingly, attention was paid to, and value placed on, the church's tradition rather than on God's Word. All kinds of current opinions were elevated to church doctrine: angels and saints became mediators; purgatory; worship of relics; miracle stories; the Lord's Supper (God's gift of grace) was deformed into the sacrifice of the mass; pagan temples became Christian churches; saints now took the place of the many gods (Mary instead of Freya); pagan religious customs were christianized (still an often-used method of Roman Catholic missionaries, a method that all too easily promotes pseudoconversion).

Gregory's ambition was to lead a universal Roman church. He was the missionary pope par excellence. Many missionaries were sent to the countries of northern Europe. But in reality, these missionaries were propagandists for the papal chair! Many carried with them a box of relics. Despite these sins and heresies, God used these people to plant His church throughout the European continent.

2.3   Among the many missionaries who came to preach the gospel, we mention:

Patrick, apostle of the Irish (ca. 430). In his youth he was snatched from his native Scotland by pirates and sold to the Irish where he became a swineherd. After his escape, he returned at a later date to Ireland as a missionary—he knew the language and the customs. Ireland became the cradle of European missions (Insula sanctorum).

Eligius, goldsmith at the Frankish court, ca. 588-660. He redeemed slaves and prisoners of war (at times as many as fifty a day) and after their conversion sent them back to their native country. Later Eligius preached the gospel in Flanders.

Amandus (ca. 584-679). This missionary went to Flanders. Twice he was thrown into the wild waters of the Scheldt River. Often Frankish missionaries were treated as spies by the Saxons and Frisians.

Willibrord (658-739). He first preached in the region south of the great rivers (Frankish Frisia). On the Island of Walcheren, he destroyed an image of the god Wodan: "If he is a (living) god, let him plead for himself, because his altar has been torn down!" (Judges 6:31). As archbishop of Utrecht, he continued his work among the hostile Frisians and their King Radbod. In the cloister of the St. John's church at Utrecht stands a statue of Willibrord.

Boniface, archbishop of Mainz, Germany (680-754). As papal legate, he strongly promoted a Roman Catholic church in the spirit of Gregory I. He always carried with him a sacred shroud. Both he and his companions were attacked and murdered in Frisia, near a place called Murmerwoude (murderer's wood). He lies buried in his monastery at Fulda.

Ludger (ca. 744-809). He was the first Frisian-born missionary. He continued the work of Boniface in Frisia and Helgoland.

Anskar, apostle of the North (801-865). He worked among the Danish people and the Norsemen and is well-known as the founder of Christianity in Scandinavia.

2.4   God used the intensive labours of these missionaries in the preaching of the gospel to create a "new humanity"; Galatians 6:15: a "new creation"; Ephesians 2:10: "For we are His workmanship." The fruit of the Spirit became manifest (Gal. 5:22). The prophecy of Simeon was fulfilled also for Europe: Christ, "a light to bring revelation to the Gentiles" (Luke 2:32). The face of the continent changed and was illumined. Until that time, Europe (ereb—land of the evening) was little more than the outer porch of Asia. Now God began to "mercifully send the messengers of these most joyful tidings to whom he will and at what time he pleases . . ." (Canons of Dort I, 3). "Listen, O coastlands, to Me, and take heed, you peoples from afar!" (Isa. 49:1; see also Isa. 42:4b). In a dream, Paul had already heard a (European) call for the gospel (Acts

16:9). Therefore, it is not because of people (popes and missionaries) that Europe became a Christian continent and became the heart of the world. God Himself remembered the European people (Romans, Corinthians, Philippians, Thessalonians). Japheth's sons would dwell in the tents of Shem (Gen. 9:27; 10:5). For all Europeans, these words are true: "But of Him you are in Christ Jesus. . . . He who glories, let him glory in the LORD" (1 Cor. 1:30, 31). For centuries, the other continents remained in darkness. The Asian and African people were not part of the development of society and culture as it took place in Europe under the illumination of the gospel, even though Christian churches had been established on these continents well before churches were established in Europe. "In (the Word) was life, and the life was the light of men" (John 1:4). Only since the nineteenth century, and particularly in the twentieth century (the age of mission), has the whole world seen great progress, and the gospel is being preached everywhere. Has Christ's judgement now come over Europe? "And this is the condemnation, that the light has come into the world, and men loved darkness rather than the light, because their deeds were evil" (John 3:19).

2.5   Charlemagne ruled over half of Europe and subjected the pagan Frisians and Saxons. Under his firm government, churches and monasteries enjoyed a time of prosperity. He attempted to maintain the scriptural preaching in the native language over against the increasingly influential Roman Catholic sacramental worship. He strongly promoted the organization of the church and the training of the clergy. He opposed the worship of images. It became a crime to hinder and oppose missionaries, who before had often been treated as Frankish spies. First they would try to win the tribal leaders for Christianity, then the people would follow in accordance with the German principle: the religion of the prince is the religion of the people. Charlemagne dealt forcibly with the rapacious and treacherous Saxons, who more than once broke their oath of allegiance. Near Bremen (Germany) some four thousand were hanged. He forced them to adopt the Christian religion and made heathendom punishable by death. This was misuse of civil authority, even though it was for the good of the church (see John 18:36: "My kingdom is not of this world. . ."). During the Christmas celebrations in the year 800, the pope suddenly crowned Charlemagne emperor. The pope claimed that this act made the Carolingian Empire (the dynasty to which Charlemagne belonged) into a Christian empire, an empire that lasted for a thousand years: the Holy Roman Empire (800-1806). The aspirations of the popes were toward a papal, worldwide church-state while the aspirations of the Carolingians were toward a mighty empire in western Europe in which the church was central, not under the pope, but under the Word of God. It is in this period that the struggle started between the Carolingians and the popes, a struggle that lasted throughout the Middle Ages.

3. THE CLUNIAC MONASTIC REFORM

3.1   The decline of the papal church reached its lowest point toward the year 900: the dark tenth century. The papal chair was occupied by the apostate Roman nobility, criminals who did not hesitate to use poison and dagger to gain and maintain power and who lived a life of lewdness and fornication. The church of our fathers had become like the people of Israel in the days of Manasseh and Isaiah: "Hear the word of the LORD, you rulers of Sodom . . . you people of Gomorrah . . ." (Isa. 1:10).

3.2   Pachomius (ca. 320) is generally considered the founder of monasticism in the Eastern churches. Benedict of Nursia (ca. 500) became the founder of monasticism in the Western churches. Benedict founded a monastery at Monte Cassino in the place of a dilapidated temple of the god Apollo (destroyed during World War II, later restored, and at present an art centre). A monastery was founded at Cluny (France) in 910 in an attempt to combat the decadence of the church. Its first abbot was Berno.

Egypt:	Pachomius
Italy:	Benedict of Nursia
France:	Cluny

The abbots of Cluny used the basic rules of Benedict very strictly: command of silence, self-chastisement, contempt for the world. The monks of Cluny were known as "the saints of the people". Starting at Cluny, this monastic reform spread throughout France and Italy. The Cluniac order became one of the most powerful monastic orders of the Middle Ages. The abbey of Cluny was the largest Christian church building in the world until the building of the St. Peter at Rome. The monastery of Cluny was destroyed during the French Revolution, and today only ruins remain.

3.3   The Cluniac monastic reform was aimed especially against simony and lay investiture while it also strictly maintained celibacy.
a.   *Simony*: the purchase of spiritual gifts for money (Acts 8:18). This practice led to bribery and a trade in ecclesiastical offices. Not only emperors but also popes sold bishops' offices for large sums of money.
b.   *Celibacy*: we read about this in 1 Tim. 4:1ff: ". . . doctrines of demons . . . forbidding to marry, and commanding to abstain from foods. . . ." The rejection of marriage and the use of selected foods and drinks and in general the rejection of material and physical things as unimportant are characteristics of Gnosticism.

However, the Cluniac reform was one of outward appearance only and did not bring a return from the papal doctrines of the church. Since this monastic order did not place itself under the supervision of bishops but under the direct authority of the pope, it soon became a powerful instrument in the hands of the papal politicians in their struggle against the emperor. This became evident when the Cluniac monk Hillebrand became pope in 1073 (Gregory VII).

4. MONASTERIES

4.1   During the Middle Ages, many monastic orders were founded and many monasteries were built. Why was this? The main cause must be sought in the straying from God's covenant of grace which He established with His people. The people did not really love the Lord (they did not know a God of love) and therefore found little enjoyment in the everyday service of the Lord. Many attempted to conquer the evil of world conformity by means of world avoidance. It was thought that a monastic life would bring a person closer to God than the everyday matters of craft, commerce, marriage, and family. Ordinary life was considered secular (unhallowed, nature). Monastic life was grace (supernature). There came about a separation and contrast between the lower life of the laity (nature, unhallowed), and the higher life of the clergy (grace, supernatural). The Roman Catholic church continues to use the terms *clergy* and *laity* while the churches of the Reformation have rejected this distinction and refused to use the terminology. (The idea of monasticism comes from the Eastern world of paganism, for instance, Vietnam. The rosary originated in Tibet.)

4.2   God's Word teaches the creation of the whole man in the image of God, "May we, Thy children here below, in all our deeds Thy image show" (*Book of Praise,* Hymn 47:2). This was replaced by the Roman Catholic doctrine that taught that the image of God is no more than an addition to natural man. As a result of the fall into sin, man lost only that addition. The "natural" man was left, weakened, but unspoiled. This Roman Catholic doctrine did not clearly recognize sin and therefore denied salvation in Christ alone. In the cities, "religious" people (the clergy) lived next to the common people (the laity). This situation demonstrated a double Christendom and a double church, one for the clergy and one for the laity. This distinction between the spiritual and the natural things has caused a great deal of damage, and in times of apostasy it reappeared even in so-called protestant countries.

4.3   God's Word teaches us the true antithesis by faith in Christ Jesus:

grace	-	wrath
obedience	-	sin
righteous	-	unrighteous
the fear of the Lord	-	rejection of the covenant obligations
born of water and the Spirit (John 3:5), through faith in Christ Jesus	-	incapable of doing any good

The fall into sin taints all of man's faculties and capacities, and the broken covenant relationship touches all of life. Our heart is evil (see Mark 7:21). And that heart came along with a person who entered a monastery! Religiosity does not save us; Jesus alone is our Saviour. During times of obedience, Israel recognized one altar only: the one at Jerusalem, with the sacrificial blood of reconciliation. In times of disobedience, Israel built altars "in the high places" and betrayed God with its pseudospirituality. Those who are truly spiritual are led by the Holy Spirit; those who are not led by the Spirit are men of the flesh, carnal people (1 Cor. 3:1; Gal. 6:1).

4.4   During the Middle Ages, many monasteries and chapels were built, with images of saints as decorations. People were very religious but hardly knew the LORD God. Religious processions were organized to bless the harvest, the ships, the tools, and the barn, and everywhere and everyday sacrifices (masses) were brought. But the unrighteousness of the people was great, and God's Word was not obeyed.

However, many pious priests and monks were a blessing to the ignorant and uncouth people. Monks regularly tilled the fields; they provided opportunities for education. Many nuns tended the sick and cared for the needy. The greatest blessing came from those monasteries where the holy Bible was painstakingly copied by hand. Because of this patient labour, the Word of God has been kept for later generations. We should not forget either that the first Dutch martyrs in the time of the Reformation (Hendrik Voes and John van Essen) were monks.

4.5   As protestant Christendom departed from God's covenant, protestant monastic communities appeared, such as:

Iona Community	- Scotland 1938
Communaute de Taize	- France 1945
Marienschwesterschaft	- Germany 1947

5. "THE LIGHT SHINES IN THE DARKNESS" - John 1:5 - Part A

5.1   Christ maintained His church also during those dark times of papal hierarchy. Again and again He raised up men who called the people back to God's Word. We name two such people from the ninth century: Claudius of Turin and Gottschalk of Rheims.

5.2   Claudius of Turin (d. 827) became bishop of Turin in 820. He was well versed in the writings of Augustine and strongly opposed the doctrine of good works, the worship of saints (the bones reputedly belonging to a Spanish saint turned out to be those of a criminal), the worship of images and relics, and the practice of pilgrimages. Claudius argued, "If we are to worship every block of wood which has the shape of a cross, then we also have to worship every crib because the Lord Jesus lay in a crib at the time of his birth. Then we should also worship all cloths, because at his birth he was wrapped in cloths. Then we should worship asses, since the Saviour entered Jerusalem riding on an ass. We should not worship the cross, we should bear it!"
  The opposition against his attacks on public opinion and hallowed beliefs was great. He was called "a serpent that destroys the church". But the emperor offered him protection; thus he lived in peace throughout his life.

5.3   Gottschalk of Rheims (Godescalus)(ca. 805-869) was the son of a Saxon nobleman, Count Bruno. He was an orphan from the age of five. He was educated in the monastery of Fulda and forced to become a monk. He finally received his freedom but was not allowed to take possession of his family's inheritance. A staunch student of Augustine, he strongly defended the doctrine of particular grace and double predestination. He fearlessly attacked the teachings of Pelagius. Condemned by two synods, deprived of his priesthood, and flogged, he was finally imprisoned for twenty years at Rheims till his death in 869.

5.4   The teachings of Athanasius (Jesus is the Son of God) triumphed in the Western Christian church, namely at the Council of Toledo (589), where Europe was saved from Arianism. But the teachings of Augustine (man cannot be his own saviour) did not triumph despite the condemnation of Pelagian doctrine at the Council of Carthage (418). Although there were many who agreed with Gottschalk, the papal church deviated more and more from the line of Augustine and became semipelagian in its doctrine.

5.5   It was not until the Great Reformation of the sixteenth century that the doctrine of God's good pleasure was again accepted in the church of Christ.

6. PAPAL POWER FLOURISHES 1073 - 1294

6.1   Gregory VII (1073-1085) was born in 1021 into a simple Italian peasant family. He became a Cluniac monk and was a strict ascetic. Later he became counsellor to the pope, and finally he himself was elected pope by popular choice. He was small of stature, uncomely, and lacked distinction in appearance.

His life's goal was to free the church from the yoke of the state and to make papal authority supreme. The pope is the sun while the emperor is the moon. Gregory attempted to reach his goals in the following manner:

a.   The pope was no longer elected by the German emperor but by the college of cardinals, that is, by the curia (see Numbers 11:24).
b.   A relentless enforcement of the principle of celibacy: "Cluny must be victorious". This decision brought enormous sorrow in many priests' families: either a father resigned his priestly office, or he was forced to leave his wife and children.
c.   Prohibition of simony.
d.   Prohibition of the appointment of ecclesiastics by laymen (lay investiture). Investiture was the privilege of the emperor in those days. The word *investiture* is derived from *investitura*, meaning to hold an office. This word is used to denote the installation of a bishop by the presentation of the staff (symbol of the office of shepherd) and the ring (symbol of marriage with the church) and sometimes a sceptre (symbol of authority).

6.2   Gregory VII strove for a universal theocracy, with the pope (himself) as Christ's representative over the whole earth. He ruled the congregation of Christ in a terrible manner and in fact opposed the Lord himself. He is the greatest church politician of the Middle Ages. "Imperial necks are of lesser value than priestly knees", said Gregory.

The church (pope) ruled over all:
-    over the living with all kinds of man-made rules
-    over the dead with indulgences to save them from purgatory
-    over the priests with the doctrine of celibacy
-    over the local churches through a hierarchical system
-    over the civil authorities with political supremacy

And all this because the church ruled over God's Word. The pope was regarded as having authority greater than that of the Bible instead of the Bible having authority over all, even the pope.

6.3   During the Middle Ages, the whole life of a Christian fell under the heavy rule of the church. The cathedral dominated the city, rising high above the dwellings of the simple villagers. The priest performed all official acts (as is done now by civil authorities): registration of marriage, births, and deaths. Bishops ruled supreme and involved the church in many things that were not its concern at all. God's Word teaches that the task of the church is the preaching of the gospel of God. Church, state, and society each have their own sphere of responsibility, and each must take note of God's ordinances for its particular sphere. This was not recognized till after the Great Reformation of the sixteenth century.

7. THE INVESTITURE STRUGGLE

7.1 Both pope and emperor were blind to the basic heresy of the Middle Ages, which claimed that ecclesiastical office bearers have political power and authority. Gregory VII prohibited lay investiture, but Emperor Henry IV did not obey this papal command. He forced the pope himself from office. At the very moment that the bishop of Utrecht, on Easter Sunday 1076, read the imperial announcement concerning the dismissal of the pope, lightning struck the church, and two days later, that bishop died. The people said, "This is God's judgement over the unlawful actions of the emperor!" The pope, in turn, excommunicated the emperor, with the result that no one supported the emperor any longer, giving Gregory a chance to journey to Germany to appoint another emperor.

Emperor Henry IV, together with his wife, was compelled to make that famous journey across the Alps to the Italian city of Canossa in the severe winter of 1077. For three days he cried for remission of his sins as a penitent sinner, standing bareheaded and barefooted before the gates of the papal castle. The pope had no other option than to rescind the bull of excommunication and accept the emperor again as a member of the church. But his dismissal as emperor remained in force. As a priest, Pope Gregory was forced to commit political suicide: Gregory lost his influence over Germany. Henry IV regained his power and influence in Germany and organized a military campaign against Rome. Eventually he was crowned emperor by a pope whom he himself had appointed. Gregory VII fled and died in exile in Salerno.

7.2 The Canossa incident seemed to have brought glory to the pope and humiliation to the emperor, but it brought the pope bitter disappointment and the emperor sweet victory, be it only temporarily. A temporary compromise was reached through the Concordat of Worms (1122): the ecclesiastical investiture (ring and staff) was the papal privilege while the royal investiture (the sceptre) was the imperial privilege. The pope selected bishops, but the emperor could veto such appointments. Despite this agreement, the basic heresy (the claim that office bearers had political authority) was not removed. To the people, it seemed as if the pope defended the things of God and that the emperor was after self-glorification only. Therefore it was almost inevitable that eventually the pope gained the upper hand, and papism was victorious over caesaropapism.

7.3   Once, when the leaders of the Jews attempted to snare the Lord Jesus with a political question (Palestine was occupied by the Romans), the Lord replied, "Render to Caesar the things that are Caesar's, and to God the things that are God's" (Matt. 22:31; Mark 12:13-17; Luke 20:20-26). This answer was not a compromise but a practical-prophetical reply that already pointed toward separation between church and state. Both church and state remain under the authority of God's Word as befits the New Testament era.

7.4   The Concordat of Worms resulted in an increasingly powerful papal court for almost two centuries: 1122-1294. The need for financial resources increased steadily, and these resources were obtained by means of simony and indulgences. The Vatican became the largest bank in the world. The lust for money has often been one of the worst sins of the papacy, contributing directly to the apostasy of the papal church.

8. THE CRUSADES

8.1   The crusade ideal was typical of the medieval mentality: to conquer the world, and first of all the so-called holy places, for Christ with the sword. A wave of enthusiasm to earn the "supernatural" grace that the church offered in her sacraments (see 1 Sam. 4:5ff) rolled over the Western church: earn the grace of God offered by the church to all those who participate in the holy crusade against the infidel—God wills it! But "seeking to establish their own righteousness" (Rom. 10:3) was a sin against the second commandment.

8.2   The popes used the Crusades as a means to strengthen their hold over the Eastern Orthodox Church as well as over the emperor at Constantinople and over the whole Mohammedan world. Often western trade interests played a major role, for instance, the commercial interests of the city of Venice. Many people participated in these crusades, driven by an insatiable longing for indulgence, riches, and adventure. A crusade is a holy war; it is not a missionary journey but a conquest. Thousands, including children, perished by the sword that they had drawn themselves (Matt. 26:52).

8.3   The Crusades strengthened the power and influence of the pope and increased superstition because of the relics that crusaders brought back from the holy land. They resulted in increased trade, especially for the cities around the Mediterranean Sea. New orders were founded, known as orders of knighthood, for instance, the Knights of St. John and the Knights Templar. The crusaders discovered the simplicity of life in the holy land: Jesus' life on earth could never have been a life of splendour! This opened many eyes to the apostasy of the wasteful luxury of the papal courts.

9. BERNARD OF CLAIRVAUX

9.1   The Cluniac reform movement developed during the tenth century, whereas Bernard of Clairvaux (1090-1153) stimulated the renewal of the monastic ideal during the twelfth century when he founded the Cistercian monastery of Clairvaux (1115).

Bernard was born into a noble family. After a sudden conversion, he joined the strict monastery of the Cistercians. Later, he founded a monastery at Clairvaux in the forbidding valley of the Saône River (France). Together with his followers, he cleared the land and created a haven for travellers and merchants (Clairvaux means "clear valley"). The Cluniac monks wore black habits, whereas Bernard's followers wore habits made of white, undyed wool.

He was an eloquent speaker and one of the chief organizers of the Second Crusade (which ended in disaster). No images or ornaments were found in Bernard's monasteries. The pope was taken aback by those bare walls and cells. Bernard promoted strict self-discipline (asceticism), with frequent bodily chastisement. He strongly opposed the persecution of the Jews. As personal counsellor of princes and popes, his influence was enormous, and he became known as "the uncrowned pope". It is said that for weeks he unselfishly fed a crowd of some two thousand persons during a period of famine.

9.2   Bernard rejected the doctrine of good works and preached justification by faith alone. In this he followed the teachings of Augustine, and he preceded the reformers who preached this doctrine even more radically. For this reason, Luther called him the Augustine of the Middle Ages. Bernard's motto was "pray (the monastic prayers) and work (on the land)". He demonstrated a typical medieval attitude: by withdrawing from the world after every journey, he tried to rule the world from within the monastery. He accepted the papacy as the legitimate authority of the church. Over against the then popular understanding of Christ as the conqueror, he showed the significance of the sufferings and the wounds of Jesus (Isa. 53), piety and devotion (not mysticism, that is, the unification of the immortal soul with God), and the following of Jesus (do as Jesus did, imitation of Jesus). However, he did not escape the medieval, legalistic belief in the gospel as a new law to do good works as opposed to the gospel of grace to believe in Christ.

10. THE PAPACY AT ITS PEAK

10.1 The reign of Pope Innocent III (1198-1216) may be regarded as the peak of papal power. He became cardinal at the age of thirty and pope at the age of thirty-seven. He was a powerful, impressive personality.
Some of his pronouncements:
- The pope is less than God yet more than a human being.
- The pope is not the vicar of Peter but of Christ.
- The pope judges all without being judged by anyone.

10.2 Thus the antichristian character of the papacy became clear. This peak of papal power was in reality a tragic low point. The papacy had brought about a distortion of the true church. Innocent III managed to subject all princes of Europe to his authority. He forced the French king to annul his divorce; he removed the king of England from the throne, allowing him to return at a later stage as a papal vassal.

10.3 In 1215, he called together the Fourth Lateran Council. This was the twelfth ecumenical council. It was a demonstration of pomp and celebration, the whole world seemed to be there. This council adopted the following resolutions:
- Severe punishment for all unrepentant heretics, especially the Waldensians and Albigensians.
- The institution of the secret Inquisition, the scourge of the church. (Judgement over the world by man: Jer. 1:10). The Inquisition was not disbanded until 1834.
- Secret confession at least once a year.
- The doctrine of transubstantiation.
   a. The doctrine of transubstantiation was a new doctrine and is certainly not an apostolic teaching. During the ninth century, the theologians at the court of Charlemagne attacked and condemned this doctrine as a heresy, but since 1215 it has been the official teaching of the Roman Catholic church. This doctrine teaches that after consecration, the wafer (used during the eucharist) becomes the host (sacrifice). Pope Innocent ordered that this "new god" (as Guido de Bres would call it later) had to be kept behind lock and key, safe from theft and vermin. A stolen host would take revenge by bleeding. Jews were often accused of such crimes, suffering terribly in the resulting persecutions brought upon them by medieval Christendom. In 1370, the host of the St. Gudule church at Brussels was found to be bleeding. Rumour had it that Jews had pierced it with daggers. The persecution was vicious. Whole families were burnt alive or banished for life without any

form of judicial process, let alone legal protection. In 1870, the pope cancelled the festive celebrations of the five hundredth anniversary of the bleeding of the host at Brussels because scientists had discovered a bacillus which caused red spots on bread as well as on potatoes under certain conditions of humidity and heat.

b. The doctrine of transubstantiation was maintained by the Council of Trent (1545-1563) against the teachings of the Reformation. The members of the latest Vatican Council (1962-1965) were asked to reaffirm, under oath, the decisions of the Council of Trent. Although many Roman Catholic theologians doubt the validity of this teaching, it remains part of the official doctrine of the Roman Catholic church.

c. Guido de Bres rejected the doctrine of transubstantiation and admonished his audience to remain faithful to the teachings of the apostles and martyrs. "I also will not refuse to seal (this doctrine) with my blood."

d. The Eastern churches never accepted the false doctrine of transubstantiation. At the Council of Florence (1439), which attempted to breach the schism between East and West, the Eastern church refused to accept this doctrine as the thirteenth article of the apostolic creed. But despite this refusal, they were not condemned as heretics.

e. The Heidelberg Catechism (Lord's Day 30) calls the popish mass "an accursed idolatry".

10.4 After 1215, it became more and more obvious that the original catholic church, which had already changed into a popish church, was now turning into a false church.

11. MENDICANT ORDERS

11.1 *Mendicare* means to beg. As the name indicates, the mendicant orders depended on the generosity of the people. These monks did not withdraw behind the walls of monasteries but lived among the common people, preaching in word and deed. The mendicant orders were characterized by the absence of personal as well as communal possessions. Historically, these orders came into being as a reaction against the wealth and excesses of the papal court. In fact, a mendicant order is organized ingratitude toward God: "For every creature of God is good, and nothing is to be refused if it is received with thanksgiving; for it is sanctified by the word of God and prayer" (1 Tim. 4:4, 5).

11.2 The Order of the Franciscans was also known as the Friars Minor, or the Grey Friars—*Ordo Fratum Minorum* (O.F.M.). Its founder was Giovanni Bernadone (1182-1226) from Assisi. He received the nickname Francesco—Francis—because at the time of his birth his father was in France on business. In his youth he was disorderly, squandering his money. Later his motto became, "poverty is my bride". He considered self-chastisement to be a work of merit. "All creatures are my friends", he wrote. He spoke to the flowers and preached to the animals. With emotional fervour, he gave himself to the work of caring for lepers. At first Innocent III refused to recognize this order, condemning its antisocial character: "Go to the pigsty, man!" Francis did just that, persevered, and finally received papal approval. The pope recognized the Franciscans in an attempt to counter the growing influence of the Waldensians. These people had gained much respect with the common people through their preaching and their simple, pious life style. Francis showed great missionary zeal in Spain, Morocco, and other places. He also joined a crusade to Egypt. His influence over the people was charismatic. Two years before his death, he received the so-called stigmata. This word is taken from Gal. 6:17, ". . . I bear in my body the marks of the Lord Jesus." Paul, however, meant something rather different; the marks in his body were the scars of ill-treatment he had suffered for Christ's sake. Within two years of his death, Francis was already proclaimed a saint because of his many good works.

During the first half of the thirteenth century, the Asian Mongols threatened European Christendom. The Franciscan monks fearlessly preached the gospel to these unbelievably cruel Asiatic hordes. Their missionaries travelled as far as the court of the Mongol Khan in China.

A society for women, based on Franciscan ideals, was founded by Clare Sciffi, a daughter of a wealthy family in Assisi. This order became known as the Poor Clares (Clarisses). The influence of Francis was also noticeable in the growing cities, and still another order was founded: the Tertiaries. Although the members of this order adhered to a set of rules similar to those of the Franciscan order, they did not profess monastic vows. Also, the Beguines, another charitable organization, did a great deal of good during those days.

11.3 Order of the Dominicans, *Ordo Praedicatorum* (O.P.), the second major mendicant order, was founded in 1216 by the Spaniard Dominic of Osma (1170-1221). His purposes were study, preaching, and mission. Many Dominicans became fanatic opponents of heretics and were among the leaders of the Inquisition. The common people nicknamed them *domini canes*, the Lord's dogs that keep the flock together. Often knights and emperors employed Dominicans as their confessors. One of the most famous Dominicans was Thomas Aquinas.

11.4 Besides the mendicant orders, mention must be made of the religious orders of knighthood which came into being during the time of the Crusades. These orders provided protection and care for pilgrims and crusaders. These orders of noblemen and knights were also based on monastic ideals.

a. The most well-known is the Order of the Knights of St. John. Since their main task was the care of the sick and wounded, they became known as Hospitallers. After having been driven from Palestine, they settled on the Island of Malta and became known as the Knights of Malta. The capital city of Malta is named after their last grandmaster, La Valetta.

b. The Order of the Knights Templar was so named because its first centre was established on the place where the temple of Jerusalem had been (1118). This order was disbanded in 1312 on accusations of heresies and immorality by order of Philip IV, king of France, who seized the wealth of this order to replenish the empty royal coffers.

11.5 Many nameless people from all ranks of life did, as New Testament Nazarenes, much to bring relief and comfort in those rough and miserable ages. With dedication and abandon, they performed miracles of charity, educated the people, and preached the gospel. In the meantime, the official leaders of the church cared for themselves only. The words of the prophet Ezekiel certainly apply to the leaders of the church of those days:

"Woe to the shepherds of Israel who feed themselves! Should not the shepherds feed the flock?

"You eat the fat and clothe yourselves with the wool; you slaughter the fatlings, but you do not feed the flock.

"The weak you have not strengthened, nor have you healed those who were sick, nor bound up the broken, nor brought back what was driven away, nor sought what was lost; but with force and cruelty you have ruled them" (Ezek. 34:2-4).

But also then, in the midst of a papal, hierarchical world church, the good shepherd Christ looked after his sheep by means of many people whose names have been forgotten.

NOTES

a. The medieval Christian was fascinated by the ascetic ideal of the mendicant orders: poverty and celibacy. These orders despised material possessions. Today the socialist ideal has tremendous appeal and influence. Socialism idolizes material possessions as the basis for a happy human life. With change in the societal situation, man also changed his thinking and philosophy. "Religion is the opium of the people." Affluence drives out the "fiction" of religion.

Absolute truths no longer exist. The socialist view eventually rejects God altogether and leads to nihilism.

b.   There is a remarkable similarity between the medieval rejection of material goods in order to serve God in a better way and the modern worship of material goods rather than the God of the covenant. Both viewpoints reject God's ordinance for society and boast that man can take care of himself. God's Word teaches food and clothing, money and goods, capital and labour, production and trade, ". . . nothing is to be refused if it is received with thanksgiving, for (these things are) sanctified by the word of God (his work) and prayer (our response)" (1 Tim. 4:4, 5). Paul typifies the rejection of earthly goods as well as their use without gratitude with these phrases: doctrines of demons, hypocrisy (1 Tim. 4:1, 2).

c.   Neither Francis of Assisi nor Karl Marx (1818-1883, the father of socialism) fought against the sins in the society of their time. Instead they fought against the sovereignty of God in society. They did not recognize and acknowledge Him as Lord over all of human life.

d.   1.   The false religiosity of the Middle Ages did nothing for the enormous poverty and misery of the people.

2.   The rejection of God's covenant by the Christian nations after the time of the Reformation provided socialism with the chance to influence the impoverished and socially oppressed multitudes in the countries of Europe, Africa, and Asia during the nineteenth and twentieth centuries.

e.   The question of our daily bread—our daily, material needs—is indeed a religious question, because the covenant in which we are allowed to live with our almighty God and Father also includes that daily bread. Francis, together with the apostate Christians of the Middle Ages, did not recognize this and rejected the idea of personal possessions. Marx, together with the godless Christians of his age, changed the matter of our daily bread into an all-encompassing issue by claiming that private ownership is theft. The major question on Mount Carmel (Elijah), however, was not "How do we get rain—wheat—bread", but "Who is God, the LORD or Baal" (1 Kings 18)?

f.   The powerful monastic and mendicant orders did not give an answer to this question. Socialism gives an answer that is totally against God's Word. It is sad to note that the Christian church in fact failed to build a truly Christian society, free of poverty and greed, because it was not aware of God's wisdom for the whole of our lives as contained in the Torah. All too often, the Bible was regarded as a book of religion and theology only.

g.   During the height of the famine in Egypt, Joseph bought all the land of the people. "Only the land of the priests he did not buy;

for the priests had rations allotted to them by Pharaoh, and they ate the rations which Pharaoh gave them; therefore they did not sell their lands" (Gen. 47:22). Also in Babylon and India, the priestly castes possessed extensive property. In Egypt the priests controlled one third of all the land, but they did not pay taxes. Just like these Eastern priests, many medieval monasteries owned enormous estates. Many Roman Catholic churches owned treasures of gold, silver, and precious stones as well as many relics. In the meantime, the population often went hungry. The Torah did not permit the tribe of Levi to own even one foot of soil in the land of Canaan (Num. 18:20; see also Num. 35:1ff) How much stronger the position of Christ's church would have been in its struggle against idolatry, also in a socio-economic respect, if the church had listened in obedience to the wisdom of the Torah.

12. "THE LIGHT SHINES IN THE DARKNESS" - John 1:5 - Part B

12.1 During the Middle Ages, the Lord kept and protected many thousands of faithful Christians as he had kept the seven thousand who did not bow their knees before Baal during the dangerous times of King Ahab. Among these were the Waldensians (Waldenses).

12.2 Peter Waldo (about 1150) probably came from the Swiss canton of Vaud, since he seemed to have been named after that place (Pierre Waldo). He was well-to-do and lived in the city of Lyons (remember Blandina and Ponticus). One of his friends died during a wild orgy. Perhaps this was the reason for his conversion; in any case, he turned to the Word of God and arranged the translation into French of parts of Scripture (the Psalms and the Gospels). He founded a community of men and women who at first occupied themselves with copying and translating Bible portions and later went out in pairs to bring God's Word to the people. Waldo gave his vast estate to his wife, and he shared the rest of his fortune with the poor. The Waldenses lived a simple and sober life and came to be known as the *Poor Men of Lyons*.

12.3 Although they were banned from Lyons, the followers of Waldo gained great influence in southern France and later also in northern Italy and Switzerland. They became well-known for their apostolic simplicity and their Bible teaching to the common folk in their native language. They were quiet, industrious citizens.

12.4 However, since they did not acknowledge the authority of the pope, Innocent III ordered a crusade against them. Throughout the centuries, they have suffered heavy persecutions—if only the valleys could speak! Whole villages were massacred under the slogan "Kill everyone, the Lord knows his own!" In Strasbourg, fifty Waldensians were burnt together at the same stake. And yet they persevered and have retained their characteristics until today. There are some seventy Waldensian congregations in Italy, still experiencing much opposition from the Roman Catholic clergy.

12.5 Their ecclesiastical logo shows a burning torch with the words, "the light shines in the darkness." And they did hold up the light of the gospel in the darkness of the Middle Ages, even though they were mistaken in their understanding of the gospel as a new law that must be obeyed rather than as the good tidings of God's lovingkindness, which allows man to walk with his God in the covenant of grace.

13. THE LIGHT OF GOD'S WORD OBSCURED BY MEDIEVAL SCHOLASTICISM

13.1 During the first centuries, the early Christians believed in and heartily confessed the Word of God. They gave their lives for it. To them it was the Truth; to them, God was Truth.

But during the Middle Ages, the church abandoned this trust in God's firm promises. The church did not keep the covenant with God. Its heart was not in it. The Bible was no longer read as the Word through which God speaks to us every day. The Bible was considered to be a book that contained various kinds of truths. Some of those truths could be accepted on the basis of intellectual reasoning rather than on the basis of God's authority. By using his intellectual powers, man could determine those truths for himself employing the philosophical methods of Aristotelian logic.

It was thought that man's intellect was not affected by sin. A Christian is an ordinary human (the level of nature) plus some additions (the level of grace). Medieval man came to put greater trust in his own power of reasoning than in divine Scripture. Scholarly thought, as practised in the *scholae* (institutes of higher learning) replaced the reverent and humble trust in the promises of God. Scholasticism is an academic discipline. The clever philosopher and the learned professor were deemed to be far superior to the ordinary church members who simply put their trust in God and gave themselves to Him with heart and mind. The terrible heresy of scholasticism attempts to explain God's Word with the help of a closed, logical, human system of thought. Scholastic learning replaces the loving respect for and trust in the Lord.

Famous universities came into existence in Paris (Sorbonne), Oxford, Cologne, and other places. Some of the greatest among the medieval scholastics were Anselm of Canterbury, Thomas Aquinas, John Duns Scotus, and William of Ockham.

13.2 Anselm of Canterbury (1033-1109). Against his will, Anselm was appointed bishop of Canterbury. He taught that God's existence could be proven in a logical, rational way. He reasoned that if God existed only in our mind and not in reality, he could not be perfect since he would then miss reality. Since God is perfect, it follows that he must exist. In his book, *Cur Deus Homo* (Why God Became Man), Anselm set for himself the task of rationally explaining Christ's virgin birth. But such rational explanations only obscure the inexplicable miracle of God's mercy in sending his Son. Anselm's motto was *"Credo ut intelligam"* (I believe so that I may understand and be able to make understandable). (And is such intellectual knowledge of God then to be followed by childlike trust in God?)

13.3 Thomas Aquinas (1225-1274). Despite the efforts of his brothers, who even imprisoned him in their parental castle near Naples, Thomas managed to escape and join the Dominican order. Later he became a world-famous professor at Paris. His most famous book is *Summa Theologiae* (Principles of Theology). For centuries, this book was regarded as the "bible" for the church, in fact replacing God's own Word. As the greatest among the church's scholars (the Calvin of the Roman Catholic church), he received the honourable title of *doctor angelicus*. But at the end of his life he admitted there is more to be learned at the foot of the cross than from scholarly treatises.

a.   Thomas distinguished two kinds of truths:

   1.   Intellectual truths, those that could be reasoned out logically (for instance, God's existence).

   2.   Religious truths, those that cannot be proven logically and therefore must be accepted on the basis of God's authority (for instance, the trinity—God is a triune God).

b.   Thomas Aquinas developed an extensive, logical system for the Roman Catholic world and life view, which has strongly influenced Roman Catholic thinking ever since.
       He spoke of a lower story and an upper story. The lower story is good within itself. Natural life unfolds to its highest level in a state controlled by kings and emperors. But only the church can give access to the ultimate, the heavenly things. The church of Rome reads the Bible through the glasses of Thomas Aquinas; Thomism is still a great power within the Roman Catholic church.

Upper Story:

POPE   So-called heavenly things:

CHURCH   - the higher
                            - clergy
SACRAMENTS   - grace

- -

Lower Story:

KING EMPEROR   So-called earthly things:

STATE   - laity
                            - nature
LIFE OF THE COMMON PEOPLE

13.4 John Duns Scotus (1226-1308) was an Englishman who belonged to the Franciscans. Little is known about his life. Scotus strongly objected to the smooth, logical system of Thomas Aquinas in which everything seemed to fit so easily and smoothly. Scotus invented another system of thought. His starting point was not God's *reason*ableness, on the basis of which everything might be explained *reason*ably, logically. Scotus started with God's will, God's absolute will and power for which there is no logical basis nor explanation. Till the present day, there is within the Roman Catholic church an ongoing dispute between the followers of Thomas Aquinas (often the Dominicans) and those of Scotus (often the Franciscans). The former have a greater influence than the latter.

13.5 William of Ockham (1280-1349). He also was an Englishman and also belonged to the Franciscan order. He was a student of Duns Scotus and later became professor at Oxford. The pope rejected Ockham's theology, and as a result, he was excommunicated. Ockham escaped from his prison at Avignon and died a victim of the Black Death.
    Following Scotus, he argued against Thomism, showing that nothing can be proven in a logical manner. Ockham claimed that we cannot prove, we can only believe. We must believe even those things that appear to go against our logical understanding. Ockham taught that we believe precisely because faith is illogical: *Credo quia absurdum.* That is the way God has ordained it. If God had wished, He could have called that which is good evil and could have commanded rather than forbidden murder and theft. God's will is pure, everything is his "unreasonable pleasure". In fact, there are two different kinds of truths: that which God reveals, however unreasonable that might be; and that which we construct

ourselves. Yes and no are standing dialectically over against each other, separating faith from reason. Therefore, Ockham could accept in faith what he rejected intellectually because the church (the pope) demanded and commanded it. Ockham placed his irrational system of theology over against the rationalist system of Thomism. But if Ockham was right, how can we then speak of absolute truths? Is it really possible to be certain about anything? Who and what may be trusted? Ockham claimed that there is no certainty in God's will; nobody is able to know what God wills from us, nor what will please him.

These ideas terrified the young Luther. He wrote, *"Ich bin von Ockham's Schule"*. Luther's major question was, How do I know for certain that God loves me?

By the end of the Middle Ages, man was losing his certainty of faith (cultural pessimism). No one seemed to remember that God does indeed transcend his own law but that he always remains faithful to that law. We can and may fully rely on his Word: He is our faithful Father.

NOTES

a. In Corinth, some members of the church claimed to have greater "knowledge" than others (Gnosticism). Paul wrote to them, "Knowledge (without love toward God and one's neighbour) puffs up, but love (with understanding and knowledge) edifies" and builds God's congregation. "And if anyone thinks that he knows anything, he knows nothing yet as he ought to know. But if anyone loves God, this one is known to Him" (1 Cor. 8:1-3). These texts speak of "bits" of knowledge, referring to unrelated truths, all sorts of pieces of information unrelated to the living God. If you think that you know a lot, you show that you have yet to learn a great deal! We may obtain true knowledge and certainty through a loving faith in God's reliable Word, and we need all our intellectual capacity for that.

b. "You shall love the Lord your God with all your heart, and with all your soul, and with all your mind" (Matt. 22:37). God's revelation is never illogical, that is, against our intellect (therefore we reject Ockham's view). It reaches far beyond our understanding (therefore we also reject the view of Thomas Aquinas). Many were "puffed up on behalf of one against the other" (1 Cor. 4:6). We cannot and we may not build a logical construct of the mighty God. That is a sin against the second commandment and is self-willed religion. Scripture speaks of the thoughts of one's heart (Gen. 6:5), of "the spirit of wisdom and revelation in the knowledge of Him" (Eph. 1:17), and the enlightenment of "the eyes of your understanding" (Eph. 1:18). Not our intellect, our *ratio*, but our heart is the centre of our humanity. Man is not primarily a reasonable-moral being; it is man's glory that he is a religious being, finding himself united with God with a faithful, trusting heart.

c. The influence of scholasticism is noticeable in expressions such as "We must maintain God as the source of all things," or "We must place Christ at the centre of our lives." If you speak in such a manner, you do not reverently acknowledge the living God, our almighty Father, and our Lord Jesus Christ, who sits at the right hand of God. Instead, you are busily building a system of thought in which you make room for your (dead) concept of God and Christ, "We must maintain. . . . We must place. . . ." This manner of speaking changes the green pastures of God's Word into a barren, intellectual wasteland; and in the meantime, the faithful go hungry. "He feeds on ashes" (Isa. 44:20). The intellectual products of man's imagination do not and cannot satisfy (see Isa. 44:6ff).

d. Thomas Aquinas belittles original sin. Original sin is merely considered the absence of the higher gifts of grace; no longer is sin regarded as the guilty transgression of God's law. As a consequence, Aquinas also belittles God's guilt-forgiving grace. He regards grace merely as the filling-in of whatever is missing in our human nature, which in itself is good. But God's Word teaches us the renewal of our whole life through regeneration, which is a new creation (Gal. 6:15). This new creation includes our intellectual abilities. Typically, Scripture speaks of the imagination of man's heart, which is evil from his youth (Gen. 8:21).

e. Scholasticism causes great uncertainty by forcing upon believers a human system of thought that replaces the gospel. The people became unconcerned and disinterested. One scholar after another invented a different system of thought. Whom could you believe anyway? The Word of the living God was rare (1 Sam. 3:1) in the time of the Middle Ages. The blessings of His covenant were not enjoyed, neither did the people understand the severity of God's covenant wrath over the evil and licentious life style of rich and poor.

f. 1. During the Middle Ages, Aristotle (Calvin called him "a blind heathen") was the teacher of Aquinas. In his *Summa Theologiae*, Thomas Aquinas does not refer to him directly by name but often writes: "The master says. . . ."

    2. During the time of the Reformation, the Lord revealed himself again through His Word to Luther and Calvin. Even though they themselves had received a thorough, scholastic education, they rejected, by the grace of God, the barren intellectual products of earlier times and listened again to the living Word of God and exalted in His covenant of grace and His lovingkindness.

3. During the Enlightenment (eighteenth century), Christianity elevated itself again above God's Word and even criticized Scripture itself. Not even the medieval scholars had dared to do that!

4. Nineteenth-century modernism removed whole pages from God's Word (for instance, miracles, the conception and virgin birth of Christ, his resurrection) and knelt down before a self-constructed image of Christ.

5. Twentieth-century theology rejects all intellectual products of the past and draws the ultimate consequence of (haughty) scholastic thought: God is dead (implying that the god of the medieval scholastics was very much alive). Faith in a living, personal God who speaks, acts, and interferes in nature and history is a total impossibility to modern man. He relies on his laboratories and space technology and, in the process, invents other gods: social awareness, humaneness. Other gods are already waiting along the sidelines for a chance to present themselves (for instance, the Eastern, mystical religions). Man cannot live without a god. Today's modernism presents Satan as an angel of light (2 Cor. 11-14), suggesting that he comes directly from before the throne of God with the (demythologized) Bible in his hands, claiming, "This is what Scripture has to say about God". And the LORD, the living covenant God who lives among his people here on earth, who loves those who fear him, who is angry over those who leave his covenant, who judges the earth, who rejoices over repenting sinners . . . that God is not acknowledged. He is placed outside and beyond the imaginations of the heart of modern man.

6. It was Isaiah who prophetically foresaw God's judgement: "In that day a man will cast away his idols of silver and his idols of gold, which they made each for himself to worship, to the moles and bats, to go into the clefts of the rocks, and into crags of the rugged rocks, from the terror of the LORD and the glory of His majesty, when He arises to shake the earth mightily. Sever yourselves from such a man whose breath is in his nostrils; for of what account is he?" (Isa. 2:20-22). "For You have forsaken Your people, the house of Jacob, because they are filled with eastern ways; they are soothsayers like the Philistines, and they are pleased with the children of foreigners" (Isa. 2:6).

7. Throughout the ages, God's Word was repeatedly obscured by Eastern Gnosticism, by Greek philosophies, by scholastic thought, by mysticism, and today by the spirit of the man of lawlessness who has gained great influence among

Christians by means of his authoritative and autonomous speaking and judging, as if he is a god (2 Thess. 2:3-12; see also Belgic Confession, Art. 2 and Art. 3).

14. THE LIGHT OF GOD'S WORD OBSCURED BY MEDIEVAL MYSTICISM

14.1 During the Middle Ages, Christ's church was not only under attack from scholasticism but also from mysticism. The word *mysticism* is derived from the Greek word *mu-ein*, which means "to close". The mystic must close eyes and ears to enable him to see God through inner enlightenment. Mystics place the inner experience of the immediate relationship with God above and in the place of the revealed, external word of God. But God's words heard in the heart are the real, the inner words of God. The mystics claim that man is in essence divine, that he is part of the godhead. By means of a series of mystical exercises, he can progress through various stages toward the highest level of mysticism, unity with the godhead. Since the immortal soul proceeds from God, it must also return to God to find rest in him. This is what the mystics call "the true peace of the soul".

14.2 Meister Eckhart (1260-1327) was the most influential and most dangerous mystic. He taught at the Dominican school of Cologne. He was a most revered teacher and confessor. He taught:
-       In the soul of every person is a spark of God; nowhere is God so really God as in the human soul.
-       The road to these divine heights goes via "holy poverty"; laying aside all earthly things (such as communion with others, with friends and relatives, the pleasures of life) and replacing these earthly things with strict ascetic abstinence, self-chastisement, self-sacrifice. Through hell to heaven! In this manner, man will grow toward unity with God; God is born in our soul.
-       Although Christ is able to assist as teacher, man does not need a saviour. Everyone should become a christ, that is, one in whom the godhead dwells in all fullness.

Eckhart's sermons on the peace of the soul were impressive and seemed quite scriptural. But he needed neither Scripture nor church; his mysticism worshipped the inner self, the "free, beautiful, and noble soul". His influence has been considerable, especially among the nuns of the Rhine valley and in southern Germany (The Brethren and Sisters of the Free Spirit).

14.3 Even the pope realized that all was not well with Eckhart's teachings. However, even though mysticism has nothing to do with the gospel of our Lord Jesus Christ, the frequent and spirited references to scriptural passages made it difficult to show fault with these teachings. Eckhart died two years before the papal verdict over his teachings was announced. His writings are still available today.

The church was forced to defend itself strongly against these heresies, especially during the sixteenth century and later (Munzer, Seb. Franck, Coornheert).

14.4 Mystical soul worship means that man, as his own saviour, concentrates strongly on his own self. This self-worship stands in direct contrast with what the Heidelberg Catechism calls, "the only comfort in life and death". The mystic rejects that we have been bought with Christ's precious blood to serve him with our whole heart and our whole life. Mysticism is in direct conflict with the covenantal relationship that we have with God in Jesus Christ. Modern-day mystics reject the Bible as meaningless and without significance.

Paul's letter to the Colossians is a continuous defence against these powerful evil spirits. Also today these spirits are powerful indeed, causing many to leave God's covenant and making them into people of "knowledge" and "experience" (but of human knowledge and human experience only—the New Age movement).

Colossians 1:13, 14: "He has delivered us from the power of darkness and translated us into the kingdom of the Son of His love, in whom we have redemption through His blood, the forgiveness of sins."

Colossians 2:3: ". . . in whom (Christ) are hidden all the treasures of wisdom and knowledge."

Colossians 2:9, 10: "For in Him dwells all the fullness of the Godhead bodily; and you are complete in Him, who is the head of all principality and power."

Colossians 2:16-23: "Therefore let no one judge you in food or in drink. . . ."

Eckhart's "dying to the world" is difficult in appearance only. "Dying unto sin" as taught in God's Word demands a daily struggle and self-denial rather than mystical self-development.

Colossians 3:1-17: "If then you were raised with Christ . . . put to death your members which are on earth: fornication, uncleanness, passion, . . . anger, wrath, malice, blasphemy, filthy language out of your mouth. . . ."

14.5 Some of Eckhart's pupils include
a.   John Tauler (1300-1361). He was a Dominican preacher in Strasbourg, drawing large audiences. He fearlessly visited the sick and the infirm during the terrible days of the Black Death. Tauler's

deeds roused the wrathful jealousy of the less-than-merciful clergy of his days. His teachings were not as extreme as those of Eckhart. Even so, he found the basis for the certainty of faith not in Scripture but in man himself. He admonished the people to "turn to themselves," since God's kingdom in truth was to be found within each person's soul. This was much better than trying to find peace in pilgrimages to Rome or Avignon.

b.   John of Ruysbroeck (1293-1381), the father of Dutch prose. He was born near Brussels and became a priest. Later he withdrew into mysticism. At Groenedaal (Green Valley) near Brussels, he founded a mystic community. Thomas à Kempis came under his influence. Scripture does not tell us to concern ourselves with mystical introspection, but we must practise self-examination, which means that we must continuously test ourselves against the norms of God's Word.

14.6 From this time dates a little booklet, written in the spirit of Eckhart's mysticism, *Theologia Germania*. The anonymous author writes about the "cross" that we have to bear. The cross is the inner experience of God's wrath. If a person has experienced this, then he has been in hell. But this hellish experience makes Christ rise within us. Adam (the understanding that we are different from God) dies within us, and Christ (the understanding that there is no difference between God and man) arises within us. In this way, the boundary between the Creator and creature is in effect removed. Luther was greatly influenced by this booklet while Calvin called it "poison which is potent enough to confuse the whole church!"

14.7 Mysticism has had great influence in Germany and the Netherlands. Mystics teach that Christ's birth, death, resurrection, and ascension are not redemptive-historical facts but are symbols of the "inner christ" in our hearts. Mysticism, therefore, is basically the idolatrous worship of the immortal soul as the place where the redemptive facts have taken place. And it is against this doctrine that Paul warns so strongly in Colossians 2:8: "Beware lest anyone cheat you through philosophy and empty deceit, according to the tradition of men, according to the basic principles of the world, and not according to Christ."

These are the spirits of this world, the demons who promote this kind of religiosity which appears to be so pious and serious but is, in all truth, from the devil.

15. MODERN DEVOTION

15.1 The influence of mysticism is particularly noticeable in a typically Dutch revival movement of the fourteenth century: the Brethren of the

Common Life. Their rather moderate mystical ideal of piety is known as the *modern devotion.*

15.2 The founder of this movement was Gerhard Groote (1340-1384). He was a magistrate's son from Deventer, Holland. While attending a fair in Cologne, a stranger asked him, "What do you seek here?" This question haunted him and eventually led to his conversion. He gave away his fortune and became a popular preacher, urging people to penitence (which is not the same as conversion). He was greatly distressed by the ignorance of the people, but he remained a faithful son of the Roman Catholic church. He founded communities of brethren living together, sharing goods, but without binding monastic vows. He promoted labour, literacy (copying Scripture), and the education of the people. The main aim of these communities was the promotion of a pious life of mystic self-examination and the practical exercise of the command to love. Groote died in 1384 after a visit to a sick friend.

The organizer of the Brethren of the Common Life was Groote's pupil and successor, Florentius Radewijns (1350-1400). He was the founder of a community at Windesheim near Zwolle (Holland). This community followed the rule of the Augustinian Canons.

15.3 The most well-known member of this movement was Thomas à Kempis (1379-1471). Born at Kempen (near Cologne), he became subprior of the monastery of St. Agnes near Zwolle. He copied the Bible four times and wrote many books. It is generally accepted that he is the author of the famous booklet *The Imitation of Christ.* This booklet does not deal with obedience in faith ("My sheep hear My voice, and I know them, and they follow Me," John 10:27) but with imitating the man Jesus. A nun at Dieperveen was bored by the daily chore of carrying wood for the fires until she discovered that this activity was, in fact, an imitation of Christ carrying the cross. In chapter 12 of his booklet (The Way of the Holy Cross), Thomas à Kempis speaks of self-crucifixion, but in a manner far different from the way that Paul speaks of the cross of affliction and persecution for Christ's sake in 2 Corinthians 6:3-10 and Galatians 6:14, 17. Thomas urged self-improvement, a task that is disheartening as well as impossible. Scripture tells us, on the other hand, that we may urge each other to believe in Christ, who has paid for all our sins and who renews us through a living faith. Mystics looked at themselves instead of looking to Christ, our Lord, who bought us. This little booklet has been translated into many languages, even into Arabic.

15.4 Johann Wessel of Gansfort (1419-1489). He was a native of Groningen and a pupil of Thomas à Kempis. A teacher of theology, philosophy, Greek, and Hebrew, he received the honourable name *Lux Mundi.*

15.5 By copying Scripture and preaching the gospel as well as a thorough study of the original languages, these brethren were instrumental in making God's Word available for the following generations. But sadly enough, they did not preach the scriptural way of faith in Christ but the way of self-invented religiosity by which the people were to gain salvation in their own strength.

16. DECLINE OF PAPAL POWER - 1294 - 1520

16.1 In their struggle with the German emperors, several popes called upon the French kings for help. This created obligations and fostered a feeling of importance and a sense of superiority among the French kings, who gradually came to regard themselves not only as equal to, but even as somewhat above, the papacy. This situation was bound to lead to conflict.

Boniface VIII (1294-1303) was an ambitious, arrogant, and vain person. He was the first pope to erect his own statues. At times he even appeared in public dressed in imperial clothes: I am Caesar! He published the famous bull, *Unam Sanctam*, in which he propounded the doctrine of the two swords (Luke 22:38). He claimed that the spiritual sword must be used by the church while the secular sword must be used for the church. This doctrine had already been taught by Pope Innocent III.

Boniface VIII came into conflict with the French king Philip IV on the question of taxation. The controversy ran high, and finally Boniface was imprisoned by the French king. He managed to escape but died shortly after "of chagrin and melancholy" (Latourette). A shockwave rolled across Europe: the pope imprisoned by a king!

Under strong pressure of the French kings, the papal court was moved from Rome to Avignon, a period known as the Babylonian exile of the papacy (1309-1377). The victory of the papacy began at Canossa (1077); its defeat was signalled by Avignon (1309). After returning to Rome, the papacy tried to break away from the French influence. The French cardinals retaliated by appointing their own pope at Avignon. In this way, the great schism of the Western church came about (1378-1415). During those years, the church had two popes, the one excommunicating the other.

16.2 Because of these developments, the latter half of the fourteenth century witnessed the end of the universal papal theocracy. Doubts arose about the divine authority of the papacy. As a result, several national churches attempted to gain their freedom from Rome. All this resulted in a new movement, known as the conciliar movement, which had as its main purpose the reformation of "head and members". This reform movement had a strong following among intellectuals, with Pierre D'Ailly (1350-1420) and John Gerson (1363-1429) from the Sorbonne University in Paris among the most well-known leaders. The great point of conflict was the question of how reformation must be achieved. Some argued that reformation must be brought about by the curia, the official body governing the church under the authority of the pope. Others maintained that it was the responsibility of a general council (conciliarism). Three such general councils were held: at Pisa (1409), at Constance (1414-1418)(John Hus, see 17.3 below), and at Basel (1431).

In the end, no one won. The conciliarists lost out, but the curia did not win either. The papacy was no longer a world power; the pope only maintained immediate control over his own church-state in Rome.

16.3 During the twentieth century, the old struggle between council and curia—between the conservative and hierarchical Vatican and the national synods of bishops demanding pastoral consultation and discussion—has renewed itself, fuelled by a modern spirit of democracy. It seems that at the moment, the curia (that is, the pope) has regained much of its power within the Roman Catholic world church.

17. "THE LIGHT SHINES IN THE DARKNESS" - John 1:5 - Part C

17.1 During the dark fourteenth century, the light of God's Word was probably seen most clearly in England through the work of John Wyclif (1320-1384). Wyclif was of noble birth and became professor at the university of Oxford. The English king was pleased with Wyclif's strong protest against papal taxation and guaranteed him a position as pastor of Lutterworth, which he held till his death in 1384.

Wyclif did for fourteenth-century England what Waldo had done for twelfth-century France: he sent out preachers in pairs to bring God's Word to the common people. Increasingly, he recognized the errors of the church: worship of relics, indulgences, purgatory, transubstantiation. Openly he condemned the papal hierarchy as anti-Christianity. But he refused to go to Rome to defend himself against the charge of heresy. The Dominicans constantly opposed and hindered him.

Thirty years after his death, the Council of Constance (1414-1418), which also ordered the execution of John Hus, condemned Wyclif's teachings and ordered his remains to be burnt and the ashes scattered.

17.2 Both the Cluniac monastic reform movement and the mendicant orders attempted to remedy many of the abuses in the church. Wyclif went further, however. He attacked the Roman Catholic doctrine. He is known as the first protestant since he accepted only the Word of God as his guide. Through his pupil, John Hus, his labours also yielded rich fruit in Bohemia.

17.3 John Hus (1369-1415) was born in southern Bohemia. Ordained as a priest in 1401, he preached in the Bethlehem Chapel at Prague. (This chapel was built from a gift that stipulated that this church was to be used only for the preaching of God's Word in the language of the people.) Hus was strongly influenced by Wyclif of Oxford. In those days, there were close ties between England and Bohemia since the English queen was a sister of the Bohemian king. The favour of the emperor, as well as Hus's own popularity with the people, protected him from the anathema of Rome. He attended the Council of Constance to defend himself but was treacherously imprisoned by the Dominicans, despite an imperial safe-conduct. The emperor's protests were countered with the argument, "You do not need to keep your word given to a heretic". Emperor Sigismund became known amongst the people as *Lugismund* (Lugen means "lie"; "a lying mouth"). Hus was burnt at the stake on his birthday, July 6, 1415. After that time, the worst of the heretics were often labelled *Hussite* (for instance, Luther). Fortunately, a century later the church was no longer as powerful, and Luther did not share the fate of Hus.

Hus was somewhat milder than Wyclif. For instance, he did not oppose the doctrine of purgatory nor of transubstantiation. But he fearlessly and fiercely attacked the doctrine of papal authority, and that was an unforgivable sin. The trial of Hus and the rejection of the teachings of Wyclif, with full consent of John Gerson, shows that also the conciliarists failed in their attempts toward reformation; they also refused to return to God's Word. The true root of the evil of the papacy was not recognized; restoration is not reformation.

17.4 The Hussite Wars (1419-1436). The treacherous murder of Hus caused great unrest throughout Bohemia. This led to open rebellion in Prague. The headquarters of the Hussites was Tabor (Taborites; see Judges 4:6). Under their skilful commander, Ziska, they defended themselves successfully against the papal troops. His successor, Prokop, turned defence into attack, and a bitter civil war ravaged southern Germany, Austria, and Hungary. The Taborites were more radical than Hus had been, and they disturbed the social order. The movement ended in fanaticism (compare this with the Anabaptists at Munster in the sixteenth century). It was thought that God wanted them to attack the Roman Catholic clergy in the same way as in Old Testament times the Israelites were commanded to destroy the Canaanites. Later, divisions arose about the negotiations with Rome and the attendance at the Council of Basel (1431).

a. It is remarkable that in the Hussite movement, for the first time, a whole nation opposed the authority of the pope. Bohemia was the first European nation that dared to openly reject the papal yoke.

b.   Later, the remaining Taborites and Waldensians formed the Bohemian and Moravian Brethren. We will meet them again on the estate of the Count of Zinzendorf as Hutterites.

17.5 The fall of Constantinople to the Turks (1453) brought great terror over Europe. Many scholars fled to safer territory, and this resulted in a renewed interest in scholarship, especially the study of the ancient languages of Greek, Latin, and Hebrew. This did not only prepare the ground for the later rediscovery of Scripture in the time of the Reformation, but it also caused a renewed interest in the suppressed secular philosophy of humanism and renaissance (a secular reformation, but the opposite of regeneration by faith).

One of the centres of these secular reform movements was Florence, the city of the Medici dynasty. A member of this family, and a later pope, spoke scathingly of the birth of Christ as "the fable of Bethlehem". Indeed, the so-called new theology of the twentieth century is not quite so young after all.

17.6 Girolamo Savonarola (1452-1498), born into a wealthy family, became a Dominican monk against the wishes of his family. As prior of Florence, the birthplace of the Italian Renaissance, he strongly attacked the social evils of his days, preaching hell and doom like a reborn John the Baptist. Attempts to entice him away from Florence with the promise of a cardinal's hat did not succeed. Savonarola's prophecies of a golden age, which would follow the city's repentance of its sins, seemed to be fulfilled when the invasion of Charles VIII of France forced the Medici rulers of Florence to flee. For three years Savonarola was the leader of the city. Florence was thoroughly purged of its wicked ways—but no more. The doctrine of the Roman Catholic church was left untouched. Savonarola did not oppose the unscriptural ideas of the Renaissance with the gospel of God's unique grace (*sola gratia*) but with a new gospel of good works. The conversion of Florence from a decadent city to a virtual monastery was a conversion under duress. He threw pearls before the swine, and they turned around and devoured him (see Matt. 7:6). Tired of the legalistic gospel enforced by espionage and secret police, the people turned against him. He was hanged and burnt in 1498. For a period of time, the societal structures of Florence had been changed somewhat, but the citizens themselves had not changed at all. Savonarola cannot be regarded as a genuine forerunner of the Great Reformation. At the time of his death, Luther was fifteen years old.

18. CHRIST'S CHURCH DURING THE MIDDLE AGES

18.1 For long periods of time, the church was under control of its enemies from within: popes, councils, false prophets (see Psalms 74 and 79). Many popes were wolves in sheep's clothing. The church was persecuted by the church! And that, indeed, is the most terrible form of persecution. Councils were often meetings of false prophets. Complicated but sterile theological systems (scholasticism) existed next to zealous piety, personal religiosity, and mysticism. There were popular preachers such as Berthold of Regensburg (ca. 1210-1272), and Johannes Brugman (ca. 1473), drawing crowds so huge that even the mighty cathedrals were barely large enough. They thundered damnation over the people because of their sins and painted vivid pictures of hell and doom to force repentance, preaching a religion of fear.

18.2 During the period of the Black Death (1348-1351), whole regions were depopulated. Deserted farms were common while at sea, ships floated about without a crew. It is estimated that 60 percent of Holland's population died as a result of this dreadful disease. Flagellants moved through the cities in large processions in futile attempts to move God to mercy. Self-chastisement (scourging) was thought to be a powerful way to persuade God. Such processions could last as long as thirty-three days (the number of Christ's years on earth) or even forty days (the number of the days of his temptation in the desert). Christ was regarded as the strict and merciless judge of the world while Mary and the saints were called upon to mediate and pacify. The churches grew rich because of the sins of the people; masses for the souls of the dead and indulgences were expensive. A simple and faithful trust in God and His Word was replaced by a typically pagan belief in a wrathful god who must be kept at bay by means of incantations, prayers, and rituals.

18.3 The ungodly who controlled the church persecuted the righteous. The papal Inquisition made use of a worldwide espionage network, placing the judgement of God over the world in the hands of man. It was claimed that the church did not thirst after blood and therefore the (often innocent) victims were delivered to the civil authorities and their henchmen for sentencing. Often the slightest deviation from the church-invented doctrine or precept could result in a death sentence. Witch hunts caused the death of many innocent widows, and pogroms against Jews occurred regularly.

18.4 One of the greatest heresies was, and still is, the doctrine that declares that the spiritual, the pious things are far removed from, and are greatly superior to, the things of everyday life (nature versus grace). The fruit of the Holy Spirit (Gal. 5) which is to be found in the daily lives of the Christians, was unknown because it was no longer recognized that the covenant of grace includes the whole of life.

18.5 Everything awaited the great act of a merciful God: the return of his Word of *sola gratia*.

IN THE BEGINNING WAS THE WORD

REFORMATION
AND
COUNTER-REFORMATION

1. THE LUTHERAN REFORMATION

1.1 With the sixteenth century, we enter a new period in history. The forces of change were powerful and many, such as the invention of printing and the discovery of America. However, the greatest force to bring renewal was the rediscovery of the Word of God. This may well be compared with the rediscovery of the Law during the reign of King Josiah (2 Kings 23:4-6). God planned great things for the continent of Europe during this period. Through the reformation of His church He caused "showers of blessing" (Ezek. 34:26)—covenant blessings—to come down, which brought welfare across the world. He broke asunder the bonds of papal hierarchy which, together with the absolutism of kings such as Henry VIII, Francis I, and Charles V, kept Europe prisoner. Pope Leo X (1513-1521), son of Lorenzo de Medici, was a connoisseur and patron of the arts, with a passion for instrumental and vocal music. But Judaism, the religion of Bethel which trusted in its own religiosity, strongly influenced the church. The reform movements of the fourteenth and fifteenth centuries had failed because they did not recognize the basic errors of the Roman Catholic church: its false doctrines. This was the situation until the glory of the Lord again shone over His church (see Isa. 60:1). God Himself is the source and the cause of every reformation; it is not the work of men. It is God Himself who calls His people back from error. *Reformation* means return to the Word of God, the renewed proclamation of the gospel as the tidings of God's grace.

1.2 During the Middle Ages, the gospel had been turned into a set of laws that demanded strict obedience. The eucharist, as an act of reconciling God with men, was the centre of the worship service. The church did not believe, and therefore could not preach, God's grace in Christ. But God gave His Word back to His church and saved it from the house of bondage of legalistic piety. The European Christian church was again placed in the marvellous light of the gospel. Luther was the preacher of that very gospel.

1.3   As a Roman Catholic, Luther tried to find an answer to the question, "How can I reconcile myself with God and appease his wrath?" Often he experienced a mortal fear of God. Although he did not want to become a monk at all, it was this fear that compelled him to enter an Augustinian monastery. The vicar-general of the order, Staupitz, tried to console him by suggesting that "whatever is missing in your works will be provided by Christ". But God kept him from achieving peace of mind in this manner. He remained uncertain, until the reformed Luther learned to ask, "How are you righteous before God?" The answer is through faith in Christ, without the works of the law". "The just shall live by faith" (Rom. 1:7). "Therefore, having been justified by faith, we have peace with God through our Lord Jesus Christ" (Rom. 5:1).

As a Roman Catholic monk, Luther literally shook with fear when reading the phrase *righteousness before God*. Was that not the wrath of God over his sins? Luther read these words through the glasses of Aristotle, believing that you get what you deserve. He had yet to learn how to read the Bible as the book of God's covenant of grace and reconciliation. Only after his conversion did he understand the scriptural meaning of this word. God's righteousness is the same as God's active lovingkindness by which He declares righteous all those who believe in Christ Jesus. "Gracious is the LORD, and righteous; Yes, our God is merciful" (Ps. 116:5). The Lord does not merely say things; He also honours His promises. That is His righteousness to all those who have their hope in Him.

a.   God's righteousness means He keeps His Word (see Ps. 31:2, 3).

b.   God's righteousness becomes visible especially in the mighty act of His mercy when He sent His Son for our salvation. He had promised this already in paradise. Indeed, the Lord is a righteous God, and a Saviour (Isa. 45:21).

c.   God also shows His righteousness by really and completely acquitting the guilt of everyone who trusts in Christ alone. He is faithful and righteous in forgiving our sins and cleansing us from all unrighteousness (1 John 1:9).

d.   "By the righteousness of our God and Saviour Jesus Christ," the Gentiles received "like precious faith" as that of the Israelites because God had already promised this to Abraham (2 Pet. 1:1).

e.   "Zion shall be redeemed with justice, and her penitents with righteousness" (Isa. 1:27). The righteousness of God is His truth and faithfulness. Since He promises salvation for Christ's sake, He will also do it.

f.   "Deliver me in Your righteousness, and cause me to escape" (Ps. 71:2). See also Psalm 143:1: "Hear my prayer, O LORD, Give ear to my supplications! In Your faithfulness answer me, and in Your righteousness." (Note the parallel between God's faithfulness and God's righteousness.) Does the twentieth-century church pray equally fervently to the Judge of the whole world for such righteousness in this age? Such a prayer requires a living faith in Christ. This is what the Roman Catholic Luther failed to see, even though he was pious and very religious. But faith in God is not the same as being religious. Therefore the author of Psalm 119 (verse 18) prayed, "Open my eyes, that I may see wondrous things from Your law." This man was not blind (neither was Luther); he could read, and yet he needed God to open his eyes.

g. The word *righteousness* does not always indicate God's faithfulness to His covenant. It often refers to our faithfulness, to our "new obedience" (Form for Baptism). Jesus urges us to keep His commands, for instance, "But seek first the kingdom of God and His righteousness, and all these things shall be added to you" (Matt. 6:33). During our life here on earth this seeking God's kingdom happens always in an imperfect way; therefore God declares us righteous by faith in Christ alone. Christ's righteousness is given to me and counted as mine "as if I never had committed sin" (Heidelberg Catechism, Lord's Day 23). Scriptures even give Christ the name, "The Lord of our righteousness" (Jer. 23:6; Jer. 33:16).

h. During the winter of 1512-1513 God opened Luther's eyes. But it took another four to five years of intensive study and meditation before he was able to publish the ninety-five theses.

1.4 Luther underwent a total change. "I felt as if I was born again. Immediately Scripture showed itself in a totally different light." One of his tasks was the supervision of the Augustinian monasteries in his region. During his travels, he was able to sow the seed of the gospel among his monastic brethren. And this seed was to bear fruit soon. Disturbed and annoyed by the scandalous practices with the indulgences, which led to careless and at times wanton conduct and life style, Luther composed and published ninety-five theses designed to invite an academic debate on these matters (October 31, 1517). (An indulgence is a document by means of which the sinner is able to purchase his salvation without repentance before the Lord.) During that same evening, he wrote a most humble and submissive letter to the archbishop of Mainz, his superior, showing that there certainly was no thought at all in Luther's mind of a church reformation.

1.5 *THESIS* 1: When our Lord and Master, Jesus Christ, says: "Repent ye," etc., he means that the entire life of the faithful should be a repentance.

 THESIS 32: Those who suppose that on account of their letters of indulgence they are sure of salvation will be eternally damned along with their teachers.

THESIS 62: The true treasure of the church is the most holy Gospel of God's glory and grace.

The Roman Catholic church regarded penance as a meritorious work which the faithful were required to perform every now and then. Luther spoke of penance as conversion and a total change of our whole life; penance is the fruit of God's love and the work of God's grace. Travelling monks and peddlers ensured that within a matter of weeks these theses were known throughout half of Europe, even in Rome. The battle began!

1.6   On June 20, 1520, the pope issued a bull against Luther: *Exsurge domine* (Arise, O Lord, and judge Thy cause. A wild boar has invaded Thy vineyard.) Luther was excommunicated. On December 10, 1520, he gave his answer by publicly burning a number of papal publications outside the gates of Wittenberg.

"Where will you go, Luther, when all men desert you?"

"*Sub caelo*," was Luther's answer, "under the heavens where God dwells."

1.7   The three great principles of the Reformation are:

SOLA FIDE	-	by faith alone: directed against the salvation through human works.
SOLA GRATIA	-	by grace alone: directed against the meritoriousness of our own works.
SOLA SCRIPTURA	-	Scripture alone: directed against tradition and ecclesiastical canon.

1.8   Some of Luther's writings:

Address to the German Nobility - August 1520. Luther makes an appeal to Emperor Charles V and the German nobility, calling upon them to reform the church since the pope refused to do this. It refuted the claims of the bishops and other clergy to political power.

The Babylonian Captivity of the Church - October 1520. Luther ridicules the empty show of the Roman Catholic church, which claims to be the mediator of salvation and therefore places a heavy burden of laws and precepts upon the believer.

The Freedom of a Christian - November 1520. Its contents can be summarized as follows: a Christian is completely free, not subject to any human being. At the same time, a Christian is also a willing servant and is willing to serve everyone. This book is a commentary on 1 Corinthians 9. A Christian does not live for his own pleasures, but he will willingly serve others so that many may be won for Christ and that one may be found to do the works of the Lord. Such is the freedom of the Christian.

The reading of these three booklets—written and published in the same year—brought light to many people who lived in the terrible darkness of uncertainty, fear, and ecclesiastical slavery.

Some of Luther's other writings include *The Bondage of the Will* (1525), written against the semipelagianism of Erasmus's *Diatribe on the Free Will*; the *Small Catechism* for the congregation and the *Large Catechism* for the pastors, both written in 1529; *Table Talk* (between 1531 and 1544); and many Bible commentaries.

2. OPPONENTS OF THE LUTHERAN REFORMATION

2.1   Soon enough, Luther was forced to defend himself against those who at first seemed to support him. One of these men was the famous Desiderius Erasmus (1469-1536). Erasmus was born in Rotterdam (Holland). The inscription on his statue in this city reads in translation: "Here rose the great sun which set at Basel". After a life of study and travel to almost all European countries, he died in the city of Basel in 1536.

At first Erasmus was sympathetic toward Luther. He loathed the papal control over the consciences of the people, exercised relentlessly with the help of the infamous Inquisition. He therefore regarded the collapse of the medieval world as a liberation; indeed, Erasmus believed that this freedom of conscience would allow man to reach full human development. He was, therefore, an optimistic humanist. The Roman Inquisition did not trust this man who ridiculed the monks and mercilessly satirized the shortcomings of the Roman Catholic church. But Erasmus never left this church. "I am not made of martyr stuff," he said. Luther commented, "He is as smooth as an eel, he wants to walk over eggs and not break any."

2.2   The disagreements between Luther and Erasmus came to a head when Erasmus, the most learned and famous man of Europe, published his book, *Diatribe on the Free Will*. The answer of the Augustinian monk in Germany was awaited eagerly and with anticipation in all the monasteries and university halls across Europe. And that answer came, passionately and fiercely. In *The Bondage of the Will*, Luther wrote, "You alone, Erasmus, have seen the heart of the matter, and you grabbed me by the throat because of it." As a latter-day Elijah, Luther turned against Erasmus, in whom he tasted not the faith of Scripture but the faith of reason. "What do you expect from man, Erasmus? Have you never read the Bible?" The father of lies used the deceitful promise of liberty to turn man against his God and in this way enslaved him again (John 8:44). For what reason did Christ come down to earth? Erasmus denied the heart of the gospel.

Even more powerful was the second part of Luther's answer: *sola gratia*. In all things man is dependent on the grace of God. Those who are Christ's are completely new creatures; they share his life and future. That is the true reasonableness of faith, and that is true morality. Let us dare to live in justification by faith alone! Indeed, the die was cast: Luther totally rejected Erasmus's humanism.

These two booklets have been of enormous influence and importance in the history of the church. They show two totally different and opposing viewpoints: Luther defended the belief in the Christ of Scripture while Erasmus propounded the belief in autonomous, free (from God) man. With apocalyptic and prophetic, clarity Luther saw the end result of that belief in man. His evaluation has been proven correct by the history of the Enlightenment of the eighteenth century and the radical lawlessness of the twentieth century.

Erasmus did not recognize this demonic struggle for what it was—a desperate attempt to retain some of that "being like God" (see Gen. 3:5). Luther, on the other hand, realized this so much the more. Erasmus was neither hot nor cold. He was lukewarm (Rev. 3:16). Luther strongly affirmed the absolute sovereignty of God's good pleasure and the dignity of the gospel over against the humanistic doctrine of the free will. This doctrine taught that Christ is indeed the teacher of humanity; but so were famous philosophers such as Plato and Seneca, who were also inspired. The gospel was not the only form of divine inspiration; it was merely of a form higher than that of the philosophers.

The Son of God used the struggle between Luther and Erasmus to gather, protect, and preserve his church in the sixteenth century (Heidelberg Catechism, Lord's Day 21).

a.   Erasmus indirectly served the cause of the Reformation by publishing the New Testament in its original Greek text.
b.   Erasmus is the forerunner of Arminianism, the Enlightenment, as well as liberal protestantism. He is highly respected in the circles of the United Nations and UNESCO.

2.3   During the period that Luther was in hiding at the Wartburg castle, two "prophets" arrived at Wittenberg during the month of December 1521: Nicholaus Storch and Markus Stubner, pupils of the fanatic Thomas Munzer of Zwickau. Not only did these men reject all human authority in the church, they also rejected the authority of God's Word, claiming that "Luther has freed us from the Roman pope, but we now also need to be freed from the paper pope!" These fanatics claimed to live according to the "inner light" but in fact followed the corrupt and sinful impulses of their own heart. Urging violence against the church, they destroyed the images in the churches of Wittenberg and disturbed public and social life in the city. Melanchthon could not contain them, and another of Luther's friends, Karlstadt, even came under their influence.

Hearing of these disturbing events, Luther fearlessly returned to Wittenberg. From March 9 through March 16, 1522, he preached his famous sermons on the theme, "I will force no one." No drastic changes in the worship services were necessary as long as the gospel was preached. The Roman Catholic superstitions and heresies must be banished. In this way peace was restored; however, these events led to Luther's rejection of medieval mysticism.

In the twentieth century, Thomas Munzer appears to have regained some of his popularity. His writings have been republished while some even claim that Munzer rather than Luther was the real reformer of the German church. A modern German play characterizes Luther as a capitalist and Munzer as the revolutionary renewer of society.

2.4   The sixteenth century was an age of poverty, particularly in rural areas. Many peasants lived as virtual slaves of their landlord. These people listened to Luther's sermons on liberty but thought that liberty meant freedom from law and authority. They openly revolted against the rich landlords and swept across the countryside, murdering and looting. The Reformation was in grave danger. Luther was forced to appeal to the princes and rulers for help to contain this wild revolution. In his sermons, he emphasized the authority of the princes (Rom. 13).

The Peasants' Revolt was suppressed in blood. It is said that some 100,000 peasants lost their lives. Munzer was beheaded. Luther recognized the social injustice that plagued the society of his days, but he maintained that the Reformation was no revolution. He sharply condemned the bestialities of the princes: "The devils which once possessed the peasants have now gone to dwell in the princes. God will punish them."

3. EXPANSION OF THE LUTHERAN REFORMATION

3.1   God's merciful return to His church is shown in the great hunger and thirst after the gospel that He caused in the people of the sixteenth century. Within a period of two months, two thousand copies of the New Testament were sold. During each of the years 1522 through 1572 (except for three of those years), a new edition of the Bible was published. Many monasteries turned into centres of reformation, especially those of Luther's order, the Augustinians.

3.2   The first edict against the new faith was issued in 1521. The first martyrs were Augustinian monks from Antwerp, Hendrik Voes and John Van Essen (July 1, 1523). The inquisitor, Jacob Van Hoogstraten, was greatly distressed because of what he thought to be the terrible necessity of the execution of these men. But did he think of Jesus' words to his disciples: ". . . yes, the time is coming that whoever kills you will think that he offers God service" (John 16:2)? The prior of Antwerp, Jacob Spreng, managed to escape to Wittenberg; his successor, Hendrik Van Zutphen, was executed in 1523. Hearing of these terrible events, Luther comforted his hearers with the words of Psalm 116: "Precious in the sight of the LORD is the death of His saints."

The obedience of these martyrs was a seed for the church. The first martyr (blood witness) in the northern Netherlands was Jan Pistorius, a parish priest at Woerden (1525). The professors of the University of Louvain and Paris were among the fiercest and the most fanatic persecutors, caught as they were in their self-made theological systems, which they regarded as God's truth.

3.3   The northern regions of Germany were mainly Lutheran while the southern regions remained under Roman Catholic control. Later, Calvinism gained influence in the western regions, including the areas of Wezel, Nassau-Dillenburg, and the Palatinate with Heidelberg as centre.

Outside of Germany, the Lutheran Reformation gained ground in the Scandinavian countries through the work of Luther's friend Bugenhagen. In these countries, the Lutheran church has been introduced by the authorities and elevated to state church. This is also the case in the German provinces around the Baltic Sea. The Lutheran state church in these countries is quite similar to the Anglican church in England; both were not willing to reject the Roman Catholic ritualistic worship services completely.

4. CHARACTERISTICS OF THE LUTHERAN REFORMATION

4.1   The most characteristic aspect of the Lutheran Reformation is the proclamation of God's grace by which the sinner is declared innocent. Calvin went much further; he taught that man must not only be freed from guilt, he must also live to the honour and glory of God. When you are involved in an accident, you must not only be saved from serious bodily harm but you must also be brought to your destination. Thus, Luther and Calvin emphasized different things in their teachings. These differences were initially not of a critical nature and could well be explained historically. Luther, living in darkness and the shadow of death, was the first to see something of the tremendous light of God's grace. Calvin, living almost a generation later, was destined to teach the church to walk in the way of peace (Luke 1:79) to the honour and glory of God. Neither Luther nor Calvin attempted to separate God's grace (in declaring the sinner innocent—Luther) from God's honour (in his sovereignty over the whole of our life—Calvin); the two elements are inseparable.

4.2 Although Luther rejected ecclesiastical hierarchy, he failed to conquer the evil of caesaropapism. During the revolt of the peasants, he called upon the princes and rulers to protect the church and suppress the rebellion. With this action, he emphasized the importance of the rulers for the government of the church. The result was that control by the pope was exchanged for control by the civil government. The Lutheran church came under state control. This relationship between church and state has had bad consequences for Germany in the events of the following centuries.

4.3 These developments were helped along by Luther's doctrine of the two realms: the spiritual realm of the gospel and the secular realm of the state. Although the office of preacher was restored, Luther failed to restore the offices of the elders and deacons. The local Lutheran church was, therefore, not ruled by a consistory but by the local civil authorities. It was Calvin who showed the scriptural interpretation of the offices in the church and restored them to their apostolic form.

4.4 Luther rejected the Roman Catholic doctrine of transubstantiation, but he went astray in the doctrine of consubstantiation.

4.5 Because of the political situation in Germany, Luther's efforts to reform the whole of life—private as well as public life—met with little success. Calvin, living almost a generation later, was much more successful in this. After Luther's death, his followers often neglected to emphasize the importance of the gospel for political as well as social life.

4.6 Luther rejected everything that proved to be in direct conflict with God's Word. Calvin accepted only those things that the Word of God teaches directly. Therefore, Luther retained altars, images, and crucifixes in the church while Calvin abolished all these things. These things show that in a number of ways, Lutheranism remained close to Roman Catholicism.

4.7 *ECCLESIA REFORMATA SEMPER REFORMANDA.* Once the church has been reformed, it must continue to reform itself to God's Word. Some of the things that Luther accepted—perhaps under duress—were accepted by his followers as statements of doctrine. (See the story of Joshua and the generations that followed him during the time of the Judges, a time of continual deformation.) For these reasons, the churches of the Lutheran and Calvinist Reformation remained separate.

5. CONSOLIDATION OF THE LUTHERAN REFORMATION

5.1   Political Consolidation

a.   1521: The Edict of Worms condemned Luther. The pope had excommunicated Luther in 1520. Now he was also outlawed by the emperor. His writings were to be burned. His followers were to be persecuted. However, this edict was virtually ignored throughout Germany because the population refused to cooperate while Charles V urgently needed the help of the German princes in his wars with the French and the Turks. (See Rev. 12:16: "But the earth helped the woman. . . .")

b.   1555: The Peace of Augsburg seemed to bring equality for the protestants. The pope was furious. Since the beginnings of the papal church, no heretic had ever been able to claim equal rights with the church. The unity of the medieval church—often maintained by force and with violence—was broken. But the unity of Christ's church was to be restored in truth, in the unity of the true faith, not by political force or agreement. The "new faith" was publicly accepted. This was an enormous gain over the Middle Ages. However, total religious freedom had not been achieved as yet. The treaty of Augsburg concerned the Lutherans only and with the additional restriction that the ruler of the territory determined the religion of the territory: *Cujus regio eius religio.*

c.   1648: The Peace of Munster brought an end to the terrible Thirty Years War. This treaty has been of enormous importance in the history of Europe since it affected European politics for centuries to come. It brought equality for the Roman Catholics, the Lutherans, and the Calvinists. It also rebuffed the offensive of the Counter-Reformation and signalled the end of the Roman Catholic dominance over Europe.

5.2   The most important confession of the Lutheran church is the *Augsburg Confession* (1530), written by Melanchthon. Despite his objections against its doctrine of the Lord's Supper, Calvin would have gladly accepted this confession if only this would have brought unity.

For some years after Luther's death (the period from 1550 to 1580), his followers were involved in intense and often bitter theological struggles which resulted in the *Formula of Concord* (1577). This concord prevented further controversies and maintained the basic principles of the Lutheran Reformation.

1580: *Book of Concord.* This book contained the Lutheran ecclesiastical documents: the Augsburg Confession, the Formula of Concord, and the smaller and larger Lutheran catechisms. The acceptance of these confessional documents made the breach between Lutherans and Calvinists in fact irreparable.

Since 1580, the Lutheran Reformation stands between the Roman Catholic church and the Calvinist Reformation. "Wittenberg" stands between "Rome" and "Geneva". "Wittenberg" looks back to "Rome" in its doctrine of the Lord's Supper and the Reformed liturgy. "Wittenberg" looks to "Geneva" in the principles of sola scriptura, sola fide, sola gratia.

6. STAGNATION AND DETERIORATION OF THE LUTHERAN REFORMATION

6.1 After 1580, confessionalism constricted the Lutheran churches. The people no longer understood that a Reformed church is a constantly reforming church: ecclesia reformata semper reformanda.

6.2 The attacks of the Counter-Reformation (the Council of Trent and the Jesuit order) resulted in the loss of territory for the Reformation, including regions of Austria and Bavaria.

6.3 Charles V did not succeed in the destruction of the Reformation. However, some one hundred years later it was the Emperor Ferdinand II (1578-1637), with his cunning and cruel generals Tilly, Wallenstein, and Pappenheim, who almost succeeded where Charles V had failed. They threatened to regain political dominance over Europe for the house of Hapsburg (Spain-Austria), a dominance that was lost in the Eighty Years War between Spain and the Netherlands.

But not even Roman Catholic France was prepared to accept such political developments. At the request of the protestant German princes and with the encouragement and support of Roman Catholic France (Cardinal Richelieu), the Swedish king Gustavus Adolphus marched against the German emperor. This Swede was destined to become the saviour of the Lutheran Reformation. He died in the battle of Lutzen (1632). It is said that in the Swedish army a man could not become rich, but he could gain his salvation. This saying characterizes the Christian attitude of both king and officers.

The struggle between the Reformation and the Counter-Reformation forms the background of and led to the terrible Thirty Years War that was fought in Germany, ravaging the country (1618-1648).

7. THE SWISS REFORMATION: ULRICH ZWINGLI

7.1 Zwingli (1484-1531), was born in Wildhaus as the son of a village magistrate. While studying at the University of Basel, he came under the influence of Erasmus. Zwingli's later life shows that he was interested not only in humanism but also in politics and (Swiss) nationalism. He strongly opposed the practice of his fellow countrymen to hire themselves out as mercenaries (a practice known as *Reislaufen*, leaving wife and children behind in poverty) to seek adventure and fortune as professional soldiers in foreign armies. Often these men returned as invalid victims of the war, if they returned at all.

As pastor of Einsiedeln, Zwingli preached forcefully against the idolatrous worship of the local statue of Mary, which was said to have miraculous powers. After reading the works of Luther, he also began to explain Scripture, often using a whole chapter as the text for his sermons. By 1523, Zwingli's influence was taking hold, and the city of Zurich moved toward accepting the ideas of the Reformation.

Zwingli's fellow reformer at Basel was Oecolampadius (1482-1531).

7.2 A civil war threatened between the Roman Catholic and the protestant cantons of Switzerland. Zwingli urged an alliance between the protestant cantons and the protestants of Germany, but he recognized that theological unity with Luther's followers was imperative in order to bring about this political goal.

7.3 Zwingli's meeting with Luther at Marburg in 1529 is known as the Marburg Colloquy. Both men brought along their supporters. The critical point was the interpretation of the Lord's Supper. With chalk, Luther wrote down the words, "This is my body" on the table and maintained forcefully, "Let these words stand!" Karlstadt, Luther's friend, explained it this way: at the very moment the Lord spoke these words, He pointed at himself. Therefore the Lord is bodily present in, with, and under the form of that piece of bread used during the eucharist (the doctrine of consubstantiation).

Perhaps Zwingli opposed Luther more with scholarly reasoning than with God's Word. He argued more or less in the following manner: "Do you really believe this, Luther? Surely you recognize this as Roman foolishness!" Luther, however, thought to recognize in Zwingli's arguments the intellectual haughtiness of Erasmus, who also sneered at the so-called miracles. Perhaps in reaction to this, Luther maintained his belief in miracles and replied, "Even if the Lord had changed into a horse shoe, I would still believe despite all the scholarship of Erasmus and Zwingli." Zwingli answered, "The words of the Lord remind us of the sufferings of Christ, and in that manner we remember Him. No more is meant!" But Luther rejected this position, arguing that if the primary meaning of the Lord's Supper was our remembrance of Christ's sufferings, we would strengthen ourselves in our faith, and the Holy Supper would no longer be God's sacrament. Although the two reformers agreed on most articles framed at Marburg, they could not agree on the explanation of the Lord's Supper, and further discussions were fruitless.

-    Zwingli did not understand that in the Lord's Supper Christ presents himself to us as a gift.
-    Luther did not understand that, "For the support of the spiritual and heavenly life, which believers have, He has sent them a living bread which came down from heaven, namely Jesus Christ, who nourishes and sustains the spiritual life of the believers when He is eaten by them, that is, spiritually appropriated and received by faith. . . . This banquet is a spiritual table . . ." (Belgic Confession, Art. 35).

7.4   Almost moved to tears, Zwingli exclaimed, "The men from Wittenberg are the people with whom I most desire to be one." Luther, speaking of Zwingli's friend Bucer said, "It is evident that we do not have the same spirit." Luther refused a handshake as a sign of unity of faith. And thus they parted.

7.5   Zwingli's fears came true; war broke out in Switzerland. The reformer died on the battlefield of Cappel on October 11, 1531. His weapons, together with his heavily damaged helmet, are kept in a Zurich museum. His brother died that same day.

Zwingli was not able to bring his work of reformation to completion. His successor, Johann Heinrich Bullinger, was strongly influenced by Calvin. Zwingli's break with Rome was perhaps not as dramatic as Luther's. He attempted to reform the church from within. He missed the deeply emotional concern of Luther, yet he did not have the broad and deep insights of Calvin.

8. THE CALVINIST REFORMATION: JOHN CALVIN

8.1   Calvin's life may be divided into four periods:
-    1509-1536: Youth and preparation
-    1536-1538: First stay in Geneva
-    1538-1541: Strasbourg
-    1541-1564: Second stay in Geneva

8.2   *Youth and Preparation: 1509-1536.* Calvin was born in Noyon, in the province of Picardy in northern France. Because of the friendship of his parents with a wealthy nobleman, the young Calvin received an aristocratic education that allowed him to move easily within the circles of the nobility. Although originally destined to be a priest, a dispute between his father and the church authorities changed these plans, and Calvin went to study law at the universities of Orleans and Bourges. After the death of his father, he continued his studies in Paris where he attended lectures in both Greek and Hebrew. During this period in Paris, he already attended secret protestant meetings.

In 1533, Calvin was forced to flee from Paris. It was thought, and most probably with good reason, that he had been instrumental in writing the rectorial address for his friend Nicholas Cop, the son of a royal physician.

A wearisome life of wandering followed. He preached in cellars and caves, celebrating the Lord's Supper by torchlight with a rock as a table. For three years he travelled between France, Switzerland, and Italy. In Italy, he was the guest of the Countess of Ferrara, the sister of the French king Francis I. Throughout his life, Calvin maintained contact with this woman who suffered so much for the sake of the gospel. His last letter was addressed to her.

Meanwhile, he continued working toward the publication of his major work: *Institutes of the Christian Religion*, with its famous dedication to King Francis I. This book was to be published in Basel. While on his way to this city, Calvin arrived at Geneva in July 1536. It was then that Guillaume Farel begged him to stay to help with the work of reformation in that city. Calvin refused, claiming that he was too young and that he needed peace to continue his studies. Farel adjured him, "You are following your own wishes, and I declare, in the name of God Almighty, that if you do not assist us in this work of the Lord, the Lord will punish you for seeking your own interests rather than His!" Later Calvin recalled this scene, "By this imprecation I was so stricken with terror that I desisted from the journey which I had undertaken." Calvin became a minister of religion in Geneva.

8.3 *First Stay in Geneva: 1536-1538 - Surveying the Difficulties.* The unknown Frenchman commenced work as a preacher in the Genevan cathedral of St. Pierre. Remuneration was not discussed. Soon Calvin's work met with opposition. Things came to a head when he tried to introduce a church order in which he wished to give the church its own authority and autonomy. Church discipline had been exercised by the civil authorities, but this had deteriorated into some kind of policing of the people. Calvin maintained that church discipline was the responsibility of a church council.

The institution of a church council and the introduction of a church order were major steps forward in the history of the Reformation. The city magistrates, however, refused to surrender their power over the church. Feelings against Calvin also ran high among the people. He was almost drowned in the Rhone River; angry fists attempted to break down the door of his house; fire arms were discharged under his window during the night. Later Calvin wrote that it was a miracle that no blood had been shed.

Both Calvin and Farel were banished from the city in April 1538.

8.4 *Strasbourg: 1538-1541 - Preparation for Further Struggle.* Martin Bucer invited Calvin to come to Strasbourg. Farel left for Neuchatel. Both the city of Emden in the north and the city of Strasbourg in the south were cities of refuge for protestant refugees from across Europe. Calvin became a minister of the French refugee church in Strasbourg, and under his preaching, many Anabaptists were brought back to the truth of Scripture, among them a certain Stordeur. Later Calvin married Stordeur's widow, Idelette de Bure.

As a further result of Bucer's and Calvin's labours, Strasbourg became a centre of Reformed liturgical renewal of the church. The beginnings of a Reformed psalter are found in this city. During this time, Calvin wrote his famous *Reply to Sadoleto*. Sadoleto was the cardinal of Lyons who shrewdly made use of Calvin's absence from Geneva to bring that city back into the papal fold.

Calvin's years in Strasbourg were among the happiest of his life.

8.5 *Second Stay in Geneva: 1541-1555 - Years of Struggle.* Much against his will Calvin finally yielded to urgent requests to return to Geneva. Calvin's motto was, *Cor meum tibi offero domine prompte et sincere* (My heart for thy cause I offer thee, Lord, promptly and sincerely). He received a most honourable reception, and as if nothing had happened, Calvin continued the exposition of Scripture at the very point where it had been interrupted some years before.

For the first time since the days of the apostles, the scriptural organization of the church with the offices of preachers and elders was restored. The *Ordonnances Ecclesiastiques* of 1541 described the authority and the responsibilities of the local congregation. The church of Geneva became a truly Reformed church, free from the influences of civil authorities and ruled by its office bearers in accordance with God's Word. There was no hierarchy, no caesaropapism, no consistorialism as in the Lutheran churches. In 1544, Calvin proposed the abolition of ecclesiastical feast days.

However, despite all these advances, he was forced at times to give in to the demands of the city fathers. It took years before all opposition in Geneva had been subdued. The Libertines in particular were strongly opposed to the Reformation. They neither accepted the political authority of the Roman Catholic Count of Savoy nor the spiritual authority of God's Word. Some of Geneva's most prominent citizens were Libertines, such as Ami Perrin and Philibert Berthelier. Perrin's father-in-law had been disciplined by the consistory for adultery and his wife because of immoral dancing. Berthelier had been refused admission to the Lord's Supper. In a mood of defiance, the city magistrates revoked these censures, but Calvin was not to be intimidated. He declared publicly, "You may kill me, but you cannot force me to hand out God's bread to those who are unworthy to receive it." That Sunday a massacre was expected, but Berthelier did not dare to come to church to celebrate the Lord's Supper.

a. Calvin and his followers had reason for fear since participation in the Lord's Supper was considered a status symbol of good citizenship, similar to the attendance of the mass during the Middle Ages. Berthelier was a citizen of good repute and could ill afford to be insulted by Calvin who was, after all, a stranger. In this case, the consistory certainly could not rely on the city magistrates to keep the public peace. The tension in the packed St. Pierre cathedral was almost visible. But Berthelier stayed at home. During the afternoon service, Calvin held what many believed to be his farewell sermon, using Acts 20:17-38 as his text. This passage is Paul's farewell address to the elders of Ephesus on the beach of Miletus. Calvin ended his sermon with the words, ". . . and now I commend you to God and to the words of His grace" (verse 32a). He then closed his Bible and went home, pale, sick, and with a bleeding heart, fully expecting to be banished from the city for a second time. But nothing happened.

b. Doumergue, one of Calvin's biographers, compares this episode with Ambrose's refusal to admit the Roman Emperor Theodosius after the massacre of the Thessalonians and with Luther's brave defiance of the most powerful of princes of his day, Charles V. Even his opponent-biographers admit that the events of that particular Sunday were decisive in the struggle between ecclesiastic and civil authority, the struggle for the freedom and autonomy of Christ's congregation and the authority of the consistory.

c. When requesting admission to the Lord's table you promise to submit yourself willingly "to the ad nonition and discipline of the church, if you should become delinquent in doctrine or life. . . ." Therefore, when the consistory exercises discipline and publicly mentions the name of a sinner, he or she cannot appeal to the civil judge on the grounds of libel. Such a person, however, may always request the advice of the sister churches.

d. Berthelier, protector of and lawyer for Michael Servetus (whose case was yet to be investigated), was refused participation in the Lord's Supper because of immorality and drunkenness. In drunken folly and together with a few armed friends, he had followed a minister of religion all the way to the door of his house, threatening and abusing this innocent man.

e. Pierre Ameaux, manufacturer of playing cards and married to a most licentious woman, openly abused Calvin. He was forced to confess his sins publicly by walking penitently through the city. A father who cursed his son during a hunting expedition was sentenced to three days in prison. Laws were introduced to combat debauchery and excessive luxury (without forcing anyone into a life of poverty!).

Calvin's strongest weapon against immorality and licence in this frivolous city was the preaching of God's Word and church discipline. "And this is to be done in all moderation so that no one is offended by its harshness; also the punishments must not be harsh, but must lead the sinner to repentance before the Lord."

The events surrounding the controversial figure of Michael Servetus are still used to heap abuse on Calvin. This Spanish physician had been condemned to death by the Inquisition. He managed to escape, unfortunately, to Geneva. Calvin had been involved with him before, and the two were fierce opponents. Servetus strongly attacked Calvin's *Institutes* by publishing his own *Restitutio Christianismi*. His attacks on the doctrine of the trinity were utterly blasphemous. He decried those teachings as *Athanasianum satanasianum*. This man, then, arrived in Geneva. The city magistrates (with a Libertine majority) ordered his arrest. Although Calvin requested clemency, Servetus was burnt to death as a heretic on October 27, 1553. Both Roman Catholics and protestants agreed with the judgement and the sentence.

The agreements with Zwingli's successor, Henry Bullinger, about the interpretation of the Lord's Supper must have been most welcome and gave moments of joy and gratitude during those difficult times of constant struggle. The *Agreement of Zurich* was signed in 1549, and the Swiss Reformation moved more and more in a Calvinist direction. Sadly enough, the breach with the Lutherans widened. In that same year, Calvin's wife died (1549). Her last words were, "Oh, glorious resurrection!"

In 1555, many refugees obtained Genevan citizenship. This resulted in a magistracy which was more favourably inclined toward the Reformation and Calvin. After his major opponents were forced from the city following an unsuccessful attack on Calvin's life, the Word of God gained the upper hand in Geneva.

8.6 *Second Stay in Geneva: 1555-1564 - Years of Peace and Consolidation.* Now that piety and godliness ruled its public life, Geneva became the lighted candle, a city on a mountain top. In 1559, Calvin founded a university, the Genevan Academy. At its opening, already nine hundred students had enrolled. The first principal was Theodore Beza, later Calvin's successor. This institution greatly influenced the Reformation in many countries. Among its students were counted John Knox, Olevianus, and Marnix of St. Aldegonde.

In addition to his major work, *Institutes of the Christian Religion*, Calvin wrote commentaries on almost all of the Bible books. Usually he dedicated these volumes to kings, princes, and other persons of importance in England, France, Poland, Sweden, and Denmark in an attempt to win them for the Reformation. He maintained correspondence with men and women throughout Europe. More than four thousand letters have been found while still more sermons are being discovered in the Genevan archives in addition to the twenty-one hundred already available. The *Institutes* has been translated into many languages, including Spanish and Japanese.

Calvin died on Saturday, May 27, 1564, physically worn out. His health was badly affected by his fierce struggles and ceaseless labours; but just before his death, he had enjoyed a few days without illness or pain. Soon after his burial, even the location of his grave site had been forgotten. Yet in the Lord, his labours had not been in vain. (1 Cor. 15:58).

Indeed, the Reformation that started in Wittenberg (Luther) and seemed to remain solely a German concern became a European movement because of Geneva (Calvin). Later, when the gospel reached America by means of England, it became a truly worldwide church Reformation.

9. CHARACTERISTICS OF THE CALVINIST REFORMATION

9.1 The major characteristic of the Calvinist Reformation is the preaching of the sovereignty of God's Word over the whole of life.

a. During the Middle Ages, the Roman Catholic church was a church of priests who controlled all of life. The great cathedrals rose high above the humblest dwellings. Every civil council had at least one priest among its members. But an open Bible was not found in the churches nor in the homes. The church controlled God's grace by means of the sacraments and was sovereign in the exercise of its authority. This was no less than antichristian papal hierarchy.

b. During the sixteenth century, God broke the stranglehold that the papal sacramental church and its priests had over the believers.

c. The Reformation brought all of life under the rule of God's Word.

d. The proponents of the Renaissance and the followers of humanism rejected the authority of the papal church. They also rejected the sovereignty of God's Word. Public life was considered neutral territory. Paganism—outlawed in Europe since the time of Constantine the Great—made its triumphant reentry in the form of humanism and the Renaissance. The Reformation succeeded in limiting the influence of these forms of paganism for a long time but eventually lost this struggle.

e. During the eighteenth century, the apostasy of the Enlightenment gained more and more influence over Europe.

9.2 Calvin's message to the postmedieval people was that the church should be free to govern itself. The church of the Reformation, therefore, received its own council, the consistory, made up of ministers and elders. The consistory organized the life of the church, maintained church discipline, and visited the church members as Christ's office bearers.

In Geneva, in contrast to the situation in Strasbourg, the civil authorities often forced Calvin to compromise on questions such as the appointment of elders, the number of feast days, and the frequency of the celebration of the Lord's Supper. But in cases of church discipline, he refused to compromise whatsoever.

Neither Luther nor Zwingli restored the church organization according to the apostolic model. It was Calvin who fought strongly for an ecclesiastical organization based on the apostolic directives found in Scripture.

9.3 Calvin taught that the church is not above the civil government and that the civil authorities do not have power over the church. Both the civil government and the church are subject to God's Word, without mixing civil matters with church matters. The Genevan Reformation showed the true scriptural relationship between church and state, a truth that had been ignored for many centuries at great cost in terms of human misery and sorrow, causing great injury to the church.

9.4 Civil magistrates often misused their authority and often did not remain obedient to their civil calling as God's Word teaches it. For example:

- Constantine the Great and his successors were guilty of caesaropapism.
- Charlemagne forced the Saxons to accept Christianity.
- Crusades were organized instead of missions.
- The murder of the Albigensians and the Waldensians who were branded as heretics.

It is the calling of the government, as God's servants, to maintain public order and justice and to protect the civil rights of the church to allow uninterrupted preaching of the gospel. Both Christians and non-Christians share equally in this civil protection.

a. David was king over Israel but also over the Moabites and the Philistines (Ps. 72) and other tribes. However, he did not force these heathen nations to accept the Jewish religion. As king over Israel (the church), he was assisted by Abiathar (the priest) and Nathan (the prophet of the Lord). David was no priest-king, neither was he an absolute monarch like the kings of the heathen nations around him.

b.   Already in the Old Testament, civil matters and church matters were separated. How much more should this be the case after Christ's church was made free.

9.5   The Word of God (". . . the sword of the Spirit," Eph. 6:17) plants and increases the church. In Calvin's days, that was not always clearly recognized. But Calvin did recognize the terrible truth of Christ's words to Peter in the garden: "Put your sword in its place, for all who take the sword will perish by the sword" (Matt. 26:52). Think also of the Munster drama of the Anabaptists. Calvin taught the believers to honour their rulers but never to worship them. Rebellion, revolution, usurpation of power, and violence are clearly against God's Word. After all, it was in the way of revolution that paradise was lost (Gen. 3).

9.6   It requires great faith and much resolve-in-grace to remain obedient to God rather than to man in the face of perilous situations when the magistrate and edicts of princes demand otherwise—yes, even though a person should suffer death or any other corporal punishment (Belgic Confession, Art. 28). It is difficult to say "no" when those powers demand from us things that are against God's Word. "For this is commendable, if because of conscience toward God one endures grief, suffering wrongfully" (1 Pet. 2:19; Matt. 10:28, 39).

9.7   In the sixteenth century, the church confessed God's righteousness. In the twentieth century, man cries for his own rights.

10. ATTACKS ON THE REFORMATION: ANABAPTISM

10.1   Anabaptism (ana = again; anabaptism = rebaptize). The Reformation was not the only movement that flourished during the sixteenth century; the Anabaptist movement also gained great influence during that time. The reformers found themselves fighting on two fronts: on the one side the Roman Catholics, on the other the Anabaptists.

10.2   The Anabaptists themselves detested that name since they did not recognize the baptism of infants at all. They opposed formal church organization and rejected any form of state interference.

10.3   Characteristics and teachings of the Anabaptists:

a.   One of the main characteristics of the Anabaptist beliefs is the so-called "spiritual life" in "the new kingdom of God". This kingdom of God was a completely new creation, not merely a recreation of the fallen earth. Anabaptists preached salvation from this world, a world which was considered to be the domain of the devil. Believers have no calling nor any business in that satanic domain.

b.   They preached the doctrine of an absolutely holy congregation, consisting of perfect and holy saints. These saints have severed all ties with "the world". Many Anabaptists denied that Christ was born of the flesh and blood of the virgin Mary (Heidelberg Catechism, Lord's Day 14), claiming that he came to earth merely by means of Mary. One of the sayings of Melchior Hoffman was, "Cursed is the flesh of Mary" (see Belgic Confession, Art. 18). Therefore they could maintain that Christ himself was also severed from this world. Rather than preach the (scriptural) struggle against sin in this world, Anabaptist doctrine presented a means of escape from this evil and sinful life. Its ideal is a life without sin. The consequences of this denial of the world can be found in the rejection of military service, the office of the government, and the legitimate use of the oath. Anabaptism is *not* reformation; at best it attempts restoration.

c.   The Anabaptists claim that the kingdom of God must be brought about either by revolution and violence (Munster) or by painstakingly avoiding all the evils of this world (Menno Simons). Anabaptists do not want to be of this world, but they do not want to be in this world either. Their "kingdom of God" floats, as it were, like oil on water.

d.   As did the teachings of Montanus and Donatus, the Anabaptist teachings replaced the proclamation of God's grace by the proclamation of a zealous saintliness based on man's own effort. This explains the harshness and relentlessness that characterized every Anabaptist group. In their efforts toward saintliness, they went to great extremes (banishments, purifications). Guido de Bres once wrote: "If it were possible, they would shave an egg!" It therefore becomes understandable that they rejected infant baptism since man is not sanctified by the promises of God's grace but by his own achievements of faith. Baptism can be administered only when faith has become evident.

1.   Medieval scholasticism distinguished between nature and grace. The former was good but needed the addition of the latter, the supernatural, that which is holy. However, the unity between nature and grace was still recognized.

2.   Medieval mysticism preached the merging with the divine. The mystic had no interest in ordinary, everyday life but attempted to rid himself of this life in order to be united with the divine.

3.   The reformers preached the struggle against sin and taught the covenant that encompassed all of life: reformation rather than avoidance.

4.   Anabaptists contemptuously referred to ordinary life as the domain of the devil and glorified the spiritual life in God's

kingdom. In fact, Anabaptists seemed to have learned little from the Reformation, and despite many differences, they remained very similar to Roman Catholicism in their search for a kind of mystic holiness. Perhaps not so surprisingly, many Anabaptists returned to the Roman Catholic fold in times of persecution (although it should be added that also many adherents of the Reformed faith did the same for fear of persecution). Many were enemies of the cross of Christ, refusing to bear shame with him. "For", says the Apostle Paul, "our citizenship is in heaven, from which we also eagerly wait for the Saviour, the Lord Jesus Christ, who will transfer our lowly body . . ." (Phil. 3:20, 21).

5. A major Roman Catholic heresy is the doctrine that teaches that the pope is lord over all and that the church is above everything. A major Anabaptist heresy teaches that "the inner light" (one's own personal insights) is lord over all, and "God's kingdom" is above everything. One might say that every (true) Anabaptist is his own pope since the true (Anabaptist) believer could detect if one was truly converted. This explains why factions developed, often excommunicating each other. Both Roman Catholics and Anabaptists looked down on ordinary life because it is not considered to be "ecclesiastical" (Roman Catholics) or "spiritual" (Anabaptists).

6. God's Word teaches that under the old covenant Israel was at times called upon to execute God's wrath with the naked sword, for instance, against the Amalekites and the Philistines (Ps. 18). Under the new covenant, the Spirit ministers through the preaching of the gospel. At times Christ himself pours out his wrathful judgements over an apostate Christendom through wars and epidemics. The believers, however, do not struggle against flesh and blood but against the "spiritual hosts of wickedness in the heavenly places" (Eph. 6:12-17). This Bible passage speaks of our spiritual armour, which never becomes outdated and which never becomes a burden to God's people. We may pray God for His blessing over the use of these spiritual weapons. But God will *not* bless the pious revolution brought about with a naked sword and violence. It is true, Christ is above all powers, but the Christians owe obedience to the civil authorities (see Rom. 13:1ff).

7. Writing to Timothy, Paul says, "Therefore I exhort first of all that supplications, prayers, intercessions, and giving of thanks be made for all men, for kings and all who are in authority. . . . For this is good and acceptable in the sight

of God our Saviour" (1 Tim. 2:1ff). The church must involve itself in politics in this way. But the church may never indulge in Anabaptist, revolutionary, or "ecclesiastical" politics.

10.4 One of the first Anabaptist leaders was Melchior Hoffman (1495-1543). He was born in Germany and was a furrier by trade. He travelled widely and finally arrived in Strasbourg. He claimed that God's kingdom would be established in this city. He even called himself Elijah (that is, "he who is to come": Matt. 11:14). However, ten years later he died in prison in that same city.

10.5 John Mattysz, a baker from the Dutch city of Haarlem, claimed to have received special visions: Strasbourg was unworthy, the German city of Munster was chosen to be "the Zion of God". He claimed to be the second Enoch (who walked with God). Mattysz preached that the time of oppression was passed and that the harvest time had arrived. Now was the time to take up arms against the ungodly. The city of Munster became the stronghold of a large group of fanatic Anabaptists. However, Mattysz was killed during an attack on the city by the troops of the bishop of Munster.

His successor was Jan Beukelszoon, better known as John of Leyden, a tailor by trade. On the basis of a prophecy, he was crowned king not only of Munster but of the whole world! As a second King David, he presided over his court on the Munster marketplace. Thousands were attracted to this Anabaptist dream and flocked to this "heavenly Jerusalem". They were urged to bring their weapons along to fight the wars of the Lord, as David had done. Private ownership was abolished, polygamy introduced (after all, David himself had many wives). The purifications of the city were terrible: all unbelievers were banished or killed. Eventually this unspiritual fanaticism led to madness which did not respect anything or anyone. In the middle of winter, during a period of bad weather, many non-Anabaptist citizens, including many women and children, were driven from the city "into outer darkness". On June 25, 1535, the troops of the bishop of Munster recaptured the city and brought it again under Roman Catholic rule. The vengeance was terrible; the mangled bodies of the leaders were exhibited from the city towers; ". . . all who take the sword will perish by the sword . . ." (Matt. 26:52).

10.6 The fall of Munster signalled the end of the revolutionary fanaticism of the extreme form of Anabaptism. However, it did not bring real changes. Menno Simons (1496-1561) became the leader. He was born in Friesland and was an ordained priest. He came under the influence of Melchior Hoffman, but Simons was certainly not as fanatic as Hoffman. The moderate wing of the Anabaptist movement is named after him: Mennonites.

During the 1680s, many Mennonites left for America. Later, the German Mennonites moved into Russia and became known as the Wolga Christians. They suffered severely from persecution during the years 1890-1910, and during the Second World War they were deported to Siberia because of their German ancestry.

10.7 It was of the utmost importance to the Reformed Christians of the sixteenth century to show that they were not to be confused with the Anabaptists.

Belgic Confession, Article 34: "For that reason we reject the error of the Anabaptists, who are not content with a single baptism received only once, and who also condemn the baptism of the little children of believers. . . ."

Belgic Confession, Article 36: "For that reason we condemn the Anabaptists and other rebellious people, and in general all those who reject the authorities and civil officers, subvert justice, introduce a communion of goods, and confound the decency that God has established among men."

10.8 The sixteenth century appeared to experience a severe crisis of authority. However, over against the Anabaptist rejection of everything on which was written "Holy to the Lord" (Zech. 14:20), the reformers maintained that there existed a crisis of obedience. They regarded obedience to all in authority (even to the hard taskmasters) as their calling. Anabaptist martyrs did not acknowledge the government, cursing those in authority. Reformed martyrs acknowledged the authority of their judges but said, "You are wrong, we are no criminals."

10.9 Anabaptism (spiritualism) is still a strong undercurrent in the secularized Western society: antimilitarism, pacifism, the theme *Church and Peace* of the World Council of Churches, the claim that religion is a personal matter, and the doctrine of the "open" canon of the Bible.

11. ATTACKS ON THE REFORMATION: MYSTICISM

11.1 Paul warned Timothy against contradictions of what is falsely called knowledge, or gnosis (1 Tim. 6:20). These "people of knowledge" offered an explanation of the gospel that differed greatly from Paul's. They said, among other things, that the resurrection had already taken place (2 Tim. 2:18). In their view, Paul's teachings were too much in conflict with the Greek philosophy and spirit of those days. But this is what God's Word calls the wisdom of this world (1 Cor. 1:20).

11.2 During the second century, the Christians (including Irenaeus of Lyons) were called to fight against Gnosticism. These "people of knowledge" used familiar words but filled them with new meanings. They spoke of God but did not mean the almighty Creator of heaven and earth. To them Christ was not a real man, born of the virgin Mary. His cross did not signify His sacrifice for our sins. They considered the soul to be the eternal part of man; man's soul was thought to be divine.

11.3   During the Middle Ages, Gnosticism was revived in the form of Meister Eckhart's mysticism. Eckhart could preach very beautifully about the rest the soul would find in God. This ancient enemy of the gospel showed itself during the time of the Reformation as well, also in the southern regions of Germany. A major proponent of the mysticism of the sixteenth century was Sebastian Franck (1499-1542).

Born in Donauworth, he was an ordained priest. He became a Lutheran in 1527, but by 1528 he was attracted to Anabaptist beliefs, and in 1529, he finally turned spiritualist. Erasmus lodged a complaint against him, and this resulted in his banishment from the city of Strasbourg in 1531. (Erasmus used this incident to demonstrate his own faithfulness to the Roman Catholic church.) As was the case with many Anabaptists, Franck lived a restless life, moving from one place to another. He finished up in Basel as a printer. He died there in 1542.

Franck disassociated himself from the Anabaptist movement because he drew the full consequences of the Anabaptist position. With him we find genuine characteristics of Gnostic mysticism: the merging of the soul with the divine. He rejected both sanctification through works (Roman Catholicism), as well as sanctification through God's Word (protestantism). He claimed that the deepest matters of the heart must be brought to the surface and that the Spirit does not need the preaching of the Word of God at all for this. The Bible is at best the scabbard but certainly not the sword itself. Franck removed the certainty of faith from God's Word, seeking this certainty in his own heart. Instead of accepting the norms of God's Word, Franck and his followers submitted to the tyranny of their own personal "gnosis". They regarded things such as the Bible, sermons, the church, baptism, and the Lord's Supper as unimportant and certainly not matters for which one should be prepared to suffer persecution.

For quite some time Franck's writings were held in high esteem, also in the Netherlands. In that country it was Coornheert who gained quite some influence during the middle of the sixteenth century. Their pious discussions of what, according to them, really mattered (the deeply devout union with God) sounded very serious and impressive, but in the meantime both Franck and Coornheert lived lives in true antinomianism; they were a law unto themselves.

NOTES

1.   It is this Gnostic mysticism that is preached so loudly in our own age of rebellion against God.

2.   It fully agrees with the "gospel" of Satan in paradise. Satan revealed to Eve what God wanted to keep secret, namely the truth of the real deliverance of man.

3.   The devil betrayed God's secret: you will not die. Satan knows that your eyes will be opened if you eat from that tree and that this knowledge will lead to equality with God because you then know good and evil (Gen. 3:4, 5).

4.   a.   By means of art, literature, films, theatre, politics, and social movements and actions, the modern antigospel acclaims that man is not a creature, that he is not dependent on his Creator. Man, it is claimed, came into being by the processes of evolution and is therefore truly independent from God. If God were our Creator, he then would have the right to demand obedience.

      b.   This antigospel states that our creatureliness is a fallacy, a strait-jacket from which man has to free himself.

      c.   Man becomes free and equal to God—even becomes God—when he himself determines what is good and what is evil. He has the knowledge of good and evil.

      d.   Only then will his eyes be opened. Therefore, away with laws and statutes, with rules and norms.
            During the student rebellion in Paris (1968), the following slogan was painted on the wall of the Sorbonne University: "It is forbidden to forbid anything". If this slogan is considered illogical, the deep things of Satan have not been noticed in this antigospel! (See Rev. 2:24).

      e.   When Gnostics speak of salvation, they do not mean the resurrection from the dead, but they mean rebellion against God. This rebellion leads to the statement, "We know . . ."; this statement, made in absolute and divine freedom (existentialism), claims the right to absolute self-gratification and to a life ruled by one's own free will and lusts.

      f.   These modern Gnostics preach freedom from all ties, including those of our own neighbour (that's hell, said Jean Paul Sartre) and marriage partners since in marriage people give themselves to their spouse. Every Gnostic and every mystic is a divine individualist, lonely and alone. Many cannot live with this demonic loneliness and commit suicide. Others turn to the mysticism of Eastern religions in order to experience some of that divinity, filling the desperate spiritual vacuum in which they live.

g.   Gnosticism is the major expression of this modern antigospel. The Apostle John saw already on the beach of the Isle of Patmos the beast of the earth rising forth from the East, from Asia (Rev. 13:11). Certainly in the East must lie the source of mysticism. The East has given us a rosary from Tibet and monasticism from Vietnam. This Gnosticism is a cancer (2 Tim. 2:17) for the Christian church and threatens to destroy it because the proud Gnostic spirit so easily infects the communion of saints. The one always knows better than the other (see Rom. 14). Paul warns against being puffed up on behalf of one against the other (1 Cor. 4:6, 7). It is this attitude that threatens unity in the congregation. And this unity in the congregation is the focus of the continuous admonition by Christ and his apostles. See John 13:35, "By this all will know that you are My disciples, if you have love for one another" (see 1 John). How destructive has been the influence of the beast of the earth, which looks deceivingly like the lamb yet speaks like the dragon!

5.   This antigospel changes apostate Christians into self-satisfied antichristians, and urges a rebellious Christendom more and more toward a conscious anti-Christianity here on earth (Ps. 2). Therefore, the three epistles of the Apostle John, as well as the epistle of the Apostle Jude, are most relevant to the spiritual situation of today. In fact, the Pharisees also decided for themselves what was to be regarded as good or evil. On the one hand, they lived a most careful life, observing every regulation of the law meticulously. This created a good impression—such holiness. On the other hand, they lived lives of avarice, harshness, and hatred. Therefore the Lord showed what they really were: you are children of Satan, he is your father, and of course you will do the wishes of your father (John 8:44; John 9:41). This truth really shook them up.

6.   This antigospel has, despite its variations, remained the same. Indeed, Satan's methods are repetitive and boring, and mankind is slow to learn. Satan uses this method to lead the rebellion against God. His followers are not in the first place blind heathens; on the contrary, his most faithful followers are apostate Christians who have ignored God's covenant of grace and reconciliation which He established with our fathers, a covenant which is still operative and leads either to eternal life or eternal death.

12. THE COUNTER-REFORMATION

12.1 The Roman Catholic church prefers to speak of the Catholic Reformation or the renewal of the church, rather than using the term

Counter-Reformation. The Counter-Reformation is primarily the work of the Order of the Jesuits and the Council of Trent.

12.2 The Order of the Jesuits (Society of Jesus). Its founder was Ignatius Loyola (1491-1556), a member of the Basque nobility. During a local war against invading French troops, he was severely wounded. The tedious and lengthy convalescence provided him with an opportunity to read about many lives of saints (for lack of better books). This led to his conversion. His ideal of chivalry now changed into chivalry for God and the church. He studied, among other places, at the University of Paris (at about the same time as John Calvin), and founded the Society of Jesus (Society Jesu - S.J.). This strict society was organized along military lines and received official papal sanction in 1540.

The purpose of this society was to promote the fame and honour of the church. The zeal and devotion of the members of this society might well be considered idolatry of the church. The infamous Jesuit attitude is characterized by:

a. Total, blind obedience (*ac si cadaver esset*); willing tools of the pope; very strict spiritual discipline; espionage of brothers; no ties of friendship with family. The pope called them the most zealous rowers aboard Peter's ship.

b. Spiritual reservations (*reservatio mentalis*). A member is not required to speak the truth always and in all circumstances; he is allowed to withhold part of the truth. He could therefore respond, "I don't know," without adding the words, "whether I should tell you."

c. "The end justifies the means". A member is allowed to commit a lesser sin in order to prevent a greater evil. Such a principle badly hinders sound character development.

12.3 One of Loyola's fellow founders of the society was Francis Xavier (1506-1552). The Roman Catholic church regards him as one of the greatest missionaries since the time of the apostles. He worked in Asia and Japan and made many converts ("My hands are tired from the many baptisms!"). Often, though, such conversions were no more than superficial. But it is also known that many Japanese Christians withstood terrible persecutions.

12.4 By means of their work as confessors as well as their educational efforts in their schools, the Jesuits strongly promoted the cause of the papacy. Their fanaticism was a major cause of the bloody religious wars that ravaged Europe.

12.5 The Council of Trent was held—with a number of interruptions—from 1545 to 1563. The city of Trent was located in the southern part of the Holy Roman Empire, close enough to Rome to satisfy the pope. The Jesuits in attendance ensured the supremacy of the pope. Papal infallibility was recognized, although this was not declared to be the official doctrine of the church until 1870, during the First Vatican Council. The major scholastic writings of Thomas Aquinas were a primary resource for those in attendance at the Council of Trent.

12.6 Trent caused the definitive separation between Rome and the Reformation.

a.   Over against the Reformed *sola fide*, Trent placed the doctrine that teaches that God's grace is administered during the liturgical actions of the priests when administering the sacraments (*ex opere operato*).

b.   Over against the Reformed *sola scriptura*, Trent maintained the importance of the traditions (pronouncements and practices) of the church. Officially those traditions were considered of equal value to Scripture. However, in practice this often meant that traditions were placed above Scripture.

c.   Over against the Reformed *sola gratia*, Trent placed the meritoriousness of good works.

1.   The Holy Spirit, given us from Christ on Pentecost, does not give new revelations in addition to Scripture. God has revealed Himself once in His Son, and that is sufficient (Heb. 1:1; Rev. 22:18, 19). The sufficiency of Scripture is denied by the Holy Roman Church (its official name) as well as by the Anabaptists.

2.   Rome acknowledges the infallibility of its popes when they speak *ex cathedra* (for instance, the ascension of Mary was announced as official doctrine by Pope Pius XII on November 1, 1955). On these occasions, the pope claims the inspiration of the Holy Spirit for such new teachings, with reference to Acts 15:28, ". . . it seemed good to the Holy Spirit and us. . . ." However, the apostle referred to the fact that also converted Gentiles would belong to the church. Anabaptists also refuse to accept a finalized canon. They claim that the Holy Spirit reveals new teachings by means of inner voices.

3.   In his monumental defence of the Reformation—his *Reply to Sadoleto*—Calvin calls both the Roman Catholic church and the Anabaptists sects, since both removed the Spirit of God from the Word of God. The Roman Catholic church does this by means of traditions, and the Anabaptists do so by means of an "inner light" and "inner voices".

12.7 From the canons of the Council of Trent:

CANON 6: If anyone says that the sacraments of the New Law do not contain the grace that they signify or that they do not confer that grace upon those who do not place any obstacles in the way—as if they were merely external signs of the grace or justice received through faith and insignia, so to speak, of a Christian profession by which men distinguish the faithful from infidels: *LET HIM BE ANATHEMA.*

CANON 8: If anyone says that through the sacraments of the New Law grace is not conferred by the rite itself (*ex opere operato*) but that faith alone in the divine promise is sufficient to obtain grace: *LET HIM BE ANATHEMA.*

> Note: This means that the liturgical, ritual act of the priest during baptism causes grace to be poured out over the child, who will then be immediately regenerated. Before this liturgical act of baptism, the child was equal to any other infidel child. The act of baptism makes it worthy to be carried back to its mother through the hallowed spaces of the church.

CANON 12: If anyone says that justifying faith is nothing else than confidence that divine Mercy remits sins for Christ's sake, or that it is confidence alone which justifies us: *LET HIM BE ANATHEMA.*

> Note: All members of the Second Vatican Council (1962-1965) were required under oath to state their agreement with and submission to the canons of Trent.

12.8 The Reformation was judged *anathema* (see 1 Cor. 16:22; see also Gal. 1:8). Although some of the abuses were condemned, the Roman Catholic church reaffirmed its apostate doctrines. "At that moment the Roman church separated itself from the true Mother church, and became an apostate sect" (Groen van Prinsterer).

12.9 The decisions of the Council of Trent provided especially the Jesuits with renewed zeal and motivation to attack the Reformation forcefully. The southern Netherlands were lost for the Reformation; in Spain, the Reformation was smothered in blood by the Inquisition. The Jesuit persecutions in Italy, Hungary, and the southern Netherlands were terrible. Northern Europe (Scandinavia and Northern Germany) remained faithful to the Reformation. Central Europe (France, England, Scotland, and the northern Netherlands) became the battlefield for bloody religious wars.

13. EXPANSION OF THE REFORMATION: FRANCE

13.1 During the decades following the Reformation, northern Europe was dominated by the Lutheran state church while the Roman Catholic church maintained its grip over southern Europe. Therefore it was in central

Europe that the struggle between the Reformation and the Counter-Reformation was felt most painfully.

The beginnings of the religious wars that battered most of Europe during the sixteenth and seventeenth centuries are to be found in the peace treaty signed between France and Spain in the year 1559. This treaty included the secret but intentional agreement to destroy the Reformation heresy. The then young prince of Orange, Prince William the Silent, heard of this treaty by chance. Philip II, son of Charles V and king of Spain, became the political leader of the Counter-Reformation.

The turning point in the political struggle between Reformation and Counter-Reformation came in 1588 when the great attack on England by the Spanish Armada came to nought after our forefathers prayed for God's curses over this satanic enterprise (see Mark 11:22-25). England's Queen Elizabeth I ordered a medallion struck with this inscription: "God's breath destroyed them". Spain's dominance over Europe came to an end in 1588, with the destruction of this infamous fleet. After that time, the Reformed churches became the leaders of the world.

13.2 Mainly due to Calvin, the Reformation gained great influence over France. The Reformed believers became known as *Huguenots*, and many congregations were instituted across the country. By 1559, there were approximately three thousand French Reformed congregations while in the city of Orleans alone some five to six thousand people attended the Lord's Supper. One-quarter of France's population was reformed while as many as 75 percent of the educated citizens (nobility, scholars, wealthy citizens) adhered to the new faith. Orleans, Bordeaux, Lyons, La Rochelle, Montaubun, Montpellier, and Rochefort were among the cities that had openly chosen for the Reformation. The powerful noble families of De Coligny and De Bourbon joined the Reformation, while the commander-in-chief of the army (D'Andelot) and the admiral of the fleet (Caspard de Coligny) were also reformed.

13.3 A secret synod was held in Paris in 1559, despite the threat of persecution and execution. The French churches adopted the *Confessio Gallicana* (French Confession) and the French church order.

But the opposition was fierce. Thousands were executed in the most gruesome manner. The faithfulness unto death of these martyrs made a strong impression on the general population. ". . . The word of the Lord grew and multiplied" (Acts 12:24).

The struggle between the Reformation and the Counter-Reformation polarized around two families. The Roman Catholics supported the family of the Guises while the Huguenots assembled around the families of De Bourbon and De Coligny. A Huguenot conspiracy—supported by a number of Huguenot noblemen—against the Guises in an attempt to gain influence over the king (1560) failed because of betrayal. Calvin was falsely accused of being one of the accomplices of this rebellion.

13.4 Year after year, Calvin received frightening news from the faithful churches in France. In a most moving manner, he attempted to comfort them and persuade them not to take revenge, otherwise there would be no more room for God's wrath. "Vengeance is Mine, I will repay, says the Lord" (Rom. 12:19). On this we may place our steadfast hope, he wrote. Calvin warned them that their weapons were their confession and their sufferings. Deliverance will come from God. Hold fast to His promises and continually remind Him of those promises (Isa. 62:1, 6, 7). We must acknowledge that the cross of oppression is put upon us as chastisement for our sins (Hos. 13:11).

During the preparation of the Ambroise conspiracy, Calvin warned Admiral De Coligny: "The first drop of bloodshed by our people will cause a flood of blood which will flow all over Europe." Calvin denied that the believers had the right to rebel against what he called "the cross of Christ". He did not encourage violence against any level of government. However, he did recognize the responsibility of every officer charged with civil authority. Therefore he encouraged lower magistrates to refuse to cooperate when persecution was ordered from higher up and urged them to protect the faithful. His *Institutes* XX:25-32 does not contain a mere theory about rebellion against the lawful authority; neither does it describe a general theory about God's help in days of tribulation. With great conviction, Calvin spoke God's words of comfort to the faithful: the LORD God is a living and almighty God, a God who helps in distress. He will grant deliverance at his time. Calvin never encouraged revolution or rebellion. He urged greater humility because of our sins before God and called on all believers to pray urgently for salvation (Ps. 37:1-11).

13.5   The Huguenot Wars 1562-1598

a.   The Huguenot wars began with the massacre of Vassy. Francois De Guise was on his way to Paris with his troops. Annoyed and embittered by the psalm-singing Huguenots, he ordered his troops to massacre the defenceless population of that village. The Huguenots answered in kind, conquering Rouen and Lyons. Calvin did not approve. He wrote to the ministers of Lyons, "It would be a betrayal of God, yourself, and the whole of Christendom if we did not speak the words which you are about to hear to our great sorrow. It is certainly not an act which behooves a minister of the word when he makes himself a soldier or a commander in battle; it is even more despicable when someone leaves the pulpit and reaches for weapons of war."

b.   A bitter and cruel civil war resulted; much blood was shed, harvests were destroyed, cattle was stolen, and possessions were confiscated. De Coligny's portrait was nailed to the gallows, and a high price was placed on his capture, dead or alive. Then, suddenly, the Peace of St. Germain (1570) brought relief. The Huguenots were allowed to meet in almost all cities, except Paris and a number of other places. De Coligny even received an invitation to attend court.

c.   But all this turned out to be a terrible deception; the wedding between Henry of Navarre and the sister of the king, Margaret, was used as bait. It had been announced as a feast of reconciliation, but it turned into a blood wedding (August 23-24, 1572 - massacre of St. Bartholomew's Day). De Coligny was murdered, and many Huguenots across France were mercilessly slaughtered. The Huguenot movement never recovered from this tragedy, which was indeed a black page in the history of the Counter-Reformation. The instigators of this massacre all died a violent death.

d.   The Edict of Nantes (1598) gave the Huguenots the right to establish churches and schools. They could also be employed in government positions. In addition, a number of fortified cities were given to them, including the city of La Rochelle. The Huguenots formed a small but influential minority in the midst of the Roman Catholic majority. They had their own armies and fortified cities and formed, as it were, a state within a state. As was the case with the Peace of Augsburg in Germany (1555), the Edict of Nantes granted political-religious freedom to heretics and recognized that more than one religion should be allowed to exist within one state. This was a most important change from medieval political and religious thought.

13.6 Under King Louis XIII, it was the notorious Cardinal Richelieu who ended this period of relative peace. He schemed to destroy the Huguenots once and for all. The political power of the Huguenots ended with the fall of their last stronghold, La Rochelle (1627-1628). Ships from both the English and the Dutch navies joined in the bombardment of this city. The ironies of European politics forced Reformed Dutch sailors to fight against their own fellow believers. Indeed, politics and trade seemed more important than religious convictions.

13.7 During the reign of Louis XIV, life for the Huguenots was almost impossible: dragonnades, murder, persecution. Finally, the official revocation of the Edict of Nantes came in 1685. Half a million refugees left France, many finding a safe place within the Netherlands. But the Camisards continued their stubborn resistance, aided by the forbidding terrain around Cevennes. The Tour de Constance, a tower near the Mediterranean Sea, was used especially to imprison women. A certain Marie Durand was held here from July 1730 to April 1768. With her knitting needles, she managed to scratch in the wall the word *resistez*. God gave these people—not in the least the women and children—great willingness to suffer, and made them "glory in their tribulations" (Rom. 5:3).

13.8 Louis XIV elevated the Roman Catholic church again to the position of state church: un roi, une loi, une foie. The downfall of the royal house in France during the French revolution also meant the downfall of the Roman Catholic church in this country.

14. EXPANSION OF THE REFORMATION: SCOTLAND

14.1 Patrick Hamilton (1504-1528) was the first Scottish martyr. He was a member of the nobility, studied to become a priest, but became a follower of Luther. He was captured, sentenced, and executed all in one day in order to intimidate others and suppress the rising tide of the Reformation.

14.2 John Knox (1513?-1572) was also an ordained priest. He was converted to the Reformed faith after witnessing the execution of heretics. For nineteen months he was a prisoner aboard a French war galley. Once, when his ship sailed along the Scottish coast in view of his church at St. Andrews, he is said to have remarked to one of his fellow galley slaves, "Look, one day I will preach in that church again." And indeed, the unbelievable did happen. To everyone's surprise, the protestant Knox was set free during an exchange of prisoners of war. He visited John Calvin in Geneva and eventually returned to his native Scotland.

It was under influence of Knox that the Scottish Parliament strongly promoted the Reformation and accepted the *Scottish Confession of Faith* (1560). Knox was of the opinion that it was wicked and unscriptural for a woman (Queen Mary Stuart) to be ruler of the land. He wanted Scotland to be like Israel. Calvin tried to moderate the ideas of this fiery Scottish "John the Baptist".

Knox severely admonished the fanatically Roman Catholic Queen Mary Stuart because of her sinful life. His epitaph reads, "Here lies the man who never feared to face anyone on earth". Especially this man has been instrumental in making the Reformed religion in Scotland become the "leaven," which, "hid in three measures of meal," leavened the whole of life (Matt. 13:33). His statue stands next to that of Farel, Calvin, and Beza on the international monument of the Reformation in Geneva.

15. EXPANSION OF THE REFORMATION: ENGLAND

15.1 The English king Henry VIII (1491-1547) wrote a booklet in opposition to Luther. The pope rewarded him for this effort by granting him the title *Defensor fidei* (Defender of the Faith), still part of the official title of the present queen of England.

Despite this show of allegiance, Henry VIII simply removed the English church from papal control when the pope refused to grant him a divorce. Henry appointed himself head of the church (1531). In this way, the English Roman Catholic church became the Anglican, or Episcopal, state church. This change was no more than a "free-from-Rome" action and had little to do with true reformation. Both Roman Catholics (who continued to acknowledge the authority of the pope) and followers of Luther (protestants who refused to acknowledge the authority of the king as head of the church) were persecuted; at times they were hanged next to each other from the same gallows.

15.2 As archbishop of Canterbury, Thomas Cranmer (1489-1556) not only supported Henry VIII in his plans for a divorce, he was also sympathetic to the Reformation and corresponded with Calvin. During the reign of the God-fearing King Edward VI, Cranmer introduced a number of reforms into the Anglican church (the *Thirty-nine Articles* and the *Book of Common Prayer*), attempting to move the church closer toward a true reformation. During the counter-reformation of Bloody Mary, Cranmer became a victim as well, and was executed. He put his right hand into the fire because with that hand he had in a moment of weakness signed his recantation from the Reformed faith.

15.3 While Henry VIII forced the people to become protestant, Mary Tudor forced them to become Roman Catholic again. The process was reversed when Elizabeth I became queen. Three (pseudo?) reformations in less than thirty years, each forced upon the people by the reigning monarch.

15.4 Many refugees from Holland, Germany, and Poland found in the England of Edward VI and Cranmer a safe place (among them John à Lasco, 1499-1560). By royal decree, the monastery of the Austin friars was given to the Dutch refugees on July 24, 1550.

Whereas during the reign of Henry VIII and Edward VI many refugees from the European continent came to England, during the reign of Mary Tudor the stream of refugees flowed the other way. And again, during the reign of Elizabeth I, many once more returned, often as former students of John Calvin and others. This strengthened the Calvinist influence in England. Further support for the English Reformation came from the Scottish Reformation.

It should be remembered that during those years England was not a well-developed country. There were some two million inhabitants (Spain had three, and the northern and southern Netherlands somewhere between two and three million inhabitants). London had about a hundred thousand citizens. Housing was poor. Erasmus commented on the floors of clay, with straw to hide the filth of beer, fat, leftovers, bones.

15.5 The Anglican church has never been a truly Reformed church, despite its breach with Rome. It remained strongly hierarchical, with two main factions:

-       the High Church - with an episcopal church government maintaining the apostolic succession; liturgical ceremonies; pelagian in doctrine.

-       The Low Church - maintaining the *Thirty-nine Articles* and the *Book of Common Prayer*.

During the sixteenth and seventeenth centuries, the High Church was the instigator of terrible persecutions. This false church persecuted the faithful because they refused to acknowledge by oath that the king had ultimate authority over matters of faith.

15.6 Although most remained, many of these Reformed believers, who became known as Puritans (pure church, pure life), left the English state church. Among the Puritans we find:

-       Presbyterians, who did not accept a church government of bishops but maintained a (regional) presbytery which had authority over local consistories.

-       Congregationalists, who allowed the local congregations much more influence than the Presbyterians were willing to give them. They were also known as *Independents* since they wished to remain independent from the influences of pope and Anglican bishops as well as from the civil government.

Over the years, groups of protestants, often persecuted in their own country, left their native country. Some came to the Netherlands and settled in cities such as Leyden and Middelburg. Later some of these people, the Pilgrim fathers, together with other refugees, sailed on the Mayflower for the New World in 1620. When the Pilgrim fathers were about to depart, they knelt down in prayer on the cobblestones of the Delfshaven quay, just like Paul once knelt down on the beach of Miletus (Acts 20:36).

15.7 During the seventeenth century, the conflict between the (Anglican) crown and the (Puritan) parliament led to a civil war (1642). Parliament called together the Westminster Assembly, which drew up what is now known as the *Westminster Confession of Faith* (1646-1648). Since this English Reformed confession was adopted by the Presbyterian churches in North America, it made the Reformation into a world event.

The reign of Oliver Cromwell (1649-1660) may be regarded as the peak of the Reformed influence in England. Protestantism was the major political force, and there existed almost total religious freedom during that time.

15.8 During the reign of Charles II, the Anglican church was restored to its role of state church. The Baptist tinker, John Bunyan, was in prison for twelve years. He is the author of the famous book *Pilgrim's Progress*, an allegory of the journey of a Christian to the heavenly Jerusalem.

15.9 As King Gustavus Adolphus of Sweden saved Lutheran protestantism in Germany from the Roman Catholic Hapsburg rulers, so Prince William III, Stadholder of Holland, saved Reformed protestantism from the Roman Catholic James II who in league with the French king Louis XIV threatened the very existence of the Netherlands (the Glorious Revolution, 1688). The Toleration Act of 1689 provided freedom of religion for Anglicans and dissenters, while Roman Catholics and Socinians were expressly excluded from its stipulations. This act protected the protestant character of the English nation.

- Dissenters or nonconformists were protestant citizens who did not belong to the Anglican state church.
- In 1960, the archbishop of Canterbury went on an official visit to the Vatican—the first since 1531.

16. THE REFORMATION IN THE NETHERLANDS: OVERVIEW

a.	1517-1530	The rise of the Reformation movement under Lutheran influences.
b.	1530-1540	Anabaptist dominance.
c.	1540-1550	Influence of Calvin and the Calvinist Reformation.
d.	1550-1566	The beginning of the institution of Dutch Reformed refugee churches in foreign countries, especially in Germany. In the southern Netherlands: persecution of the Reformed churches.
e.	1566-1572	Persecution of the Reformed churches in the northern Netherlands.
f.	1572-1586	"The LORD is righteous; He has cut into pieces the cords of the wicked" (Ps. 129). God moves the power in the northern Netherlands from Spain to Orange. Increased freedom for the Reformed churches. Struggle with the Libertines.
g.	1586-1619	Struggle with the Arminians. National Synod of Dort, 1618-1619.

17. THE REFORMATION IN THE SOUTHERN NETHERLANDS

17.1 Like the Pharisees in the days of Christ, so also the Roman Catholic leaders in the sixteenth century were blinded by their own doctrinal system. They had taken away the key of true knowledge, that is, God's grace by which he declares all those who believe in Jesus Christ righteous without payment (Luke 11:52). These leaders were able to read the Word of God only as a book of commands and prohibitions. Their own heresies forced them from one terrible decision to another, chastising the people mercilessly with the whip of the law.

17.2 Caught in the spell of scholastic systems of thought about God and the church, the inquisitors, especially the theologians of Louvain, acted with blind cruelty and with no regard for anyone or anything in executing the edicts of Charles V. "Woe to you lawyers! For you have taken away the key of knowledge. You did not enter in yourselves, and those who were entering you hindered" (Luke 13:14).

17.3 The monasteries of the Augustinian order (to which also Luther had belonged) were centres of reformation. In particular, the Augustinian monastery of Antwerp became a leader. In these monasteries the grace of God in Christ Jesus was preached. "For Christ is the end of the law for righteousness to everyone who believes" (Rom. 10:4). Thousands joyously professed his name, rescued from the devilish snare of Roman Catholic Pharisaism. By His Holy Spirit our Saviour poured out heavenly gifts of joyfulness and steadfastness unto death on the martyrs of the sixteenth century, as He had done during the persecutions under the Roman emperors (see Heidelberg Catechism, Lord's Day 19).

17.4 The reformer of the Netherlands was Guido De Bres (1522-1567). He was born in Mons in what is now the southwestern region of Belgium. He was forced to flee to England, and later he also visited Germany. Eventually he became a student of Calvin in Geneva and a pastor of the congregation at Tournay. Since the magistrates were annoyed by the singing of psalms in public gatherings (the so-called chanterie, a practice against which Guido de Bres had warned strongly for fear that it would remind people of Anabaptist practices), they dealt harshly with the Reformed citizens. On the night of November 1, 1561, a copy of the *Belgic Confession* (of which de Bres was the chief author) was thrown over the castle walls at Tournay in the hope that the governor would realize that the Reformed congregations were not groups of revolutionary Anabaptists. But persecution was heavy. Together with his fellow office bearer Peregrin de la Grange, De Bres was hanged at Valenciennes in 1567.

a. De Bres's mother had already before his birth fervently prayed that Guido would be permitted to become a priest. This motherly prayer was the result of a fiery sermon of a monk. Her prayer was heard, but not in the manner she expected. Before his death, De Bres wrote a most moving farewell letter to his mother.
b. An instigator of the chanterie, a weaver by the name of Du Four, considered the Reformed pastor De Bres too fearful and too lax. Yet when the soldiers came, De Bres remained with his congregation while Du Four fled for his life.

17.5 The Roman Catholic church, which was originally the church of the apostles, had become the whore who sat on the scarlet beast (Rev. 17:3), the unfaithful magistrate. She drank the blood of the saints (Rev. 17:6).

17.6 Together with Guido de Bres, some of the organizers of *the Churches under the Cross* (as the Reformed churches were known in those days) were:
a. Caspar van der Heyden - for some time minister at Antwerp.
b. Franciscus Junius - first an atheist, later a travelling preacher in Flanders, chaplain for William of Orange, and professor at Leyden.
c. Petrus Dathenus (1531-1588) - a travelling preacher in Flanders, pastor of the congregation at Ghent. He greatly influenced the life of the churches in the Netherlands by translating the Heidelberg Catechism and by publishing a psalter in the Dutch language. This psalter has been used for a number of centuries.

17.7 During the sixteenth century, the city of Ghent was larger than the city of Paris. It had been won for the Reformation in 1577. Groen van Prinsterer called the citizens of this city extremely reformed. They wanted to force all of Flanders to follow their example. Under the command of Burgomaster Hembyse and with the blessing of their pastor, Dathenus, acts of violence were committed against peaceful Roman Catholic citizens in a number of villages of the Flanders countryside. Churches were burnt down, monks tortured, monasteries destroyed, all in reckless and senseless wantonness. Stolen goods were sold to benefit the city coffers; churches were changed into army camps and stables. Dathenus wanted Prince William of Orange to force the pure religion upon the Roman Catholic counties with military force, if necessary. The church should make use of the sword of the magistrate to bring about conversion, Dathenus claimed.

Dathenus was under the mistaken impression that his task was the same as that of King Josiah in Jerusalem, who destroyed all the altars of the idols. Twice Prince William visited the city, but twice Dathenus refused to meet with him. Burgomaster Hembyse turned out to be a traitor who wanted to hand over the city to the Spanish general Parma.

He was sentenced by his own followers. Later Dathenus recognized the errors of ways.

a.   Dathenus made a serious error in comparing himself with King Josiah: Josiah was a foreshadowing of Christ in his church. Within the church, idolatry must be removed by means of preaching and discipline.

b.   It is not the task of the magistrate to plant the church with force. Groen van Prinsterer commented that it is good to oppose a false religion, providing the means are right. The church is not founded by the weapons of war; truth is not planted by violence. Those outside are to be won by the sword of the Spirit and by the fulfilment of the commandment of love by those within. God's blessings may be expected over righteous actions only. The magistrate is called to use the sword to protect its citizens against evildoers who threaten to disrupt orderly civil life (see Rom. 13:4—"for good"). The magistrate must use its sword to protect the political right and freedom of the church of Christ to preach the gospel.

c.   Calvin was one of the first to acknowledge the distinction and separation between state and church, between civil and ecclesiastical matters. This insight is, indeed, a fruit of the Reformation. Also, Prince William recognized this much better than did the extreme Reformed citizens of Ghent under the leadership of Hembyse and Dathenus. However, the moderate view of the prince was understood by few, and many did not trust him.

d.   Dathenus admitted, "Too often I used the examples of Gideon, Joshua, and David to justify the civil war in Flanders over against Orange. Now I have come to realize that this is not the true way in which religion is to be planted. I also emphasized too much the external ceremonies, forgetting the main point, which is to preach to my congregation the true conversion of the heart."

e.   Lydius, pastor of Bruges and later professor at the University of Franeker (Friesland) commented, "These people (Dathenus and his followers) have caused the loss of Flanders and Brabant for the Reformation."

17.8 *Iconoclasm: the destruction of images - 1566.* Starting in Flanders, fanatical protestants swept across the countryside, destroying images, pictures, and shrines in the local Roman Catholic churches. This fanaticism was driven more by Anabaptist ideas of purity than by reformed-scriptural principles. People robbed the Roman Catholic citizens as well as the churches and monasteries. Anyone daring to oppose them was violently dealt with. In fact, these actions amounted to civil rebellion. The prince of Orange ordered three of the chief instigators to be hanged in Antwerp. The Spanish general Alva used these uprisings as an excuse to order the suspension of all privileges of the population. The counts of Egmond and Hoorne, leaders among the lesser nobility and champions for the rights of the common citizens by petitioning to government, were accused of complicity in this revolution and were beheaded in public. While already on the scaffold, Egmond recanted and kissed the crucifix; Hoorne maintained his innocence till the end, decrying the injustice of the government.

17.9 Rome regained its dominance and authority over the southern Netherlands by means of military power. Many of the citizens fled to the northern Netherlands. Antwerp, one of the most important cities in the South, lost its commercial importance to Amsterdam, which became one of the largest trade cities in the world.

18. THE REFORMATION IN THE NORTHERN NETHERLANDS

18.1 No Lutherans were martyred in Germany because the Edict of Worms (1521) was largely ignored by the German rulers. The persecution in the Netherlands, on the other hand, was so severe that by 1530 the Lutheran Reformation had all but disappeared. Anabaptism swept into the Netherlands, gaining great popularity. After the fall of Munster, this movement lost much of its external strength but remained an undercurrent noticeable even in the present-day society.

18.2 By 1555, Calvin's influence became the most noticeable in the northern Netherlands. This influence came in the form of Calvin's writings (*Institutes*), his students (Marnix of St. Aldegonde), and the Reformed refugees from the southern Netherlands.

The situation in the Netherlands was rather different from that in Germany where Calvinists were forced to flee from city to city pursued by Lutheran pastors. Although not more than 10 percent of the Dutch population joined the Reformation initially, its influence in the Netherlands was enormous. This was not because the Dutch nation was more suitable than others to become God's field where the seed of His Word could grow most abundantly. The kind of religious fervour with which the Spaniards attended autos-da-fe in their country was unknown in the Netherlands. On the contrary, it was Groen van Prinsterer who, in a later century, noted a rather different type of fervour, namely, the intense interest of the Dutch nation in trade and commerce. He asked, "Is not mammon the Dutch Baal?" Indeed, the great significance of the Reformation in the northern Netherlands can only be explained on the basis of God's sovereign good pleasure.

18.3 The blessings of the gospel have been granted in great abundance to the Dutch nation. To state this is not haughty; it is gross ingratitude to deny it. But next to the great riches of divine lovingkindness, the depths of human depravity were also revealed in Holland. Dutch history shows many parallels with the history of Israel (Ps. 106:7ff).

The Lord has brought many plagues over Holland: wars, floods, famine, disasters, deadly sicknesses, often called *the plague*. People realized that these calamities came from the Lord, and special days of fasting and prayer were held to still God's wrath. "If there is a calamity in the city, will not the LORD have done it?" (Amos 3:6).

18.4 The year 1566 was a year of miracles. People attended open-air gatherings armed to protect themselves against ambush or attack, for instance, at Alkmaar (Jan Arendsz) and Amsterdam (Pieter Gabriel). The terrible consequences of iconoclasm brought this period of relative peace to an end. With the arrival of the Spanish general Alva, a new wave of bloody persecutions swept over the land.

18.5 The first Dutch Reformed churches were not instituted in the country itself but on foreign soil. These first churches were refugee churches.

a.   London (England): The congregation met in the former monastery of the Austin Friars (1550).

b.   Emden (Germany): This city became known as "the inn for God's oppressed". The church's crest shows a little ship on a wild sea with the Dutch inscription: "Godts kerck, verstroyt, verdreven, heeft Godt hier rust ghegheven" (God's church, ousted and scattered, found rest here). In the winter of 1560, some 350 refugees arrived across the ice. A baker offered to look after 30 of them.

c.   Wezel (Germany).

d.   Frankfurt (Germany).

18.6 The organization of the Dutch refugee churches in foreign countries became more detailed:

- 1568 Convent of Wezel
- 1571 First National Synod at Emden. Article 1 of the acts of this synod reads: No church shall lord it over another, no minister of the Word, no elder, nor deacon shall lord it over another, but everyone will guard against any suspicion and enticement of lordship (at present Article 74 of the church order of the Canadian Reformed Churches).

18.7 Forty years of martyrdom were followed by eighty years of war (Groen van Prinsterer). God's church in the Netherlands did not rebel against the authorities because it could no longer allow itself to be slaughtered. God's church did not reach for weapons of war to defend itself. The LORD Himself rose to save His people, in His time and in

His way, in answer to the many supplications sent before His throne by the heavily persecuted church.

The Eighty Years War was fought by the Reformed believers not as a struggle to promote Christ's church, as advocated by the Anabaptists; nor as a struggle to gain mere freedom of conscience, as the Libertines wanted. It was a struggle with cold steel for the political-religious freedom for Christ's church; not *pro libertate* (Libertines) but *pro religione*.

God's Word does speak of religious freedom for all. No one is free to serve God as he pleases. There cannot be religious freedom within Christ's church; there must be religious freedom for Christ's church. Political freedom of religion is a great gift of God. During the first centuries of church history, Christians did not possess this gift. In today's world there are many regions where Christians still do not have this freedom or where they have lost it. This gift of freedom may well be taken away from us; however liberal the World Council of Churches may appear, in essence this council is as tyrannical as the Roman Catholic church.

18.8 In 1572, the snare broke (Ps. 124). In compassion over His oppressed church, the LORD God moved the political power from Philip II (king of Spain) to William of Nassau (prince of Orange). Orange did not start an armed rebellion, but as sovereign prince of Orange, he received strength and opportunity to use his political power and authority in the defence of God's church. His efforts were richly blessed. As sovereign prince in the Netherlands, he was able to guarantee the political rights and freedoms of all Dutchmen, especially those of God's church in these regions. As a Christian prince, he applied the apostolic word: be more obedient to God than to men (Acts 5:29). He had always honoured his lord, Philip II, king of Spain, but when he was ordered to persecute the church he received grace to refuse. As sovereign prince—and not as a rebel or guerrilla fighter—he recruited troops in agreement with constitutional law as it stood in the sixteenth century. In this way, God intervened for His oppressed church. He made the States of Holland and Zeeland willing to support the prince of Orange (Dordrecht, July 1572).

The Dutch Reformed churches were not set free as a result of revolution but because of God's compassion. God gave William of Orange the opportunity to exercise his duty and office with great blessings for the church. Before 1572, all the military plans of Orange failed, and he himself was forced to live as a fugitive in his father's castle. After 1572, he returned to give political leadership to the northern Netherlands.

18.9 The years 1572 - 1586 saw a rapid growth of the Reformed churches in the Netherlands. For the first time in Dutch history, the church offices functioned as instituted by Christ Himself. A national synod could be convened on Dutch soil: the National Synod of Dort, 1574. More cities joined the Reformation, but for a long time much of the countryside remained under the influence of the Roman Catholic church.

18.10 During the first meeting of the States of Holland in Dordrecht (1572), it was decided to adhere to the principle of freedom of worship for all. Unfortunately, this good start floundered in the following year when the Roman Catholic religion was prohibited. The Reformed church became the ruling, and therefore the most privileged, church.

18.11 The Libertines fought side by side with the Calvinists, but they were driven by the belief in *libertas* (freedom) of conscience and national freedom.

One of the most influential Libertines was Dirck Volkertszoon Coornheert (1522-1590). He started his career as a notary, later became town secretary in Haarlem, and finally became secretary to the States of Holland. He was considered the "Sebastian Franck" of Holland, being strongly anti-Calvinist. He tried to find peace for his soul in God's, as well as in his own, goodness. He believed that God would not spoil His own good creature. He did not find his comfort in the redemptive blood of Christ Jesus.

Coornheert is regarded as the father of Arminianism, the heresy which considered God's reconciliation through Christ's redemptive work only partly of value to sovereign man. The Libertines rejected the Belgic Confession and the Heidelberg Catechism, claiming that these documents contained only dead doctrine and dry letters.

18.12 The Struggle with the Arminians - Background
a.   Arminius (Jacob Hermandszoon Arminius, 1560-1609) was an orphan who had been able to study because of the generosity of the city of Amsterdam. As a minister in Amsterdam, he came into conflict with another minister, Petrus Plancius. Later, Arminius was promoted to professor at the University of Leyden where he became a colleague of Gomarus. Before the year 1600, only a few ministers in cities and provinces based their preaching on humanist (semipelagian) teachings, but after 1600, these heresies permeated also Arminius's lectures at the University of Leyden.
b.   Gomarus (Francis Gomar, 1567-1641) was the chief opponent of Arminius. He was born in Bruges (southern Netherlands) and studied in Strasbourg and other places. He was a student of Ursinus and became professor at the University of Leyden and later at the University of Groningen.

c.   Gomarus's struggle against Arminius is the same as the struggle of
        Augustine against Pelagius and Luther's struggle against Erasmus.
        The heart of Arminian teaching (also known as Remonstrantism)
        can be summarized as follows:
        1.   If man by his own free will elects to do good, then God
                elects such a good man.
        2.   If man wishes not to choose for God, then God cannot give
                him His grace either.
        3.   If man chooses for God, then God's grace can function.
d.   The struggle became even more difficult because the government
        interfered.
e.   The development of this struggle:
        1.   1608: Arminius and Gomarus met before the High Council.
                Gomarus claimed that he would not dare to appear before
                God's throne of judgement if he was of Arminius's opin-
                ion. Further, ecclesiastical matters must be dealt with in an
                ecclesiastical manner.
        2.   1609: Arminius died of tuberculosis. Johannes Uytenbogaert
                became the new leader. Uytenbogaert was chaplain for
                Prince Maurice of Orange.
        3.   1610: Uytenbogaert and forty other ministers presented a
                remonstrance to the States of Holland.
        4.   1611: Festus Hommius and other defenders of the Re-
                formed faith answered with a *contra-remonstrance*.
        5.   The struggle between the two parties became vicious and
                violent because of deep-seated religious hatred.
        6.   1617: Prince Maurice took sides and ordered his solemn
                oath of office which he pledged in 1586 to be read again.
                He restated his intention to protect the Reformed religion.
                With full retinue, he attended a church service in The
                Hague. The nation's secretary of state, Van Oldenbarnevelt,
                was imprisoned and later executed for high treason.
        7.   The congregation of Amsterdam was the first church that
                freed itself from the influences of caesaropapism (by the
                members of the States of Holland) and the teaching of
                Arminianism.
        8.   1618: A national synod convened on November 13 in the
                city of Dordrecht (Dort).

18.13 The Struggle with the Arminians: The Synod of Dort
a.   Its president was Reverend Johannes Bogerman, minister in
        Leeuwarden (Friesland) and friend of William Louis, a cousin of
        Prince Maurice. Many foreign theologians were present as well as
        eighteen commissioners of the States-General. The English king
        (who persecuted the faithful in his own country) was represented by
        a bishop.

b.   Synod decided to publish a new Bible translation. This transla-
       tion—the *Staten Vertaling*—was published in 1637. This translation
       has been a great gift of God to his church in the Netherlands,
       especially because of its marginal notes (commentaries). It has
       greatly influenced the life and culture of the Dutch nation. But the
       title page of this translation shows that a scriptural separation
       between church and state had not yet been achieved (compare this
       with the King James Version).

c.   The Remonstrants were ordered to appear before synod. But they
       refused to recognize the authority of the synod. They considered
       themselves a party that happened to be in opposition to the Re-
       formed party. To them, the synod was no more than a convention,
       and they refused to justify their position on the basis of God's
       Word. They demanded that the government decide in this dispute.
       Synod listened to them with much patience, but finally dismissed
       them.

d.   1.   May 6, 1619: Canons of Dort - the Five Articles against
          the Remonstrants:
          - Article 1:   Divine election and reprobation.
          - Article 2:   The death of Christ and the redemp-
                                  tion of man by it.
          - Articles 3-4:   The corruption of man, his conver-
                                  sion to God, and the manner in
                                  which it occurs.
          - Article 5:   The perseverance of the saints.
     2.   Dort maintained the scriptural doctrine of God's sovereign
          good pleasure. Those of the Remonstrant ministers who
          refused to stop preaching were banished from the country.
          Many left for France, often returning to the Roman Cath-
          olic church. In 1619, a Remonstrant brotherhood was
          formed in the city of Antwerp.
     3.   The church order, the confessions, and the liturgical forms
          were revised.

e.   The States-General never approved the church order of Dort. Full
       freedom for the church had not been achieved as yet. The church
       remained dependent on the state to some degree.

f.   After Dort, 1618-1619, no national synod was held until 1816.

THE CHURCH IN CONFLICT
WITH RATIONALISM AND ENLIGHTENMENT

1. INTRODUCTION - THE ENLIGHTENMENT

1.1 Overview
- 3d century: Paganism dominates
- 4th century: Paganism outlawed in Europe (380)
- 14th century: Revival of Greek-Roman paganism in humanism and Renaissance
- 16th century: Return to God's Word in the Reformation
- 17th century: Emphasis on man's piety
- 18th century: The evolution of rational man
- 19th century: The age of autonomous man
- 20th century: The age of postchristian and antichristian man

1.2 During the period between the time of the Reformation and the French Revolution, a renewed interest was shown in the Renaissance. The basic idea of the Renaissance is in essence the deepest self-actualization of fallen man. During the eighteenth century, this development became known as the Enlightenment (in German, *Aufklärung*). The famous German philosopher Immanuel Kant (1724-1804) described man's position before the Enlightenment in the following words: "The Enlightenment is man's conscious movement away from ignorance in which he dwelt due to his own fault and shortcoming. Ignorance is man's impotence to use his own intellect independently. This ignorance is not due to lack of intellectual power, but is due to lack of courage". Kant was one of Europe's greatest philosophers, but he abused his enormous intellectual talents by radically denying the authority of God's Word.

a. The medieval scholastics, while subjecting themselves to the authority of God's Word, attempted to make God's Word under-standable and acceptable to the human mind. These rational expla-nations would make it easier for unbelievers to accept that Word, suggesting that unbelievers were simply too ignorant to be able to understand God's Word without such help.

b. The Enlightenment, on the other hand, went much further, accept-ing the autonomy of reason and the sovereignty of intellect and science. This movement did not merely elevate itself above the

Word of God; it totally rejected any authority but its own. Its slogan was *sapere aude*—dare to be wise, use your own intellect and do not rely on God's Word, or on the confessions of the church. The men of the Enlightenment are the great destroyers of religion; they are the freethinkers who dare stand alone.
- Descartes   (1596-1650)
- Voltaire   (1694-1778)
- Rousseau   (1712-1778)

1.3   The Enlightenment accepted reason as the basis for the only acceptable worldview and the only workable philosophy. The remarkable scientific and technological developments (Galileo, Newton, Kepler, and others) promoted an almost unlimited trust in the power of the human mind. Insofar as eighteenth-century man accepted religion at all, his thoughts were far from scriptural. Some of these unscriptural ideas:

a.   The heart of all religions is the same. This statement denied the absolute truth of the Christian religion and led to relativism and scepticism.

b.   Jesus is a great teacher of virtue. Natural man is good but must become humane and tolerant over against those of different views.

c.   Christian refers to what is natural and what is truly humane. The new, reasonable religion is cleansed from the supernatural revelation of God's Word with its impossible miracles.

d.   God - virtue - immortality: these basic concepts could still be accepted since these were "natural" and therefore "Christian". The Christian faith was reduced to *deism*, the natural religion that claimed that God made this world like a clock and does not need to care for it any more. God no longer had significance for daily life. The fear of the Lord out of love for Him was lost; the truly Christian piety in daily communion with the Lord was gone. God no longer reigned from day to day; He was replaced by man the great organizer—also in the church. The general feeling of the people was one of optimistic humanism.

e.   However, when in the year 1775 a terrible earthquake and flood ravaged the city of Lisbon (Portugal), leaving fifty thousand dead, the deists panicked. A so-called *theodicy* was put together to explain the problem of evil and suffering in this world. Leibnitz suggested that evil was only a shadow to allow the light to shine even more brightly. In this way the need for adversity and sufferings was explained, but man's blind reasoning no longer saw God's curse, wrath, punishments, and judgements over this earth. People talked a great deal about God, but they did not know Him as their Father.

1.4   In 1717, the movement of *freemasonry* was established in England. Its basis was the absolute autonomy of the human mind. Its slogan was "Know thyself, control thyself, and ennoble thyself". God is the master builder of the cosmos. Freemasonry is a universal religion based on the most radical kind of humanism.

a.   Influenced by the tremendous scientific and technological developments of the nineteenth and twentieth centuries, many considered the whole notion of the existence of a god rather old-fashioned. The contrast between God's Word and man's thoughts became so great that the latter could not conceive of a place for the former; modern man no longer needed a god. The sovereign God of the Christians was declared dead, and His death was no great loss. He never existed anyway! Modern man only accepts what can be measured, tasted, and scientifically proven.

Centuries ago, the ancient Egyptians believed in their gods Isis and Osiris; the ancient Greeks believed in their gods such as Zeus on Mt. Olympus; the Romans had their gods such as Jupiter; the ancient Germans believed in gods such as Donar, Freya, and Wodan.

All of these gods had been abandoned, and now it was the Christian god's turn to be added to this historical-religious mausoleum of gods!

b.   Behind these pagan religions and gods stand demonic powers. The Bible does *not* say that these things are nonsense. The Apostle Paul writes, "What am I saying then? That an idol is anything, or what is offered to idols is anything? But I say that the things which the Gentiles sacrifice they sacrifice to demons and not to God, and I do not want you to have fellowship with demons. You cannot drink the cup of the Lord and the cup of demons; you cannot partake of the Lord's table and of the table of the demons" (1 Cor. 10:19-21).

c.   The Lord gives names to these demons: Chemosh, the detestable idol of Moab; Molech, the detestable idol of Ammon (1 Kings 11:7). The prophecies of Ezekiel clearly show God's anger with His church for serving those wretched idols. Certainly this divine damnation of the religious convictions of nonchurch people is considered intolerant and offensive to many. But consider the depths of evil to which the service of these idols led the children of Israel. In the very soil of the promised land, many earthenware jars have been found that contain the remains of small children— sacrifices to the gods of the Moabites and the Ammonites. It was Noah, the man with whom the LORD God made the new covenant of the new earth, a covenant that included the historic place for each of the earth's nations, who cursed Canaan. This curse was fulfilled when the Israelites were commanded to destroy all the

Canaanites with their abominable religions and bestiality. The demonic spirit of sexual perversity had already been present in the manner in which Ham and his son had shamed Noah (Gen. 9:24, 25).

d.   It was to preserve His Hebrew church that God commanded the total destruction of Canaan and its inhabitants. But Israel was not always obedient. Kings such as Ahab and Ahaz did not only permit the Canaan religions to be practised, they strongly promoted them. It can be shown from history that Canaan has been an accursed source of evil filth that has marred the world, in particular the countries around the Atlantic Ocean. Throughout history there has been a constant flow of seductive eroticism through the licentious idol worship of the Canaanite Baal and Ashtaroth, the Egyptian Isis and Osiris, as well as the abominations of the Greek goddess Aphrodite and the immoral Roman goddess Venus to the present-day European and American sex clubs with their erotic amusement which are no less than legalized brothels.

e.   One could only wish it to be true that these gods of evil had really been entombed in a historical-religious mausoleum, dead and long gone! Although these ancient gods are no longer mentioned, they are still very much alive in the modern man of lawlessness who wallows in the crimes and filth that came his way from Canaan through Hellenism and the Renaissance. The children of the covenant have never been so badly deceived as in our age. Why then should our God and Father in Christ Jesus not thunder His wrath against those who wallow with evil pleasure in abomination and filth?

f.   Never enter into a debate about the existence of God. Such a debate assumes that a justification of God's existence is necessary, and therefore it accepts, in essence, the basic position of the rebellion in paradise. The first words of the Bible do not state: There is a God. . . . Genesis 1 starts majestically with, "In the beginning God created. . . ." God starts by telling us what He has done even before there was anything or anyone. Never enter into a debate about the trustworthiness of Scripture. That is the demonic question posed by proud humanity, fallen away from God precisely because of that very question, "Has God indeed said. . . ?" (Gen. 3:1). We learn obedience only through listening. God gives certainty of faith in the way of obedient listening.

g.   Postchristian man is autonomous, free, *existential*. There is nothing beyond this world. The word *pagan* no longer has a contemptuous connotation as the word *barbarian* still has. Originally the word *barbarian* indicated a person who could not speak Greek (see 1 Cor. 14:11). After all, a reasonable and rational human being cannot be a Christian. For the first time since Emperor Constantine the Great, *pagan* has again become a respectable word.

h.   The modern "Philistines", with their self-made gods of science and technology and with their modern worldview, rule mightily over modern Israel (baptized Christendom), which is being deserted by God because it has deserted Him. The God of Israel is again imprisoned in the temple of Dagon, until He will again remember His people according to His Word.

i.   The prophecies of the Apostle Paul as well as those of the Apostle John are being fulfilled. Christendom in the countries bordering the Atlantic Ocean is consciously changing more and more into a willing anti-Christianity.

j.   With the Reformation, by means of which Christ, the light of this world, stimulated such tremendous growth and development of the European nations, came the ideology of the Renaissance, which influenced those countries by means of the powers of demonic darkness in the shape of the light of reason, the Enlightenment (Satan is Lucifer, the prince of light).

k.   In the sixteenth century, God sent a power so that many might believe the truth. During the twentieth century, God sent the people "strong delusion, that they should believe the lie" (2 Thess. 2:11).

1.5   The period following the end of the struggle between the Reformation and the Counter-Reformation saw the development of all sorts of individualistic movements that emphasized piety as life's central concern. These piety movements came about in reaction to dead orthodoxy and the rebellion of paganism of the Renaissance and Enlightenment.

in France   - Jansenism
in Germany   - Pietism
in England   - Methodism
in the Netherlands   - Reformed Mysticism

1.6   These post-Reformation movements may well be compared with the pre-Reformation movement of the Modern Devotion. None of these movements was truly reformational since they did not bring the people back to the living Word of God in faith.

These piety movements were a reaction to the deadly "reasonable" religion that had caused the church to fall short of the grace of God (Heb. 12:15). These movements shunned dead doctrine, emphasizing the pious life as the way back to God. However, Scripture does not make a distinction and contrasts between piety and confession. Such a contrast is the evil result of scholastic reasoning. The Reformation had managed to halt these teachings temporarily, but during the eighteenth century they returned, overpowering God's people.

a.   Often Christians claim that they believe that the Bible is true and that God certainly exists. But they are often blind to God's works

of blessings and punishment. They live from day to day in complacency, undisturbed by personal and communal sin. Such Christians
practice deism without recognizing it. They live in total self-
assurance, for all practical purposes without God (Eph. 2:12). Such
deistic Christians deny Belgic Confession, Article 2, which states
that we (believers) know Him (God) by two means: by His Word
and by His work. Although facts and events are not the norms for
our life (God's Word provides those norms), God's works do speak
to us also.

b.   Note how Scripture admonishes us to consider our ways (Hag. 1:5,
      7; Hag. 2:16, 19, 20). Also note the precise dates mentioned by the
      prophet: "In the second year of King Darius, in the sixth month, on
      the first of the month, the word of the LORD came. . . ." Using a
      modern calendar, that date has been identified as August 29, 520
      B.C.   Other dates of Haggai's prophecies have been calculated as
      September 21, 521 B.C.; October 18, 520 B.C.; and December 18,
      520 B.C.   We may notice the hand of the LORD God at work in
      the events of every day. "Heed the (swishing of the) rod and the
      One who appointed it" (Mic. 6:9 NIV; see also Isa. 42:25).

c.   We may recognize the LORD God through His Word, and then we
      may recognize Him in His work.

d.   During the period from Adam to Abraham, the nations were never
      without the proclamation of His spoken Word, and during the
      period from Abraham to Christ, God spoke to Israel in particular.
      Since Pentecost, His Word goes out to all creatures. Already from
      the time of paradise God has permitted man to know Him by
      means of His self-revelation. Man knows God's justice. There is no
      excuse for anyone. Neither are there "bare" facts (facts without the
      revelation of the Word, see Rom. 1:18-32; Rom. 2:14-15).

e.   We maintain against scholasticism that God's Word is never
      without his work.
      We maintain against deism that God's work is never without his
      Word.

f.   Read Paul's speech to the Athenians on the Areopagus about the
      guilty ignorance of the people (Acts 17:15-34). Paul recognizes the
      ignorance of these people, but he does not excuse them because of
      it. Speaking scripturally and church-historically, every person is a
      covenant breaker since paradise, because he was willing to listen to
      the antigospel of Satan.

2. FRANCE - JANSENISM

2.1   Cornelius Jansen (1585-1638) was of Dutch birth and became
bishop of Ypres (in present-day Belgium). His most well-known book,
Augustinus, was published after his death. It made quite an impression.

Jansen strongly opposed the teachings of the Jesuits and defended the doctrine of grace as taught by Augustine.

2.2 The monastery at Port Royal de Champ became the centre of this movement. The Jansenists counted among their followers the famous Blaise Pascal (1623-1662), the great mathematician. Pascal's *Provincial Letters* forcefully and brilliantly exposed the morals of the Jesuits. His *Pensees* (still widely read) contained a defence of the Christian religion in the form of a series of aphorisms.

At the instigation of the Jesuits, the monastery at Port Royal was closed; later even the buildings were demolished.

2.3 In 1713, the pope officially condemned the doctrine of grace as taught by Augustine and by implication therefore condemned the teachings of the Jansenists. Semipelagianism triumphed in the apostate Roman Catholic Church.

2.4 Many Jansenists fled to the Netherlands. Partly due to their views and partly due to the antagonism of the Jesuits, the Jansenists separated from the Roman Catholic Church to form the Old Catholic Church (1765). This church has some twelve thousand members in thirty parishes, with about thirty priests, three bishops, and the archbishop of Utrecht as the head of the church. Celibacy is not compulsory for the clergy. This denomination has its own seminary at Amersfoort (the Netherlands). Since World War II, attempts have been made to reestablish contact with the Roman Catholic Church through the Dutch Roman Catholic cardinal. The Old Catholic Church has also joined in the ecumenical movement.

2.5 One of the greatest victories of the Enlightenment was achieved when the Roman Catholic Church was forced to disband the Jesuit order in 1773. However, in 1814, this order was reinstated.

3. GERMANY - PIETISM

3.1 Pietism is a typically German movement, coming out of the Lutheran state church of the seventeenth century. This movement came about in reaction to the rationalistic and intellectualistic heresies that were eroding Christianity during that time.

3.2 Philip Jacob Spener (1635-1705) was a Lutheran minister. He organized separate meetings for believers who wanted to share their religious experiences with each other (collegia pietatis—this led to the nickname pietists). In his major work, *Pia Desideria* (Pious Desires), Spener sharply criticized the uninspiring, deadly atmosphere that prevailed in the churches of his days. He urged training in godliness, emphasizing not doctrine, but life. The leaders of the Lutheran orthodoxy fiercely opposed him.

Spener's work resulted in the founding of a pietist faculty at the University of Halle (Germany), which became the centre of the pietist movement, almost forming a church within the church (ecclesiola in ecclesia).

3.3   August Herman Francke (1663-1727) was the organizer of German pietism and the founder of the famous *Franckesche Stiftungen*—schools, hospitals, and orphanages for the neglected youth of his days. This work of mercy spread throughout Germany and became known as *home mission*, an extension of the work of the deacons.

Francke strongly emphasized the importance of the religious experience and the sudden conversion (the believer should be able to name hour, date, and place). His legalistic attitude, strict educational views, and a very grave outlook on life (children's games were folly) may be understood best as a reaction against the self-complacency of the Christians of his time.

Halle became the centre for the German pietist mission into India.

3.4   The wealthy Nicolas Ludwig Von Zinzendorf (1700-1760) was a pupil of Spener and Francke. The Moravians (followers of Hus) found refuge on his estate at Berthelsdorf. This community became known as *Hernhut* (under God's care) and is known for its deep mystical, spiritual-experiential faith.

3.5   There is quite a difference between Francke (Halle) and Zinzendorf (Hernhut). Francke emphasized the importance of the serious penitential faith experience of pious man. Zinzendorf rejected sudden conversion, and pietist legalism but beamed forth a childlike (although at times almost childish) joy about Jesus' love for sinners.

3.6   The Moravian Brethren (the United Brethren) were zealous missionaries. At their own risk they went to Greenland, the Gold Coast, Surinam, Russia, and South Africa. By the time of Von Zinzendorf's death (1760), some two hundred missionaries had already been sent out. Their often lonely gravestones are found in the wildernesses around the world.

Against the wishes of Von Zinzendorf, the Moravians founded their own church—without a confession and with only a "Saviour theology".

3.7   The power of the "spiritual experience" was unable to withstand the onslaught of the power of reason (the Enlightenment), which managed to replace experiential faith with a "reasonable religion".

4. ENGLAND - METHODISM

4.1   Many persecuted European Christians found refuge in North America. Therefore protestantism gained quite some influence in the New World. Already in 1646, John Eliot (England) preached among the Indians, but sadly enough, throughout the years, many of these American natives died at the hands of protestant *pale faces*. Hans Egede (Denmark) preached the gospel among the Eskimos of Greenland (1721).

4.2   The Quakers were English Baptists. George Fox (1624-1691) was their leader. He relied on inner voices rather than on God's Word. The Quakers gained great influence in North America, especially through the work of William Penn, the successor of Fox and the founder of the Quaker state of Pennsylvania. The Quakers have the honour of being the first to arouse the world against the church's gravest sin, slavery. Often, runaway slaves were assisted by Quakers wherever and whenever possible. Today, many influential Americans belong to the Quaker movement and provide help across the world in many works of mercy.

4.3   *Methodism*
a.   The founder of Methodism was John Wesley (1703-1791). His conversion, as reported by himself, took place on May 24, 1738, at a quarter to nine at night. "My work is to save souls. I look upon the whole world as my parish."
b.   Originally the term *Methodist* was a nickname given to Wesley and his friends because of their very strict rules for their lives. Later they adopted the name, and the method of conversion recommended by Wesley became the rule. The brothers Wesley (John and Charles) travelled widely throughout England and became known as "the cavalry of protestant Christendom". Wesley was an Arminian revivalist, and the Methodist movement is characterized by a strongly legalistic idea of sanctification. They concerned themselves mainly with the common (often neglected) people, and they became the comforters of the poor, the prisoners, and the destitute.
c.   George Whitefield (1715-1770), a Calvinist and a friend of the Wesleys, also gained fame as a preacher. He preferred to speak in the open air, rather than in a church building, to reach the lost souls of his days. There are many different kinds of Methodist groups in England as well as in America. Methodists have noticeably influenced the whole of the Anglo-Saxon world on both sides of the Atlantic Ocean.
d.   This typically British form of revivalism resulted in:

- The British and Foreign Bible Society which was founded in 1804. Through the work of this society, the Bible became the world's most read book.
- The centre of world mission shifted from Germany (Moravians) to England and America (Methodists), particularly in the work of William Carey.
- The Salvation Army was founded by William Booth (1829-1912).

e. One of the best known revivalists of the nineteenth century was Charles H. Spurgeon (1834-1892). He preached in the Metropolitan Tabernacle (London), especially built for him, to audiences often in excess of five thousand.

5. THE NETHERLANDS - REFORMED MYSTICISM

5.1 By God's grace, the Dutch Republic received both political and religious freedom so that this country became a place of refuge for persecuted Christians from all of Europe. These refugees found comfort in the words of the Lord Jesus himself, "Assuredly, I say to you, there is no one who has left house or brothers or sisters or father or mother or wife or children or lands for My sake and the gospel's, who shall not receive a hundredfold now in this time—houses and brothers and sisters and mothers and children and lands, with persecutions—and in the age to come, eternal life" (Mark 10:29, 30). Many foreigners found religious freedom and employment in Holland.

a. Before 1648, many people arrived from the southern Netherlands and England (the Puritans).

b. After 1648, many Lutheran refugees and refugees from Hungary arrived. It was the Dutch admiral De Ruyter who at one time freed twenty-six Hungarian ministers from the war galleys of the Turks in the Mediterranean Sea.

c. A great deal of money was sent to Switzerland to help the Waldensians. November 28, 1733, was declared a public day of rejoicing when many destitute Waldensians arrived in Amsterdam.

d. The French Huguenots founded their own *eglises Wallones* and brought with them an upsurge in industry. The city of Amsterdam grew well beyond the confines of its city walls.

e. Many Jews, especially those from Spain and Portugal, found refuge in Holland. Among them was the well-known philosopher Baruch Spinoza. The wealthy Jew Lopez Suasso offered Stadholder William III one million *gulden* to help him finance the invasion of England in 1688 (the Glorious Revolution). He remarked, "If you are successful I'll get my money back; if not, well, then I've lost it. . . ."

5.2   It is humiliating to discover how blind these richly blessed Reformed churches have been to the sins of the society of their days. While great sums of money were gladly offered to help persecuted brothers and sisters in foreign countries, at the same time enormous profits were made in the most wretched of all trades, the slave trade.

By the end of the Middle Ages, slavery was known only in the city of Venice. But the voyages of exploration brought back this evil. African negroes were snatched from their homelands by the thousands and shipped to America.

The greatest evildoers and profiteers were the British (the country of Knox and Cromwell), and the Dutch traders (the nation that honoured Calvin and held Guido de Bres's confession high). The Dutch were the best: only 30 percent of their slaves died aboard their ships as they crossed the ocean. The Dutch traders were most ingenious in devising loading plans that would guarantee the greatest profits.

It is strange that this inhuman trade was never a point of discussion or dispute in the struggles between the Roman Catholic Church and the followers of the Reformation nor was part of the struggles between Remonstrants and Contra-Remonstrants. Not only did the Christian nations of Europe (both Roman Catholic and protestant) commit human plunder they were also guilty of the genocide of the Indians of North America, the Aztecs, the Incas in South America, and the Aborigines of Tasmania. In the meantime, at home the common people lived under social corruption and oppression.

a.   Already in the book of the covenant (God's own first commentary on the ten words of the covenant) it is clearly stated: "He who kidnaps a man shall surely be put to death" (Ex. 21:16). Forty years later, Moses repeated this commandment in the much broader explanation of Horeb's law (Deut. 24:7). Paul also refers to this evil in his discussion of the eighth commandment to Timothy (1 Tim. 1:9, 10). Despite the confession of the depravity of man, the meaning of these words of God was not understood. Despite the fruits of the Reformation, avarice caused a return to the old sins of social oppression that had been almost eradicated in the Middle Ages.

b.   The wealth of the Golden Age of the seventeenth century rested partially in the blood of slaves and in social injustice (James 5:4). Many a wealthy merchant ordered a painting of himself and his family from one of the great masters, often with a brown slave in the background. These paintings can now be viewed in museums around the world.

c.   As late as 1788, the Dutch slave trade was booming, with some two hundred thousand "items of merchandise" per year!

d.   Natives of the islands of the Dutch East Indies were also used as slaves, especially the physically strong Sudanese. Holland was one of the last nations to abolish the slave trade (1863). As late as 1905, an advertisement appeared in a Dutch East Indian church paper drawing attention to wares for sale such as strong and cheap coolies and healthy cattle.

e.   In our days, the negroes of the southern states of the United States have not forgotten the Dutchmen who transported their forebears from Africa.

f.   The twentieth-century negro rebellions, the hatred against the whites (for instance, in Africa), and the insolvable racial problems across the world are the terrible results of these historical sins against millions of black and coloured people in European colonies.

g.   But the revolutionary cry for human rights often results in an untimely granting of political autonomy and self-rule. Many of these young nations are unable to handle such freedoms and responsibilities. Cruel and vicious tribal wars and religious battles are often the result. Revolution never fulfils its promises. Man remains what he is, a slave to sin. "Therefore if the Son makes you free, you shall be free indeed" (John 8:36).

5.3   It is true that the Dutch people were primarily interested in trade and commerce; but it is equally true that the Dutch Reformed churches of the seventeenth century also recognized their missionary calling. Traders were almost always accompanied by missionaries and lay preachers. Churches were established around the world, and the results of these mission efforts may still be seen today, for instance, in the Reformed Churches of Sri Lanka and Taiwan.

5.4   But during the seventeenth and eighteenth centuries, our forefathers did not obey the laws of the covenant (Deut. 32:15). Church membership was often no more than an obligation, perfunctory, the thing to do. The magistrates had great influence in the church. The admonitions of Amos apply to them, "Woe to you who are at ease in Zion, and trust in Mount Samaria, notable persons in the chief nation, to whom the house of Israel comes!" (Amos 6:1). What self-sufficiency, complacency, and conceit in the church of Jesus Christ. In later years, such government control had a disastrous effect. Political tolerance (public freedom of religion) became religious tolerance (freedom of doctrine). The church was powerless against these heresies because of its own false religiosity. The church no longer lived by its confession but joined in the worship of the goddess of reason.

5.5   Rene Descartes (Cartesius, 1596-1650) was the father of rationalism in Holland. He accepted reason as the only certain, firm basis of knowledge. *Je pense, donc je suis—cogito ergo sum—I think therefore I am.* Descartes claimed, "I can think, I am conscious, and this fact rises above all doubt". This is an example of the typical pagan basis of Renaissance thought.

Descartes's slogan typifies autonomous, sovereign man in all his pride and independence, denying the very idea of dependence as a creature. However, Descartes forgot to ask, Who is this "I" that thinks? Believers confess that they are God's creatures and that therefore they can think (*creatus sum ergo cogito*). Descartes attempted to construct all truth on the basis of a rational argument, relying on man's rational intellect rather than on faith in God's revelation.

This lying spirit took the church by storm. The covenant was denied, and the basis of man's certainty and sure knowledge was found within himself and not in God. This philosophy was the beginning of modern subjectivism that eventually ended with the twentieth-century existentialist philosophy of despair. Therefore Descartes may be seen as the forerunner of the eighteenth-century Enlightenment and of the humanist rationalism of the twentieth century.

5.6   This Cartesian rationalism invaded the church, with these results:
- The Word of God was reduced to at best a Reformed philosophical system of thought.
- The confessions became the ecclesiastical law.
- Instead of a living faith, the believers heard about a faith based on reason, which needed to be supplemented by piety.
- These developments reduced the preaching to dry, scholastic, learned discourses.

No longer was man's surety found in God's faithful promises and his truths; the basis of man's faith became his reasoning ability.

5.7   Gijsbert Voetius (1589-1676) was one of the leaders of the typically Dutch Reformed mystical movement (de Nadere Reformatie). He was a pupil of Gomarus and a member of the Synod of Dort. For more than forty years, he was professor of theology at Utrecht.
a.   He was a fierce opponent of the followers of Descartes, who, in effect, opposed the Word of God with their scholarly and scholastic theological approach. But Voetius's position was badly and sadly weakened because he himself also reduced Scripture to a dry system of Reformed thought. Voetius was considered an old-fashioned scholastic, whereas the Cartesians were the modern rationalists who deviated much further from Scripture than did Voetius. Both sides tried to prove that the reasoning of the other was wrong.
b.   In reaction to the scholastic teachings of Voetius, which badly stifled Christian life, Johannes Cocceius (1603-1669), a Frisian professor of theology, countered with an almost libertine view of

Christian freedom. The result was a bitter struggle between the followers of Voetius and those of Cocceius. But neither of them recognized that the wisdom of human reasoning was foolishness before God (1 Cor. 1).

c.   In its haughtiness and pride, rationalism caused deafness to the Word of the sovereign God. The scientific objectivity of the dry and dead systems of doctrine attracted many but also forced many others to seek spiritual nourishment in a subjective faith experience (conventicles).

-    Religious subjectivism suggested that it was possible to experience God's Word. This experience was then proof of the reality of God's speaking to the individual.

-    Religious objectivism suggested that it was possible to take distance from God's Word and to talk about it in a scholarly fashion (rather than listen to it) without becoming personally and emotionally involved.

-    The Bible rejects such subjectivism and objectivism in Hebrews 4:12: "For the word of God is living and powerful, . . . and is the discerner of the thoughts and intents of the heart." God's Word is always living and active.

d.   Voetius himself was both objective (scholastic) and subjective (puritan-pietist). Therefore he was in a weak position when called upon to defend the Reformed teachings over against the Labadists, the followers of Jean de la Badie (1610-1674). These people were appalled by the lack of simplicity and sincerity of faith in the church. The criticism of the Labadists was not without grounds, but these people were mystic and Anabaptist rather than reformed in their views. They founded communes dedicated to a simple life style and a sharing of earthly possessions.

5.8   The adoration of human reason and the emphasis on personal feeling and emotion severely hindered the development of truly scriptural devotion and piety. Voetius praised Thomas à Kempis as a man whose writings were simple, strong, and pious. Certainty of faith was sought in the signs of faith. Constantly those signs were observed and examined to determine whether true faith was indeed present. This obsession with one's own faith was the result of the rejection of God's promises. Not God's grace but constant self-examination was thought to be the road toward spiritual wholesomeness.

5.9   Was there still a faithful Reformed church in the Netherlands? In the eighteenth century, the apostasy of the Reformed Churches in the Netherlands seemed complete. Everyone was orthodox; everyone was religious; yet little of the true worship of God was visible. The people were religious, but they were not faithful (full of faith). In fact, the

Reformed scholastics worshipped the image of reason and lived by a Reformed system of thought only. The mystical-pietist attitude permeated the whole church. It was as in the days of Manasseh, king of Judah, who persecuted the faithful, including Isaiah (2 Kings 21:16). The disputes between the rationalists and those who believed in experiential faith were fierce. The situation in those days was identical to that at the end of the Middle Ages with the scholastics opposing the mystics in bitter debate.

Eventually the government was forced to interfere and proclaimed the Act of Tolerance (1694)—as if such an act would have any effect on servants of idols! What was needed was repentance. The people needed to learn again to listen in obedience to the living God who speaks to us in His Word, and is never silent!

With this Act of Tolerance, the road was open for the entry of the ideas of the Enlightenment into the church. The leaders of the church had an attitude similar to that of the Pharisees, as legalistic as that of the Scribes, as haughty as that of the Sadducees, and as harsh and cruel as that of the leaders of the synagogue. The people were without scriptural norms, and the true believers were without shepherds. The Remonstrants had triumphed after all.

5.10 Mystic revival movements appeared in a variety of forms, but all with a strong emphasis on personal virtues and piety. Alexander Comrie (1706-1774) was one of the few who continued to call for true reformation in his book, *The ABCs of Faith*. But his opposition to tolerance in the church went largely unheeded.

In 1773, the government imposed upon the churches a new psalter which strongly breathed the spirit of deism, pietism, and mystical experience.

5.11 The generation of the sixteenth century was allowed to return to the Word of the Lord. They were permitted to suffer for the sake of their God.

The generations of the seventeenth and eighteenth centuries became disobedient and apostate. "People will call them rejected silver, because the Lord has rejected them" (Jer. 6:30). These generations committed the sins of Jeroboam, namely Bethel worship. Compare the paintings of men of the sixteenth century (Rembrandt) with portraits of the eighteenth-century people: lifeless faces with powdered wigs. Little work was done. The wealthy enjoyed their wealth while the poor relied on the poor house. Truly Reformed literature (the writings of Calvin and De Bres) was largely unknown, while pietist writings of people such as Sebastian Francke filled gullible minds. Relativism, nurtured by endless debates, eventually turned into indifference.

5.12 The situation within the Dutch Reformed Churches of the eighteenth century may well be compared with the situation in the papal church at the time of the Reformation. The final hour had arrived for these churches. The Lord came with his judgements and commanded the cultures to gather because the church had reduced itself to carrion (Luke 17:37). The blessings of God's covenant (the Golden Age) were replaced by the curses of that same covenant (the French Revolution).

Stadholder William V recognized this. When he was forced to flee to England, his final words spoken on Dutch soil have been recorded as: "The true source of our misery does not lie in the betrayal of our friends and allies, but in our national sins and unrighteousness: God has a quarrel with the Netherlands."

THE STRUGGLE TO BE
AND TO REMAIN TRUE CHURCH

1. SEPARATED FROM THE STATE, BUT NOT YET FREE

1.1   During the eighteenth century, Europe sank into a deistic religion. The people did no longer know their LORD, the God of the covenant. Deism is atheism in disguise since it removes God from everyday life. (See Eph. 2:12, ". . . having no hope and without God in the world.") The French Revolution turned out to be an unrighteous deception (2 Thess. 2:10), announcing the arrival of "the man of sin" (2 Thess. 2:3). Ever since the time of the first Christian Roman emperor Constantine the Great, the enmity against the LORD and his anointed (Ps. 2:2) had been restrained by the gospel, but the enemy now strove for power with even greater audacity. Groen Van Prinsterer called this revolution a total change in thought and attitude. It started in France but eventually engulfed all of Christianity. In essence, the causes of the French Revolution should not be sought in the social problems of those times but in man's evil desire to become autonomous, independent from his Creator. The actress Candeille was placed on a throne in the cathedral of Notre Dame at Paris as the goddess of reason.

1.2   Never before in history was the rejection of all law and authority considered to be a basic principle in society and a legal right of its citizens. Revolution is systematized unbelief. It preaches the rights of man and can only be countered by the preaching of the rights of God.
   Groen Van Prinsterer writes in his *Unbelief and Revolution*, "The significance of the revolution for the history of the world is the reverse of the significance of the Reformation for Christianity. Just as the Reformation saved Europe from unbelief, so, in reverse, the Enlightenment has thrown civilization back into the abyss of unbelief. Like the Reformation, so the revolution touches every area of life and study. With the former the principle was subjection to God; with the latter the principle became revolt against God. Therefore there continues to be in the church, in the state, and in study of the scholar a general and holy struggle about the question concerning the unconditional subjection to the laws of God".

1.3 The terrible realities of the revolution were discovered by the Dutch nation when it was occupied from 1795 - 1816 by the French revolutionary forces. Holland became a separate republic under French control (*De Bataafse Republiek*—the Batavian Republic). The last Dutch stadholder, William V, fled to England in 1795. When he boarded the fishing vessel that was to take him and his household to safety, he spoke of the calamity that had come over Holland. "God has a quarrel with the Netherlands, and shows this in the failure of all attempts to prevent the French from invading the country. The severe frost even made the rivers into highways. If God throws down, who shall lift up?"

While the stadholder sailed across the North Sea to safety, so-called patriotic ministers welcomed the French as the liberators of mankind. But these servants of the church were blind to the wrath of the LORD of the church. They organized prayer services in the churches to thank God for the frozen rivers and for the arrival of the defenders of the rights of man. They did not discern what was really happening. "Hear, O earth! Behold, I will certainly bring calamity on this people, even the fruit of their thoughts, because they have not heeded My law, but rejected it" (Jer. 6:19). Indeed, it was a frightening time for all who feared the LORD and acknowledged the rights of His covenant.

Napoleon was not the defender of man's rights, as many thought, but he was a scourge in the hands of God.

1.4 During those fearful years, many parents fervently prayed to God for their (baptized) sons who were conscripted by the French. Many did not return from Napoleon's bloody campaigns, including the invasion of Russia. Some years ago, Dutch coins were found during excavations near the Berezina River. The LORD brought upon the people a sword that executed vengeance for the covenant (Lev. 26:25). He brought "great and prolonged plagues" (Deut. 28:59) on His European church. Young Christians died gruesome deaths and became refuse on the ground (Jer. 16:4; Jer. 25:33).

But in the end, "His soul could no longer endure the misery of Israel" (Judges 10:16). He remembered His covenant and rescued His people.

1.5 One result of the French occupation of the Netherlands was the separation between church and state. The material goods of the churches were declared to be the property of the state. Many ministers of the Word fell into poverty; some were forced to sell their books, their furniture, or even their clothes.

Much of the material goods of the Dutch churches (for instance, estates and buildings) had originally been the properties of the old medieval church and monasteries. Ever since the Reformation, the profits of those properties were used to pay the salaries of the Reformed ministers.

1.6   There was no longer one privileged denomination. Tolerance prevailed, following the slogans of the French Revolution: liberty, equality, and fraternity for all. References to the Synod of Dort and to the confessions were not permitted since this synod, as well as the old confessions left no room for the ideas of others (including the ideas of the Remonstrants). The church was not free to govern itself; there was no opportunity to hold ecclesiastical meetings—the last synod was held in 1618-1619. Ministers were forced to swear allegiance to the state. Those who refused were dishonourably dismissed.

Despite the threats, some refused to pledge allegiance to the state. Reverend Nicolas Schotman (1754-1822) was one of them. He was suspended by the (French) authorities. Later his suspension was lifted. However, after the return of King William I, things did not improve.

1.7   After the return of the son of Stadholder William V as King William I (1813) and the final defeat of the French (Battle of Waterloo, 1815), life in Holland returned to normal. In 1815, the ministers were again placed on the payroll of the state. This right (that ministers of the church were to be paid by the state) was even enshrined in the constitution. However, the question remained which churches should benefit from this regulation. But even more sadly, the church remained under the rule of the state (caesaropapism), and tolerance was the declared doctrine. Indeed, things did not improve.

In the bicentennial year of the Synod of Dort (1818-1819), officially ignored by the state church, Reverend Nicolas Schotman published two addresses entitled *Monument in Commemoration of the National Synod Held Two Hundred Years Ago in Dordrecht, Erected by Nicolas Schotman*. Of course the (Dutch) authorities could not tolerate such a publication. How did Schotman dare to bind the church to those despicable decisions against the Remonstrants! This aging pastor was scorned and vilified. But Willem Bilderdijk, the father of the Dutch *Réveil* movement, defended him publicly in a preface to the second printing of this *Monument*.

2. THE NETHERLANDS REFORMED CHURCH 1816 - 1834

2.1   One of the first acts of William I, king of the Netherlands, following his coronation in 1815, was to provide for the material welfare of the ministers of the Dutch state church, mainly from his own estate. However well meant, with this deed the king showed that he did not understand the civil rights and freedom of the church to govern itself. The king did not merely provide the necessary finances; he wished to control the church.

King William I should have been advised to follow the example of his illustrious forebear, Prince Maurice, who defended the civil rights and freedom of the church against the Arminian magistrates. That is the task of the government. As a result of the actions of Prince Maurice, the church was able to meet in the Synod of Dort (1618-1619). But King William I prevented the church from exercising its own task, even robbing the church of its right to meet in its major assemblies.

2.2 On January 7, 1816, legislation was passed that regulated the organization of the Reformed Church in the Netherlands. These regulations replaced the Church Order of Dort, which was accepted by the Synod of Dort, 1618-1619. Legitimate protests (after all, the king had no right to regulate the affairs of the church) against this legislation were denied. The protests of the Classis Amsterdam were not even considered since under the new regulations this classical district no longer existed.

2.3 Some of the main points of these royal regulations:
a.   The official name of the church became the Netherlands Reformed Church (singular!).
b.   The highest authority in the church was a national synod. Members of the first synod were appointed by the king. The chairman and secretary of each subsequent synod were also royal appointees.
c.   The organizational structure of the church consisted of provincial and classical boards, with the local consistories at the bottom of this hierarchical structure.

2.4 The results of the royal restructuring of the church can be summarized as follows:
a.   With the abolition of the Church Order of Dort, the Reformed churches had become an association with national, provincial, and classical (regional) boards. The local congregations were local branches of this association. The local churches with their Christ-instituted offices lost their rights and were no longer governed in a truly presbyterian manner but by a hierarchy of ecclesiastical boards.
b.   Although old names were retained, the church came under even greater state influence and hierarchical control than ever before.
c.   And worst of all, freedom of doctrine remained.

2.5 The new formulation of the form to be signed by ministers, the so-called Form of Subscription, contained a subtle change. Ministers were no longer required to teach the doctrine that was in agreement with God's Word. The new phrasing allowed this interpretation: in as much as (according to one's own insight) the doctrine was in agreement with God's Word. This formulation resulted in an unofficial but nevertheless effective removal of the Three Forms of Unity as confessions of the true and complete doctrine of salvation. This permitted thieves and robbers into the sheepfold (John 10:1).

The road was now open for individual decisions regarding what was and was not to be considered the doctrine of God's Word. No longer the Word of God but the word of autonomous, enlightened man was the authority in the church. This practice received an official and legal place in the church. By 1854, ministers were asked to declare that they agreed to maintain the spirit and the main points of the doctrine of the church. One hundred years later, in 1954, the Netherlands Reformed Church confessed its faith together with, but not necessarily in agreement with, the teachings of the fathers. Although this church wants to confess its faith, the confessions are no longer considered of any value.

2.6 Later, the state withdrew its direct involvement in church matters, and the church was ruled by the synod. Since all denominations received equal rights, the Roman Catholic Church was able to reestablish its ecclesiastical hierarchy in Holland for the first time since the Reformation (1853), resulting in some strong but ineffective protests.

2.7 Groen Van Prinsterer commented about this time that it was amazing that despite apostasy and deterioration in the church, there was a general sense of satisfaction and resulting complacency. The state of the nation was considered to be quite excellent, especially when compared with other nations. Elsewhere nations were troubled by confusion and quarrels, but in Holland there was peace and unity. How blind the church was, as blind as Israel had been so often! Many lived by the law and religious precepts. Respectability was the hallmark of the church. Few lived by faith in Christ. It was left to individual ministers which baptismal formula was used in the church: I baptize you in the name of the congregation. . . . I baptize you in the name of faith, hope, and love. . . . I baptize you so that you may be incorporated into Christianity. . . .

3. THE *RÉVEIL*

3.1 *Le Réveil* (awakening, revival) is the name given to a European religious movement of the first half of the nineteenth century. By God's grace, this movement came about in several European countries and resulted in a strong witness against the spirit of apathy and self-righteousness that prevailed in the mainline churches.

3.2 In Switzerland (Geneva), many liberals opposed the scriptural preaching of Reverend Cesar Malan, who himself had been an unbeliever.

In Belgium (Brussels), Reverend Merle d'Aubigne was drawn to the gospel, and under his preaching the well-known Dutch historian and politician Groen van Prinsterer and his wife became faithful Christians.

In Germany, the *Réveil* focused mainly on the social misery within a harsh world of dead orthodoxy.

3.3   One of the fathers of the Dutch *Réveil* movement was Willem Bilderdijk (1756-1831). He witnessed against the secular spirit of his age, using every opportunity to fight against the proponents of the revolution. As a latter-day Samson, Bilderdijk began "to deliver Israel out of the hands of the Philistines" (Judges 13:5; 14:4).

The main leader of the Dutch *Réveil* was Isaac Da Costa (1798-1860), a poet and preacher of note and a disciple of Bilderdijk. His booklet, *Objections to the Spirit of the Age* (1823), was hard hitting, leading many back to God's Word. However, the police kept track of the followers of Da Costa. It was obvious that tolerance and acceptance knew limitations; everyone could say and preach whatever he desired, except those who spoke of sin and guilt and urged repentance. Da Costa's Bible readings on Sunday evenings in Amsterdam became well known.

The politician Groen van Prinsterer also belonged to the Dutch *Réveil* movement.

3.4   The *Réveil* was a reaction against the prevailing rationalism and materialism of the nineteenth century, emphasizing the importance of and the need for personal fellowship with God by faith in Jesus Christ. These people often gathered together during evening meetings for Bible reading and prayer.

There was much division among those who struggled for the reformation of the church. Da Costa, who considered the church to be a sick patient, disagreed with Groen van Prinsterer, who urged the church to return to the truth of God's Word as confessed in the Three Forms of Unity.

3.5   Many of the followers of the *Réveil* were members of the upper class in society. They were genuinely concerned with the social plight of the common people; much was done to remove all kinds of social ills, and much help was provided for the poor, widows, and orphans.

But the *Réveil* was no true reformation. This movement emphasized individual piety and was not directed toward the scriptural functioning of the church in its biblical offices. Rather than a national movement, it remained an effort for reform by some members of the aristocracy and the rich, who met at home and not in the church. By 1854, the *Réveil* as a revival movement had lost its impact.

4. THE SECESSION OF 1834

4.1   In 1827, a certain Reverend D. Molenaar wrote an anonymous brochure against the freedom of doctrine, which by that time was officially accepted in the church, *Address to All My Reformed Fellow Believers*. He attacked the ambiguity in the Form of Subscription, exposing its unbiblical and unreformed character. He urged his fellow believers to reform the church. This brochure caused a great stir. The police became involved, and even the king himself interfered since it was claimed that Reverend Molenaar had prophesied against the "king's sanctuary" and the "royal residence" (Amos 7:12, 13). Under such pressure, Reverend Molenaar recanted, and publicly expressed his regret for writing that brochure. Later, he was honoured by King William II at the occasion of the latter's coronation, an indication of the king's most tolerant attitude.

However, despite the royal disapproval, this booklet became tremendously popular—nine reprints in 1827 alone! Many people, realizing the decadence and the apostasy of the church, turned to it for encouragement. The LORD again began to search for his sheep, according to Ezekiel 34:11.

4.2   Reverend Hendrik De Cock (1801-1842) was minister in Ulrum (Groningen, the Netherlands). One of his own (older) catechism students, Klaas Pieter Kuipinga, once commented, "If I would have to add only one sigh to my own salvation, I would be eternally lost." This remark started a process of change in the young, modernist minister De Cock. He had never heard, let alone considered, words like those of Kuipinga. Slowly the LORD made him recognize the self-sufficient spirit of his time for what it was, but it took a long time before he was fully ready to boast in the only comfort of Lord's Day 1 of the Heidelberg Catechism. He needed to learn the depth of his own misery and the necessity of truly looking up to Christ's cross. He certainly had much to learn yet when he started to read Calvin's *Institutes* by 1831.

His preaching became more and more scriptural. He started to proclaim sin and grace to the people. He urged regeneration by faith instead of regeneration by means of virtue and religiosity. This kind of preaching attracted many people. At times, as many as seventy horse-drawn carriages could be seen in front of the Ulrum church building. He baptized children of parents who did not want their children to be baptized by a modernist minister in their own congregations. (It should be noted that this action was not in itself unlawful.)

De Cock also started to publish. He republished the Canons of Dort, and with his *Compendium of the Christian Religion for Those Desiring to Come to the Lord's Holy Supper*, he attempted to improve catechetical instruction.

Opposition came, in particular after De Cock publicly attacked two of his modernist colleagues. The title of this publication deserves to be given in full: *Defence of the True Reformed Doctrine and the True Reformed Believers, Attacked by Two So-called Reformed Ministers, or: The Sheepfold of Christ Assailed by Two Wolves and Defended by H. De Cock, Reformed Minister at Ulrum.* Indeed, De Cock's intent was quite clear.

Ordered by higher authorities to do so, the classical board started proceedings against De Cock. Without a hearing, he was (illegally) suspended from his office of minister of the Word, and eventually he was deposed by the provincial board. De Cock appealed to the general synod, which allowed him six months to change his opinion. An appeal to the king was also in vain. During the presentation of this appeal, the king tried to browbeat the simple village minister. De Cock himself related how the LORD gave him courage in the face of royalty. But he did not think at all of separating himself from the church; he obeyed the orders of the church authorities and did not preach.

But the Lord reigns, and by his grace, things developed rapidly during October 1834:

October 5: Janette De Cock died, age three years.

October 9: Reverend H.P. Scholte visited De Cock. What comfort amidst such misery!

October 10: Reverend Scholte preached and baptized in the Ulrum church.

October 11: The funeral of De Cock's daughter.

October 12: Because he was locked out of the church, Reverend Scholte conducted a church service in a field behind the manse.

October 13: After the departure of Reverend Scholte, Ulrum's consistory decided to separate from the Netherlands Reformed Church, "in order to remain a true Church".

October 14: The congregation came together in the home of the widow Hulshof. After prayer, most of those present signed the *Act of Secession or Return*: 136 signatures or marks (not everyone could write), 250 persons in all.

This was the beginning of a true reformation—a return to the living Word of God. "In the beginning was the Word", also in Ulrum. "And the light shines in the darkness", also in Ulrum (John 1:1, 5).

4.3 The *Act of Secession or Return*, signed during that memorable congregational meeting of Tuesday, October 14, 1834, reads in part as follows, "We, the undersigned, overseers and members of the Reformed congregation of Jesus Christ at Ulrum, having long been aware of the corruption in the Netherlands Reformed Church in the mutilation or denial of the doctrine of our fathers which is based on God's Word; as well as in the degeneration of the administration of the holy sacraments according to the instructions of Christ in his Word; and in the almost complete neglect of ecclesiastical discipline, all of which according to our Reformed confession, Article 29, are marks of the true Church. . . ."

After this introduction, the document enumerated the blessings enjoyed by the church of Ulrum under Reverend De Cock's preaching and pastoral care. But it also exposed the unlawful treatment accorded to him by the boards of the church. It compared these ecclesiastical bodies with the papal church because these bodies rendered God's Word impotent by their man-made regulations and demanded unconditional obedience to their regulations without showing that these regulations were founded on God's Word.

The document then continued, "Considering all this, it has now become more than clear that the Netherlands Reformed Church is not the true Church according to God's Word and Article 29 of our Confession. Therefore the undersigned hereby declare that, according to the office of all believers, Article 28, they separate themselves from those who are not of the Church. They do not want to have fellowship with the Netherlands Reformed Church any more until it returns to the true service of the Lord. They also declare themselves willing to exercise fellowship with all true Reformed believers, and to unite with any assembly based on God's infallible Word, in whatever place God has gathered it. They testify herewith that in all things they bind themselves to God's holy Word and our venerable Forms of Unity, namely the Confession of Faith, the Heidelberg Catechism, and the Canons of the Synod of Dordrecht held in the years 1618 and 1619. They will arrange their public worship according to the time-honoured Ecclesiastical Liturgy. And with regard to the ecclesiastical ministry and government they bind themselves for the present to the Church Order drawn up by the aforementioned Synod of Dordrecht."

4.4   Worldly judges are often more honest and logical than those in the church. Complaints were brought in against Reverend De Cock because he baptized children of parents who belonged to another congregation. But that had never been forbidden. Reverend De Cock was suspended because of a pamphlet he wrote against two of his modernist colleagues. However, the original complaint against him was not about that pamphlet. He was deposed because he opposed the use of hymns in the worship service. Does all this add up to ecclesiastical justice?

Secession or Return did not mean "we seceded because we were forced to do so, but if the situation were to improve we will return to the Netherlands Reformed Church". *Secession or Return* is two sides of the one and the same decision: "we seceded from the false church in order to return to God's Word and the confessions which are based on that Word".

4.5   For almost a year, Hendrik De Cock continued to acknowledge the authority of the ecclesiastical organization imposed upon the church by the king. As a consequence, he suffered much abuse and injustice. But he did not remain silent. Already in 1832, he started to correspond with his predecessor in Ulrum, Dr. Hofstede de Groot, who was now professor at the University in Groningen and became the father of the Groninger School of Theology.

Basically, this school of theology revived the old heresy of Arius, who denied that our Saviour is the Son of God. The Groninger theologians were of the opinion that the doctrine of Dordrecht (reconciliation by satisfaction) was a doctrine of blood that taught that God wanted to see blood before He was willing to show His love. Indeed, Dordrecht, it was claimed, had constructed a cruel, unloving God. Instead, these theologians taught that Jesus was given to us as an enlightened example. Jesus did not die for our sins. On the contrary, His death was the great sacrifice that brought about the opportunity for mankind to reach its full human potential. Christianity is a training ground for a higher level of living. We need Jesus in order to achieve these ideals of true humanity.

Hofstede de Groot had preached to the congregation of Ulrum in this manner, seemingly very scriptural, warmly personal, and loving. But this kind of teaching was completely false. However, who—in those days—recognized that the heart of the gospel had been removed by these theologians?

Scripture teaches that, ". . . God so loved the world that He gave His only begotten Son, that whoever believes in Him should not perish but have everlasting life" (John 3:16). Is the God of the Reformed confessions a harsh God? 2 Corinthians 5:18-21: "Now all things are of God, who has reconciled us to Himself through Jesus Christ, and has given us the ministry of reconciliation. . . . For He made Him who knew no sin to be sin for us, that we might become the righteousness of God in Him".

Again, the Remonstrant doctrine of self-sufficiency based on the virtue of man's goodwill replaced the scriptural doctrine of the justification of the godless and the regeneration of dead sinners through faith in Christ. These modernist, enlightened Christians claimed, with reference to the Bible, of course, that they fought against unbelief and rationalism. Professor Hofstede de Groot put it this way: "First I called the people away from the dead confessions to the Bible, and now I call them away from the words of the Bible to the living gospel in the Bible".

As the Groninger School gained influence, its Arian, Remonstrant, and modernist glorification of man and its blatant rejection of Dordrecht became more and more obvious. This urged Reverend De Cock and his followers even the more to preach the living Word of God and his sovereign grace in Christ for lost sinners. Such preaching brought many to profess the certainty of their faith and the joy of the Holy Spirit. Also Klaas Pieter Kuipinga publicly professed his faith.

4.6   But the enemy did not rest. On July 13, 1835, the general synod of the Netherlands Reformed Church requested the government to take measures against these seceders. The local and provincial authorities decreed all sorts of regulations, involving even the police and the army! An old law from the time of Napoleon that forbade gatherings of more than twenty people was used to break up the meetings of the seceders. The seceders were forced to billet soldiers in their homes; they received heavy penalties; the possessions of those who could not pay were auctioned off on Sundays to prevent other seceders from buying these goods back. Many were imprisoned. At times, the people tried to escape the authorities by sailing away on the Zuyder Sea and conducting worship services at sea. But the government condoned, even encouraged, the injustice and cruelty against the seceders.

The Apostle Paul was permitted an appeal to the emperor in Rome, but King William I abused his office by persecuting the believers of Ulrum and elsewhere. Jews and Roman Catholics enjoyed the protection of the law of the land, but not so the seceders.

4.7 Because of political troubles with what is now called Belgium, the Belgian revolt of 1830-1839, which led to the founding of the kingdom of Belgium, King William I could do well without a division in his state church. However, the harsh actions against the seceders were not motivated in the first place by politics but resulted from the modernist philosophy of tolerance. Religious divisions must not jeopardize the unity of the country, but even more importantly, there should be equality and freedom of doctrine which allowed all—truth and lie—an equal place.

Despite many requests, the general synod stubbornly refused to deal with the complaints against the modernist interpretation of God's Word. The general regulations placed on the church by the king were binding on all; but the confessions of the church were not considered binding on anyone. De Cock and his followers were condemned not because of their teachings but because of their civil disobedience and the disorder their secession caused in the land.

Already in 1834, the French ambassadors secretly reported to their superiors that the old disputes between the teachings of Arminius and those of Gomarus, decided upon by the Synod of Dordrecht in 1618-1619, had again flared up. Indeed, that was the truth that was suppressed in unrighteousness (Rom. 1:18).

In 1839, an article was published in a French periodical that announced for all the world to read, "Holland, which owes its praise and prosperity especially to the fact that it received in its bosom with great compassion all Christians persecuted for their faith, now furnishes a spectacle of savage persecutions for the faith. It is deplorable to witness such events taking place under the rule of the House of Orange-Nassau which has performed so many services for the gospel and religious liberty".

But king and counsellors, as well as the ecclesiastical leaders in the Reformed Church, took little notice. All conspired to crush, if at all possible, the new movement that spread throughout the land.

4.8   Few people dared to support the seceders or defend their political rights to freedom of religion. Mr. Groen van Prinsterer, who was secretary and historian of the royal house, and Mr. A.M.C. van Hall, who himself eventually joined the Secession, were among the few who dared to speak out. Van Hall, a lawyer, defended the rights of the seceders in court while Van Prinsterer wrote a booklet condemning the actions against them as being totally against the laws of the land.

However, the men of the *Réveil* did not agree with the Secession. To them it was a road into the desert, leading away from the love of God. Van Prinsterer and van Hall were, therefore, remarkable exceptions in their public support for the Secession, although Groen Van Prinsterer never left the state church, despite his harsh and incisive criticisms.

4.9   The movement of the Secession grew rapidly despite persecution and injustice. In 1836, the seceders numbered about twenty thousand out of a population of approximately 2.5 million. From 1850 to 1890, Holland's population increased by 47 percent, whereas the number of seceders increased by 369 percent from forty thousand in 1850 to one hundred and eighty-nine thousand in 1890.

Other important men of the Secession were:
- Reverend H.P. Scholte (1805-1868). He separated himself without awaiting the judgements of the ecclesiastical courts.
- Reverend S. Van Velzen (1809-1896).
- Reverend A. Brummelkamp (1811-1888).
- Reverend G.F. Gezelle Meerburg (1806-1855).
- Candidate A.C. van Raalte (1811-1876). The Provincial Ecclesiastical Board rejected him as a candidate for the ministry. The first synod of the seceded churches accepted him into the ministry.

The leaders of church and state were amazed at the explosion of the Secession. Within a year, there were more than a hundred congregations. Many of these congregations used to be conventicles. Conventicles were private religious gatherings of believers who thought that the state church did not bring them faithful preaching of the Word of God. The Secession brought these believers back into the church. These churches continued to grow despite the actions of the government. The authorities justified their actions by claiming that the authority of the ecclesiastical laws must be maintained, that the honour of religion and morals must be defended, and that the peace within society had to be enforced. The general synod never acknowledged that the real struggle was between the false teachings of Arminius and the scriptural teachings of Gomarus.

Paul had written concerning the Jewish leaders that they did not understand the wisdom of God, "for had they known, they would not have crucified the Lord of glory" (1 Cor. 2:8). These words also apply to the leaders of the Dutch state church of the nineteenth century. If they had understood God's wisdom, they would not have dared persecute Christ in their persecutions of the seceders.

4.10 In contrast to the *Réveil*, the Secession is a true reformation of the church. Characteristic of the Secession—as of each reformation—is the acceptance of the absolute authority of the Word of God in the church.

The Secession was no schism. The church of those days had become a false church because it misled the believers with humanistic, rationalistic, and mystic preaching. Neither was the Secession an unlawful, Anabaptist separation, but it was a return to the doctrine, service, and discipline of the original Netherlands Reformed Churches of the sixteenth century, as summarized in their confessions and Church Order. The Secession was certainly no sectarian movement but a trumpet call to reform, addressed to all in the Netherlands Reformed Church.

4.11 God's covenant people have often left the Lord, and at times the gathering of God's people became a false church, for instance:
a.   Solomon left the Lord, not as king, but as an individual believer (1 Kings 11:1-3). Jeroboam made Israel sin (1 King 22:53) and established a state church, golden calves and all, in Bethel and Dan. Jeroboam II persecuted Amos (Amos 7). The young prophet from Judah (1 Kings 13) prophesied against this false church.
b.   During the days of Ahab and Jezebel, the situation became even worse. The service of the Lord was replaced by the service of Baal, and the true prophets were killed (1 Kings 19:10; Belgic Confession, Art. 27).
c.   Also, the kingdom of the two tribes often broke the covenant with the Lord, for instance, during the reign of Manassah, who used the temple of Jerusalem to serve idols (2 Kings 21:1-19).
d.   The national Jewish church under the leadership of Caiaphas was utterly sinful (Rom. 7:13) when it crucified the Lord Jesus on the basis of God's law. The devil in paradise misused God's law in a similar fashion. "We have a law, and according to our law He ought to die . . ." (John 19:7).
e.   The Roman Catholic Church showed itself to be a false church, especially during the sixteenth century.

In the same way, the Netherlands Reformed Church, which persecuted the seceders, became the false church of Article 29 of the Belgic Confession, demanding submission to the synodical regulations without showing that these were based on God's Word. Because of this, the Netherlands Reformed Church acted in the same way as did the Roman Catholic Church in the sixteenth century.

4.12 The Secession was not only of importance to the life of the church itself but also to the nation as a whole since it was a struggle for the freedom to serve God according to His Word. Just as the Eighty Years War against Spain resulted in the free state of the Netherlands, so the struggle of the Secession resulted in freedom for the church of Jesus Christ to serve Him according to His Word. This is the only basis for all true freedom: a free nation, a free church, a free school, and political freedom for the citizens of the country.

4.13 The Secession also had ecumenical importance, born as it was out of concern for the holy catholic church of God. There was true ecumenical intention in the Act of Secession of 1834: "They also declare themselves willing to exercise fellowship with all truly Reformed believers, and to unite with any assembly based on God's infallible Word, in whatever place God has gathered it".

The churches of the Secession had contact with the men of the Swiss *Réveil*, for instance, Merle d'Aubigne and Malan. In 1857, they sought ecclesiastical fellowship with the Free Church of Scotland. In 1858, Reverend Dirk Postma went to South Africa to assist the reformation of the church in that part of the world. And as time went by, more international contacts were established.

The Act of Secession reminds us quite clearly and scripturally of the church's holiness and its catholicity.

5. CONFLICT AND UNITY: FROM 1834 TO 1886

5.1 Although since Pentecost the covenant of God with Abraham included the Christians from among the Gentiles as well, the congregation in Jerusalem found it rather difficult to accept those uncircumcised Christians in their midst. In Antioch, the Apostle Paul was forced to admonish the Apostle Peter about this. Luther never succeeded in leaving behind all medieval scholasticsm and mysticism. The forces of apostasy seemed to be strong, even in those who again professed full obedience to God's Word only. The churches of the Secession also suffered from sad disagreements between Reverend De Cock and his friend and fellow soldier, Reverend Scholte. These disagreements ended their personal friendship, causing both men to grieve deeply for each other.

5.2 At the synod of the churches of the Secession, held in Utrecht in 1837, Reverend Scholte proposed that the Church Order of Dort be preceded by a number of articles. He proposed a new Article 1: "All those who profess their faith and live in accordance with the confession must, together with their children, be recognized as members of Christ's church". Reverend Scholte explained this article as follows: "I do not want to baptize a child of members who do not dare to profess that they are regenerated. Those who cannot profess this do not belong to the church, and therefore cannot have their children baptized". Reverend

Scholte suggested that a person's profession of faith means making a statement about his conversion and regeneration. By means of self-examination and observation of your soul and your religious experiences, you can become certain of your conversion and regeneration. On the basis of such self-examinations and self-observations, you will know whether you are a child of God and whether you may claim God's promises.

Reverend De Cock, on the other hand, proposed a rather different article: "All those who have professed their faith in the church of Jesus Christ must be accepted, together with their children, as members of the visible church of Christ, which extends farther than the invisible church of Christ, which invisible church is described in our Catechism, Lord's Day 21, which many fail to appreciate".

Among the members of Reverend De Cock's congregations were many pious and God-fearing people who dared not profess their faith publicly. These people lacked the truly scriptural preaching that did not focus attention on the person and his own piety but called upon the believers to put their trust in Christ alone. These older noncommunicant members were uncertain about their own faith and therefore did not dare to profess their faith even though they feared God and lived truly as Christians. In Reverend De Cock's view, these faithful members who wholeheartedly believed the doctrine of the Word of God but had as yet not found the courage to profess this, also belonged to the congregation of Christ.

Reverend De Cock accused Reverend Scholte, "You want a church which consists of saints and perfect people only".

5.3 These disputes again highlight the dangers of subjectivism, so prevalent in the previous century; this subjectivism searched for certainty within oneself rather than outside oneself in the promises of God's covenant.

a. Both De Cock and Scholte did not sufficiently realize that God Himself speaks to us directly in His promises. The Word of God is not a message of truth without obligations; the Word of God is not distant; it is not objective. We can never separate the Word of God from God Himself. He speaks to us, and with His covenant promises, He urges us to believe.

Reverend De Cock wanted to count those as members of the church who on the one hand desired to believe the Word of God (the objective side) but who did not as yet dare to respond by accepting those promises (the subjective side).

In contrast, Reverend Scholte, under pietist, perhaps even Anabaptist influence, definitely closed the door to those "seeking souls". Reverend De Cock was more realistic and was willing to accept them, although he was not able to clearly show them their error.

In judging the thoughts of these men, we must remember their background and spiritual environment. Reverend De Cock came to scriptural insights and assurance of faith while in prison!

b.   Both men did not understand the nature of true faith, which rests only on the truth and trustworthiness of God. We cannot believe God's Word without at the same time having confidence that not only to others but also to us God has granted His promises. Those who distrust God and do not repent remain uncertain and without comfort. The Holy Spirit works sorrow to the point of repentance which leads to salvation (2 Cor. 7:9ff).

c.   Both men sharply discerned the religious smugness of the majority of people of their days who were proud of their Reformed religion and were fanatically opposed to Roman Catholicism. The scriptural preaching of De Cock and Scholte directly opposed the prevailing attitude of the church, emphasizing with great power the sovereign, free grace of God in Christ Jesus for lost sinners. That was the *credo* of the Secession; that was God's work of grace in His church in the Netherlands during the first half of the nineteenth century.

5.4 Sadly, disagreements among the seceders increased with sharp polemics, distrust, and even disagreements about minor things such as the use of gowns in the worship services. Some churches appointed preachers who were not recognized in other churches.

In order to escape further persecution, Reverend Scholte requested the king to grant the liberty to hold meetings as the new Christian Seceded Congregation. Others followed his example, but many churches refused to admit that they were a new church. They continued to call themselves the Reformed Churches (under the cross). For years these two groups opposed each other; indeed, it was a sad and sombre time. During one of the synods, Reverend De Cock was unable to control his emotions and cried like a little child because of the harshness of the brothers. Although Reverend Scholte was suspended by the synod of 1840, he continued to preach. The churches of the Secession were plagued by sin and an unchristian life style. Reverend De Cock found it necessary to admonish J.J. Beukema, the first man to sign the Act of Secession or Return, because of public drunkenness!

Ministers who tended to be more mystic in thought and teaching first joined the churches of the Secession but later left again to form yet another denomination (Gereformeerde Gemeenten - Reformed Congregations; in North America: Netherlands Reformed Congregations).

Despite the good intentions, the seceders were often ignorant of the devices of Satan (2 Cor. 2:11).

5.5   Individualism and subjectivism wreaked havoc in the churches of the Secession. Division followed division, and preservation of the group replaced the calling "with which you were called, with all lowliness and gentleness, with longsuffering, bearing one another in love, endeavouring to keep the unity of the Spirit in the bond of peace" (Eph. 4:1-3).

"But God, who is rich in mercy, because of His great love with which He loved us, even when we were dead in trespasses, made us alive together with Christ (by grace you have been saved) . . ." (Eph. 2:4, 5). If God would not have done this, the whole work of the Secession might have been destroyed. He made the hearts desirous for unity.

In 1854, the theological college was founded in the city of Kampen. There the leaders of the Secession found each other again. By 1869, the miracle of unity became reality. The churches of the Secession became known as the Christelijke Gereformeerde Kerk (the Christian Reformed Church). Note the singular! The local churches were known as Christian Reformed congregations. A *Regulation of Governance and Organization* was adopted to satisfy the demands of the government, but these churches continued to abide by the Church Order of Dort. The *Regulation* of 1869 was abandoned immediately with the Union of 1892.

6. FROM THE OLD WORLD TO THE NEW WORLD

6.1   The Lutheran Reformation was mainly a German concern; the Calvinist Reformation was mainly European. After the Reformation moved from England (Puritans) to North America, it became a worldwide concern.

The secession that began in the small Groninger village of Ulrum was mainly a Dutch concern. But because of the emigration of hundreds of seceders to America, the Secession gained international importance.

6.2   The reasons for this emigration of the seceders were:
a.   The great poverty of the farm labourers. Many of the seceders were also impoverished by the many heavy penalties.
b.   In 1846, the whole potato harvest was ruined because of disease. This was a truly national disaster.
c.   The government did not permit the Christian schools of the seceders to operate.
d.   Many people were fearful of the future in the Netherlands because of apostasy and unbelief. With this in mind, Reverend Scholte named his settlement in the state of Iowa after the small Jordanian village of Pella. During the Jewish War (66-70), the Christians fled from Jerusalem to this village, remembering the words of Jesus (Luke 21:21).

6.3   Many would have preferred to emigrate to the Dutch East Indies, but the government did not allow that. Consequently, many left for North America. Reverend Van Raalte settled in the forests of Michigan (Holland), and Reverend Scholte selected the prairies of Iowa (Pella).

These settlements have a long and moving history of hardship and danger: a voyage across the ocean of some six weeks in small sailing ships, fever and sickness, wild animals, prairie fires, snow, storms, locusts, dangerous natives, huge herds of buffalo. Yet they grew and prospered.

6.4   Reverend Scholte failed as a leader of the church. He was active in American politics; he was even considered for an appointment as ambassador to the Netherlands, but the Dutch government objected to his appointment. He was a farmer, postmaster, and school inspector. He owned sawmills, lime kilns, and quarries. Even the church building belonged to him. But his religious individualism caused unfortunate estrangement and eventually separation from his followers.

Within three years, Reverend Van Raalte joined the Dutch Reformed church (the old Reformed church from the seventeenth century, founded in New York, earlier called New Amsterdam). But the seceders found that this church was too much like the apostate Netherlands Reformed Church. Among other things, it allowed its members to join the movement of Freemasons. Many separated again from this church, but Reverend Van Raalte remained.

The separation from the Dutch Reformed Church (1857) resulted in what is now known as the Christian Reformed Church, and it may be said that the faith of the seceders was retained in the Christian Reformed Church.

Reverend Van Raalte founded a training college in Holland, Michigan—Hope College. He became well known and influential. The vice-president of the United States was present at his burial. The Christian Reformed Church founded its own training school in Grand Rapids, Calvin College. During the second half of the nineteenth century, these churches grew rapidly in size.

The arrival of the seceders has been of great importance to the United States.

6.5   During the nineteenth century, the English government attempted to anglicize the church of Cape Colony (South Africa). The intense desire of the Afrikaners to retain their own identity, political as well as religious, was the reason for the *Great Trek* toward Transvaal, approximately at the same time as the persecution of the seceders in the Netherlands. The *Voortrekkers* found themselves not only in conflict with the English government of South Africa but also with the natives. Over a period of three years more than one hundred farmers were murdered, and more than six thousand head of cattle and almost eighteen thousand sheep were stolen. In one year fifty-four thousand sheep died of sickness and exhaustion.

These Afrikaners received the seceder, Reverend Dirk Postma, with great joy (1857). Under his guidance, the Dopper Church was founded. Paul Kruger was one of its members. A training institution was established, which later became the famous University of Potchefstroom.

Worthy of special mention is the beautiful translation of the Bible in Afrikaans and the Afrikaans psalter, prepared by Dr. J.D. Du Toit (Totius), the son-in-law of Reverend Postma. Bible translation is at the same time language reformation. As the King James translation enriched the English language, so the Totius translation enriched the Afrikaans language.

However, far fewer seceders emigrated to South Africa than to North America.

7. THE AGE OF DECHRISTIANIZATION

7.1   Large numbers of European Christians turned away from the godliness which has promise of the life that now is and of that which is to come (1 Tim. 4:8). They allowed themselves to be influenced by the zealously proclaimed ideals of the revolution that reduced Christianity to a mere insurance policy for eternity.

7.2   The Industrial Revolution and the growth of huge cities created large masses of people who turned—often in despair—to the new gods of rising socialism (Karl Marx, 1818-1883). The Western colonial powers enriched themselves through colonial warfare and trade. An enormous flow of cheaply gained raw materials reached Europe, all too often by exploiting the colonies.

a.   Already in 1493, Pope Alexander VI decided to divide the known world into a Portuguese half (the East) and a Spanish half (the West) to bring peace between these quarrelsome competitors. For centuries this papal decision determined the course of events for Christianity in Europe. This decision encouraged the European nations to become colonial powers, forever searching for increased power and wealth. Therefore we find Spaniards in South America and Mexico and the Portuguese in Africa and Asia. This papal decision, then, is one of the causes of four hundred years of colonial warfare, from 1500 to the Vietnam War (Vietnam was a French colony).

b.   For centuries there remained in India a small Portuguese colony. One-half of the island of Timor, part of the Indonesian archipelago, is still under Portuguese rule. Even communist China still has a small Portuguese enclave. The protestants simply took over the trade privileges of the Portuguese.

c.   These developments were started by the "stadholder of God", who claimed authority over the kings of the earth. The Apostle John saw all this already on the Isle of Patmos: "And the woman whom you saw is that great city which reigns over the kings of the earth" (Rev. 17:18). The papal church, as well as the protestant churches of Western Europe, "has drunk of the wine of the wrath of her fornication, the kings of the earth have committed fornication with her, and the merchants of the earth have become rich through the abundance of her luxury" (Rev. 18:3). The Apostle John even listed the goods of the merchants, "merchandise of gold and silver, precious stones and pearls, fine linen and purple, silk and scarlet, every kind of citron wood, every kind of object of ivory, every kind of object of most precious wood, bronze, iron, and marble; and cinnamon and incense, fragrant oil and frankincense, wine and oil, fine flour and wheat, cattle and sheep, horses and chariots, and bodies and souls of men . . ." (Rev. 18:12, 13). The bride of Christ allowed herself to become the great whore, and apostate Christianity with her colonial power and wealth became the great Babylon.

d.   Although these things do not deal with doctrine but with trade and shipping and wealth and power, this is certainly also church history. Those visions of the Apostle John describe in a most remarkable way the developments ever since that haughty decision of 1493 by the superpower Rome. Today little is left of the greatness of these colonial nations, except in names—for instance, San Francisco, San Diego, Santa Cruz. Their ships often carried Christian names, such as the *Holy Virgin* and the *Holy Trinity*. Once a fleet of twelve ships received the names of the twelve apostles. Crosses were painted on the sails; often the first thing done in a new country was the planting of the holy cross. The Spaniards and the Portuguese zealously tried to convert the pagan natives, but mission zeal and mammon service went hand in hand.

e.   Large sections of Europe's population suffered horrendous poverty, for instance, the miners in Germany and the weavers in Bohemia and England. Child labour was considered an acceptable necessity. In Wales, the beds of the children were never cold; as soon as one child, deadly tired after a night's work at the looms or in the mines, came home on his father's back, the next child started another day of slave labour from five in the morning until eight at night.

f.   The Christian nations did not always live up to their God-given responsibilities. During a conference on social issues held in 1891, Dr. A. Kuyper concluded his speech with the prayer, "May it never be necessary to admit that it is the fault of the Dutch Christians, because of their lukewarm faith at all levels of society, that the nation was not saved and the blessings of God the Father were forfeited".

7.3   The men of the *Réveil* were not blind to these social abuses. "Indeed the wages of the labourers who mowed your fields, which you kept back by fraud, cry out; and the cries of the reapers have reached the ears of the Lord of Sabaoth" (James 5:4).

Willem Bilderdijk spoke against social injustice. Philanthropy (handing out gifts) is a humanistic concept; the Bible speaks of the rights of the poor and oppressed. Groen van Prinsterer considered poverty the greatest scourge of his days. Reverend H. Scholte wrote, "It is certainly not a sign of Christian love when the poor are fed like birds in a cage." Dr. A. Kuyper organized the first Christian Social Congress, a conference on social issues. During this conference, he sketched out Christian principles for society (1891).

Not the official public statements of all kinds of ecclesiastical boards but the prophetic and scriptural witness of many faithful believers from all levels of society has brought much improvement to the Dutch as well as English societies of the nineteenth century. The excellent social care available in the Netherlands is certainly not due in the first place to the efforts of socialism. In fact, Marxism, with its atheism and class struggle, was more a hindrance than a help in bringing relief to the poor of the late nineteenth and early twentieth centuries. Why? Because social improvement would make the class struggle redundant.

7.4   Although the preaching of the gospel and the individual efforts of many brought much relief, the basic source of the societal misery of the nineteenth century was not removed. The majority of the people, and in particular the leaders of the church and state, refused to acknowledge God's precepts for society and His sovereignty over all of man's life. God's wisdom of the Torah for Israel (both as church and as nation) was not acknowledged and therefore not preached from the pulpits. Of course, the law of God, given in the fifteenth century before Christ, should not be blindly taken over, but "the Helper, the Holy Spirit, whom the Father will send in My name, He will teach you all things" (John 14:26), and He will teach us how we should live, as far as our socio-economic life is concerned also.

"Surely I have taught you statutes and judgements, just as the LORD my God commanded me, that you should act according to them in the land which you go to possess. Therefore be careful to observe them; for this is your wisdom and your understanding in the sight of the peoples who will hear all these statutes and say, 'Surely this great nation is a wise and understanding people'. For what great nation is there that has God so near to it, as the LORD our God is to us, for whatever reason we may call upon Him? And what great nation is there that has such statutes and righteous judgements as are in all this law which I set before you this day?" (Deut. 4:5-8).

7.5   The liberal Dutch government tried to remedy the problems by placing the poor and the destitute in institutions. This was often done indiscriminately and without compassion so that families were broken up merely because the father was out of work. Was this the solution? How harsh, cruel, and unfair. The wealthy citizen bathed himself in self-right-eousness and religiosity, the wealthy farmer lived on his royal farmstead, but the labourers were sent home empty-handed when the weather made work impossible.

7.6   In the Middle Ages, the rich and powerful monastic orders did not bring real relief to the common people. In the nineteenth century, the protestant Christians were also blind to their responsibilities. Dechristiani-zation resulted in an increased rejection of Him who delivered us from the domain of darkness and transferred us to the kingdom of the saints of light (Col. 1:13).

8. THE AGE OF MISSIONS

8.1   The nineteenth century was also the century of mission to the continents of the Gentiles. In previous centuries, both the East Indies and the West Indies trade companies contributed great sums of money to missions. Until 1795, the East Indies Company sent out approximately nine hundred ministers and also financed a great deal of Bible translation work. Indeed, the company organized everything and paid for everything, church included. But trade interests had priority over religious interests. A trade agreement (spices) was signed with the Moslem Sultan of Ternate. One of the stipulations was that each native Christian convert would be handed over to the sultan. The sailors aboard ships bound for Japan were not allowed to let any one know that they were Christians.

   The rise of the great nineteenth-century colonial trade empires opened the world, also for missions.

8.2   Fortunately, many Christians responded to the missions mandate. England sent missionaries to India and Africa (Moffat, David Living-stone). The German missionaries worked on Sumatra. One of the best-known missionaries was Ludwig Ingwer Nommensen, the apostle of the Bataks, one of the fiercest tribes of natives in the Dutch East Indies. Missionaries sent out by the Dutch Mission Society brought the gospel to the Moluccas and Celebes. Since 1896, missions has been considered the full responsibility of the Reformed Churches rather than of independent mission societies.

   Today almost all mission fields where the gospel of God is preached report a great harvest, and many more workers are needed in God's vineyard (Matt. 9:37, 38). Are we perhaps approaching the day that the gospel of the kingdom shall have been preached in the whole world, and shall the end come soon? (Matt. 24:14).

9. GROEN VAN PRINSTERER
AND THE DUTCH STATE CHURCH

9.1   One of the most important figures in nineteenth-century Holland was Guillaume Groen van Prinsterer (1801-1876). He was a student of Bilderdijk. He was not merely against revolution but he was fully anti-revolutionary. Bilderdijk respected the French emperor Napoleon as the tamer of the revolution, but Groen van Prinsterer considered Napoleon as son and protector of the great revolution, as dictator and tyrant.

As did few others, Groen van Prinsterer exposed the ideas of the revolution as a rebellion against God. His writings (*Unbelief and Revolution* and *Handbook of the History of Our Nation*) witness to his scriptural insights as well as to his courage in warning the Dutch nation. His often lonely struggle was eventually rewarded with the defeat of liberalism and the rise of Kuyper's Christian politics. He is, in fact, the father of the Antirevolutionary Political Party, organized and led by Dr. A. Kuyper.

For many years, Groen led the struggle for the freedom of Christian education, begun with the Secession. The seceders wanted to educate their children in the doctrine of the church, in obedience to their baptismal promises. Nowhere else in the world has Christian education been recognized and blessed as it has been (and still is) in the Netherlands.

Although he strongly supported the Secession, and although he often attended a worship service of the seceders, Groen was and remained a man of the *Réveil*, seeking to bring about reformation from within the state church. He never formally joined with the churches of the Secession.

9.2   Groen became known for his defence of the confessions of the church, the so-called Three Forms of Unity (Belgic Confession, Heidelberg Catechism, and the Canons of Dort). But his attempts to restore these to their rightful place in the Netherlands Reformed Church were in vain.

Under the influence of the revolution ideology that swept Europe in 1848, the bond between state and church was finally severed in 1852. But although the direct influence of the king over the church came to an end, the Netherlands Reformed national church remained the church of the tolerance of Erasmus. All parties and all views were welcome as long as all accepted unity above division. Pietist and mystic beliefs emphasized man's religious emotions and experiences; modern views based on Bible criticism, as well as the reduction of the biblical gospel to a series of basic truths—all of this was allowed in the church. The Bible was no longer acknowledged as God's Word; miracles were explained away scientifically; the resurrection was denied. Even the ideas of evolutionism were used to explain Scripture.

All in all, within the Dutch state church the lie and the truth had equal rights. But instead of increased peace, the church saw an increasingly fierce struggle between the modernist left and the orthodox right.

Although many left the church, Groen remained and continued to attack its modernism. In 1864, he founded a Confessional Society, urging the return to the confessions of the church. But all to no avail.

9.3 In Jesus' days, the Jewish national church accepted all kinds of parties and views (Pharisees, Sadducees, Herodians, Zealots), but there was no room for Jesus, the greatest reformer of all times. They crucified Him. Similarly, the Dutch state church accepted all kinds of teachings but considered the seceders troublemakers.

Groen and his followers fought for the acceptance of God's sovereign Word and for the rights of the truly ecumenical confessions based on God's Word. They met with fierce opposition. Often Groen found himself without supporters. He became known as "the general without an army". His motto was, "Not a politician, but a confessor". When he died in 1876, all seemed lost. Kuyper was removed from active participation, recuperating from a severe depression in southern France.

Groen was not only a blessing to the seceders. He also influenced those who remained in the Netherlands Reformed Church. Especially in the work of his successor, Dr. A. Kuyper, who was to break loose from the bonds of the royal church regulations of 1816 and the snare of the antichristian gospel of tolerance (the Second Secession of 1886), Groen's efforts bore great fruits.

10. DR. ABRAHAM KUYPER - 1837-1920

10.1 Dr. Abraham Kuyper (1837-1920) was born in the parsonage of the Netherlands Reformed Church at Maassluis (near Rotterdam, the Netherlands). At Leyden, he studied classics and theology under modernist professors such as Professor Scholten of the Groninger School of Theology. Kuyper himself has related how these studies robbed him of the faith of his parents. He compared his own faith with the seed that fell in shallow soil and dried up under the constant attack of the spirit of doubt of modernist theology. Although he did not abandon religion nor leave the church, little was left of that old treasure of Reformed faith. In a later publication, he confessed his sin of denying his Lord and Saviour in his modernist theology.

10.2 He demonstrated his academic ability when he won an essay competition organized by the University of Groningen. This essay dealt with the concept of the church as found in the writings of Calvin and the Polish reformer John à Lasco. The story of how he managed to find material and resources for this essay is remarkable in itself. Kuyper considered those events to be God's direct interference, and he was so impressed by it all that he again began to pray. Indeed, it was not an old wives' tale for him to speak of the finger of God in his life.

10.3 During those days, the young Kuyper was reading Charlotte M. Yonge's *The Heir of Redclyffe*, published in 1853. This novel made a deep impression on him. It deals with two greatly different characters who clash and struggle stubbornly. The two brothers are finally reconciled not through the strength of the one brother but through the strength of faith of the apparently weaker brother. Kuyper was deeply impressed by the powerful climax of this novel and later wrote, "What I lived through in my soul in that moment I fully understood only later, yet from that hour, after that moment I scorned what I formerly esteemed, and I sought what I once dared to despise". Such events left a lasting impression.

10.4 In his first congregation in the village of Beesd, Kuyper learned to know the piety of the common people in their conventicles (Pietje Balthus). The certainty of faith of this young woman moved Kuyper from a half-hearted to a full interest in the gospel. He started to read Calvin in a different light. While serving the church at Utrecht, he moved away from modernism, maintaining that the Bible *is* God's Word and does not merely *contain* God's Word, as taught by the modernist theologians.

10.5 After his move to the church of Amsterdam, Kuyper's great gifts and talents became even more apparent. He succeeded Groen van Prinsterer as leader of antirevolutionary politics, and in 1872, he founded the Antirevolutionary Party. He was also a tremendous fighter for free Christian education (the so-called school struggle). He was a prolific writer, and his weekly, *De Heraut* (The Herald), reached many homes. This weekly was instrumental in the revival of the Reformed faith within the Netherlands Reformed Church. He fought against the tyranny of political liberalism, theological modernism, and the glorification of the sciences at the state universities.

10.6 A milestone was reached in 1880 with the opening of the Free University of Amsterdam. At this occasion, Kuyper delivered his majestic oratory, *Souvereiniteit In Eigen Kring* (Sphere Sovereignty), in which he proclaimed, "There is not one inch within human life which Christ does not claim for himself".

In 1891, he delivered the opening address at the first-ever Christian Social Congress. His topic was *The Social Question and the Christian Religion*. Often he publicly defended the importance of the Christian faith for the life of society, often in intense debate with the followers of socialism and capitalism. One of his famous statements is, "If there is anything which is social, it surely is the Christian religion!"

Kuyper's rectorial address of 1899 for the Free University of Amsterdam dealt with evolution. He stated, "Our nineteenth century dies under the hypnosis of the evolution-dogma", and, "Evolution is a newly contrived system of thought, a newly formed dogma, a newly arisen faith which wants to encompass and control all of our life in direct opposition to our Christian faith. It wants to erect its temple on the ruins of the Christian confession!" He concluded his speech by emphasising, "What always has been, still is, and shall remain the starting point of the confession of the whole Christian church here on earth must be maintained over against the evolution, namely the first of all the articles of the Christian faith: I believe in God the Father Almighty, Creator of Heaven and earth".

10.7 The climax of his political career came in 1901-1905 when he was prime minister of the Netherlands. Because of his gifts as orator and journalist, he was well qualified to lead the Dutch nation almost in all aspects of societal life. Although he had his faults like all human beings, under his leadership the Dutch nation experienced an extraordinary social, political, and ecclesiastical Calvinist revival during the latter part of the nineteenth and beginning of the twentieth century. Kuyper truly was a leader of the faithful common people of God.

11. THE DOLEANTIE - A SECOND SECESSION

11.1 The first secession and return from Babylon was led by Joshua and Zerubbabel. Many Jews remained in Babel, for instance, Daniel. The second return from Babel was led by Ezra. Nehemiah remained in the service of the king of Persia. Later, Nehemiah also returned to Jerusalem because there was yet much to be reformed among the Jews of the first return; the walls of the city of God needed restoration.

Similarly, the first secession of 1834 was followed by the second secession of 1886, the Doleantie. Again, the Lord remembered His covenant and rescued many who had remained in the Netherlands Reformed Church after 1834. Among them was Abraham Kuyper, who as a little boy was baptized in the false church of Maassluis in 1837 and who since 1880 served the church of Amsterdam as an elder because he was professor at the Free University.

11.2 *Toward the Doleantie.* Two major issues stood out in the struggle of the Amsterdam consistory against modernism.

a.   *The Attestation Issue.* The Amsterdam consistory objected to the practice that made it possible for catechism students who wished to be admitted to the Lord's Supper and therefore wished to profess their modernist faith to do so in a neighbouring church with a modernist minister. The home consistory was forced to issue an attestation concerning the good conduct of such students and then found itself compelled to readmit them at a later date as communicant members. Catechism students often went to church in the neighbouring city of Koog aan de Zaan for that very purpose.

This matter came to a head in 1885, when the orthodox consistory of Amsterdam refused to issue these attestations because it no longer could cooperate with such deceit. It was impossible to take action against the modernist ministers who encouraged these practices, and therefore it was decided to refuse requests for such attestations. Complaints were lodged against this decision, and the classical board ordered the Amsterdam consistory to cooperate, and to do so before January 8, 1886.

It would have been so much better if the attestation issue had been the only disputed issue. After all, this struggle concerned the Word of God and the confession of faith in our Lord Jesus Christ. Alas, another issue muddied the ecclesiastical waters.

b.   *The Ownership Question.* The Amsterdam consistory anticipated the far-reaching consequences of its conflict with the classical board, and in its meeting of December 14, 1885, it was decided that the church wardens (the committee in charge of the church buildings) would remain directly responsible to the consistory, "which sought to keep the congregation together in obedience to God's Word". Of the one hundred and thirty-six consistory members, eighty voted in favour: five ministers (there were twenty-eight ministers), forty-two elders (including Dr. Kuyper), and thirty-three deacons.

On January 4, 1886, these eighty members were suspended by the classical board. This board issued the attestations that the Amsterdam consistory had refused to issue and claimed ownership of all the buildings. Although the main issue was the maintaining of the Reformed doctrine and not the ownership of church property, unfortunately these events moved the dispute from the spiritual to the material: who owns the buildings? This caused a great deal of confusion.

11.3 The suspended office bearers appealed these actions and decisions of the classical board. But in its judgement of December 1, 1886, the general synod rejected these appeals, upholding the suspensions. Throughout the year 1886, these office bearers did not exercise their office; instead they organized Bible study sessions.

In its meeting of December 16, 1886, the Amsterdam consistory decided to reject the yoke of the synodical hierarchy. They called themselves the *Nederduits-Gereformeerde Kerk (dolerend)* (Dutch Reformed Church, dissenting).

The leaders of the Second Secession in Amsterdam were Dr. Kuyper, Dr. F.L. Rutgers, and Mr. A.F. De Savornin Lohman (who later founded his own political party).

11.4 The root of the Dutch word *dolerend* can be found in a word such as *condolence* and means sorrow, or making a complaint. These seceders appealed to the courts because their legal possessions had been taken from them. They maintained that they were the legal continuation of the traditional Reformed Church in the Netherlands. These appeals were largely rejected because the courts judged that the seceders had separated themselves from the national organization and had formed a new denomination. After these court procedures had come to a conclusion, the designation *dolerend* (dissenting) was no longer used.

11.5 Already in February 1886, the consistories of the congregations at Voorthuizen and Kootwijk had broken with the synodical boards. Soon the second secession gained momentum, and many consistories followed the example of Amsterdam and broke with the state church. As was the case after the first secession, now the government was called upon to help the synodical boards. By far the majority of the people were strongly, if not fanatically, opposed to the seceders, who experienced persecution and defamation. Yet they were steadfast in their belief that the Reformation was a work of God's grace over the church.

11.6 Who rules the church? The royal regulations for the church, issued in 1816, considered the local congregation simply a division of the national church, with the national synod as its highest board of control. In contrast, the churches of the secession maintained, in agreement with Scripture, the independence of the local church as body of Christ under the government of Christ as its head (1 Cor. 12:13, 27). The seven churches of Asia Minor are seven separate lampstands (Rev. 1), and not one lampstand with seven arms as it had been in the Old Testament.

The seceders of 1886 considered the local churches to be under the yoke of a synodical, revolutionary organization that had held the churches captive. To them, reformation meant the rejection of the synodical yoke while remaining part of the Netherlands Reformed Church.

In 1834, many individuals seceded from the church that had become false, according to Article 29 of the Belgic Confession.

In 1886, many consistories (office bearers) freed themselves from the hierarchical regulations of the ecclesiastical boards, as was their right and responsibility to do. However, many (including Kuyper) claimed that it was possible as a true Church to remain within a false organization. But this claim could not be maintained, as its argument was rather artificial and not in agreement with the facts. All the same, it has greatly hindered the reconciliation between the seceders of 1834 and those of 1886.

The main issue of 1834 and 1886 was whether Christ and His Word alone govern the church. The basic principle of all true reformation is indeed the return to God's Word.

12. THE UNION OF 1892

12.1 True to their promises of 1834, the churches of the First Secession (Christelijke Gereformeerde Kerk) sought contact with the churches of the Second Secession (the Nederduits Gereformeerde Kerken). The latter admitted their guilt that they had tolerated the sins of the Netherlands Reformed Church for so long.

12.2 Basic points of difference between the churches of the First Secession (1834) and those of the Second Secession (1886) were:
a.   The relationship with the Netherlands Reformed Church:
    1834:   Declared this church false in accordance with Article 29 of the Belgic Confession.
    1886:   Declared the organization of this church in its royal regulations of 1816 to be false.
b.   The training for the ministry:
    1834:   Ministers must be trained by the church for the church.
    1886:   The training of ministers is the work of an (independent) theological school.

12.3 Unity was achieved on the basis of unity in faith in the Word of God and the confessions (the Three Forms of Unity), which are based on God's Word. It was agreed that a radical break with the Netherlands Reformed Church organization was necessary, although it was left to one's individual judgement whether this denomination was to be considered a false church. Further, both the theological school in Kampen as well as the Free University of Amsterdam were accepted as training institutions for future ministers.

    The synods of the Christelijke Gereformeerde kerk (the churches of the First Secession of 1834) and the Nederduits-gereformeerde kerk (the churches of the Second Secession of 1886) met in joint session on June 17, 1892, in Amsterdam. The only surviving father of the Secession of 1834, Reverend S. Van Velzen, was carried into the meeting. His son read his address to the combined synod. The handshake between Reverend W.H. Gispen and Dr. A. Kuyper sealed the unity, and these churches became known as the Reformed Churches in the Netherlands.

    It took quite a long time before the unity at the local level between church A (a church of the Secession of 1834) and church B (a church of the Secession of 1886) became a reality everywhere.

12.4 Not all joined the Union of 1892. Many had strong objections to Kuyper's teachings concerning regeneration and baptism.

    But the union had not come about because everyone was of the same mind but because there was unity in faith and confession. However influential Kuyper may have been, his ideas and teachings were not the basis for the union between the churches of 1834 and those of 1886.

Many feared the influence of Kuyper's teachings, which they considered not to be in full agreement with God's Word and the confessions. Unfortunately, the history of the (now united) Reformed Churches in the Netherlands has shown that this fear was not unfounded. Many members of the churches of the First Secession wished to remain what they had been since 1869: members of the Christelijke Gereformeerde Kerk (in North America, the Free Reformed Church). Their training school for the ministry was established in the city of Apeldoorn.

13. OBJECTIONS TO SOME OF KUYPER'S TEACHINGS

13.1 Soon after the Union of 1892, objections were raised against certain teachings of Dr. Kuyper. Even the great Kuyper was not able to escape fully from the influence of rationalism and intellectualism that so strongly influenced the Christian churches in the nineteenth century.

Paul was fully aware of the severity of the struggle to destroy speculations and every lofty thing raised up against the knowledge of God; he knew how difficult it was to bring every thought into captivity to the obedience of Christ (2 Cor. 10:5). The apostle warned the divided congregation of Corinth "not to think beyond what is written, that none of you may be puffed up on behalf of one against each other" (1 Cor. 4:6). In these texts, Scripture points to the basic cause of much ecclesiastical misery and arrogance, namely going beyond the Word of God.

13.2 Already medieval scholasticism did not fully subject itself to the authority of God's Word. All too often it placed itself in its scholarship above and beyond that authority. Continuation on this road eventually placed man's "reasonable" findings in the place of God's revelation in His Word. Human imagination began to rule over Scripture, and the theological-scholarly systems and terminology tended to replace the living Word of God.

Scriptural scholarship must always remain reverently subject to Scripture; it uses language and terminology that is as close as possible to the scriptural language and terminology; above all, scriptural scholarship must serve the churches. Scholastic theology itself does not unite but brings division and often separation.

13.3 Kuyper's Calvinism as a Reformed system of theology reminds us of the methodology of his own liberal teacher, Professor Scholten, who went so far as to use scriptural and confessional terminology but with different meanings. But the question should be asked, "What does Scripture say?" We should be extremely afraid of a situation where the believers, who accept Scripture and the scriptural confessions, find themselves dependent on the concepts and ideas of a rational system of theology.

The Synod of Dort had already recognized and dealt with this danger. Maccovius, a professor at the University of Franeker, was admonished because the terminology of his teaching was not close enough to the language of Scripture. The synod admonished him to use the language of the Holy Spirit so that peace may be retained within the church.

Objections were raised against three of Kuyper's teachings: his ideas about justification, regeneration, and baptism.

13.4 Kuyper taught the doctrine of justification from eternity. According to him, the believers only need to be aware of this gift of God in their lives; they do not need to pray for true forgiveness, only for the awareness of the forgiveness of their sins.

It was in particular Dr. Lucas Lindeboom (1845-1933) who exposed the scholastic nature of Kuyper's theological system. This theologian was a minister in the seceded churches of 1834 and later became professor at the theological college at Kampen. His own ministry was characterized by his great zeal for the preaching of the gospel, and his work was blessed remarkably. He was instrumental in establishing various Christian organizations for the care of mentally handicapped children and adults. He clearly saw the crucial importance of the Christian faith for psychiatry, and in this regard he was far ahead of his time.

Professor Lindeboom pointed out that neither God's Word nor the Reformed confessions speak of *justification from eternity*; rather, both speak of the gospel declaration of justification that we accept by faith. He pointed out the rationalism of Kuyper's thought by showing how easily a person may go farther in his own thinking than God has revealed in His Word. The danger is very real that such philosophical, such scientific thinking eventually brings man to probe the secrets of God. The foolishness of the cross must become the wisdom of the scholar; scholarship that disregards the Word of God detracts from the power of the cross.

Professor Lindeboom was deeply disturbed by Kuyper's teachings. He wrote, "God have mercy upon us and our children, and may He bring Dr. Kuyper and all the brethren who allow him to continue in his ways back to the simplicity which can be found in Christ! If this does not happen—what shall be the future of the Free University and the Theological College of the Reformed Churches? A frightening thought! One may ask, is there hope for repentance of these important men? What is impossible with men, is always possible with God".

These were emotional and prophetic words that proved to be very accurate: today the Free University of Amsterdam promotes modernist ideas. Professor Lindeboom put the finger precisely on the main reason of much ecclesiastical struggle: thinking beyond what is written (1 Cor. 4:6).

13.5 The second of Kuyper's teachings that raised grave objections concerned *regeneration*. Kuyper considered regeneration to be a seed of the new life in man, implanted directly by the Holy Spirit without the means of the preaching of the gospel. This new germ could well lay dormant for years before being awakened by the preaching of the Word of God. Kuyper's son, Dr. A. Kuyper, Jr., went even further than his father and suggested that therefore in essence Paul was already regenerated at the time that he was persecuting the congregations of Christ.

Professor Lindeboom pointed out that this reasoning went against God's own Word and the Reformed confessions. He accused Kuyper of practising a theological scholarship that did not obediently subject itself in all things to God's Word. Such teachings divide, cause dissension, and are altogether arrogant (1 Cor. 4:6).

a.   Why did the disciples understand the preaching of Jesus while the Pharisees did not understand it at all? Because the latter read the books of Moses with a veil over their heart (2 Cor. 3:15, 16). They turned away from the living God of Israel and did not keep His covenant. In their hardened minds they did not know their Father who is in heaven, the Father of whom Jesus spoke and to whom the disciples found themselves so strongly and intensely attracted. They wanted to hear more and more about Him, and continued to listen to Jesus and learn from Him. "No one can come to Me unless the Father who sent Me draws him" (John 6:44). But to the Pharisees Jesus said, "Why do you not understand My speech? Because you are not able to listen to My word. . . . He who is of God hears God's words; therefore you do not hear, because you are not of God" (John 8:43, 47).

b.   The phrase *he who is of God* does not refer to some mysteriously present germ of regeneration to be awakened by the preaching of Jesus. Jesus' words refer to the believer who accepts the gospel that God Himself first revealed in paradise and that He caused to be proclaimed by patriarchs and prophets in later ages and that was foreshadowed by the service in the temple. Jesus was referring to the believer who lives from the grace proclaimed by that gospel. Such a believer recognizes that Jesus speaks the same words of God's grace and understands that the Father is at work to fulfil the promises of that old gospel in Jesus Christ, the Messiah. Such believers are God's gifts to His Son. They are reborn in the Spirit of faith on the basis of the Word of grace from the Old Testament (John 8:37ff). The disciples were among those believers in whom there was no guile (John 1:47). But the Pharisees were so blinded by their own theological reasoning and had placed themselves so far above Moses' Old Testament that the Pharisee Nicodemus did not even understand the meaning of regeneration.

c.   Jesus used the word *regeneration* for the first time, but Nicodemus could have known the idea itself from Ezekiel 36:24-27: "For I will take you from the nations, gather you out of all countries, and bring you into your own land. Then I will sprinkle clean water on you, and you will be clean; I will cleanse you from all your filthiness and from your idols. I will give you a new heart and put a new spirit within you; I will take the heart of stone out of your flesh and give you a heart of flesh. I will put My Spirit within you and cause you to walk in My statutes, and you will keep my judgements and do them. . . ." It was necessary also for Nicodemus, the proud Pharisee, to join the line of tax collectors and sinners who wanted to be baptized, humbly and with a repentant heart.

d.   Regeneration is not awakened in us; it is worked in us by the preaching of the gospel (Belgic Confession, Art. 24). Regeneration is not a sudden planting of the seed of eternal life; it is a daily submission to the words of God. The Lord even admonished His own disciples because they were foolish and slow of understanding. If they had only understood Moses, they would have expected that the Lord had to suffer and die in order to enter His glory. After His resurrection, the Lord opened their minds to understand Scripture (Luke 24:45).

e.   The Jews, hardened by their self-invented, extrascriptural systems of thought within which there was no place for the grace of God, crucified Jesus.

13.6 The third of Kuyper's teachings that greatly influenced the Reformed Churches but that was also strongly opposed by many concerned *baptism.* Kuyper taught that baptism seals the regeneration that is already present in the child. Baptism presumes the implanted ability to believe, an ability that was given us at birth in some mysterious way.

However, Professor Lindeboom and many others with him maintained that baptism does not seal something that may be presumed to be present in the child. Baptism signifies and seals the trustworthy promises of the covenant of God in which also the child may share. Baptism is not administered on the basis of an uncertain, presumed regeneration, but it is administered because it is commanded by the LORD God.

Professor Lindeboom asked how it might be possible to seal a presumed regeneration. "What is the meaning of baptism to children who are not regenerated? According to Scripture and the confession, we are not to presume anything, but we must be obedient to Him who caused both regenerate and unregenerate children to be born within the covenant and who commands us to administer the sacraments of baptism, that is the sacrament of His promises, to all those children. Imagine, if we knew that a child was not regenerated, would we baptize such a child? Many shout, No. But because I do not know this, I will baptize all of them, and consider them all to be regenerated. What a backward theory; what didactic wisdom produced by the servant! How obvious are the errors and dangers of such a subjective reasoning!"

13.7 Professor Lindeboom greatly desired to return from this philosophical wisdom to truly scriptural theology. The congregations should no longer be taught with words of human wisdom that forge the living Word of God into a sterile system of abstract concepts, but they should be taught with the words from the Holy Spirit, "comparing spiritual things with spiritual" (1 Cor. 2:13). Lindeboom maintained that the Reformed Church confesses that each word of Scripture is inspired by God's Spirit, and no one is allowed to change the language. Any such changes will always cause great damage.

He wrote, "Each true Christian wants to submit to the Word of God. God's Word speaks with power and majesty, and although it throws us down in the depths of shame and guilt, it cleanses and sanctifies and is to the believer the source of all comfort. In contrast, human theories and systems might well impress, but they never result in genuine, holy zeal; they never put psalms on your lips, they never unite hearts. Today people are depressed; there is little evidence of a joyful spiritual life. We say, the main reason for this is the tyranny of intellectualism which seeks to influence the Reformed Churches so strongly with philosophical scholarship and theology. It is therefore our undeniable duty to admonish all congregations: Be free, and remain in the Word of God!"

13.8 Professor Lindeboom clearly recognized the destructive influence of the glorification of science and scholarship on the Reformed Churches of the nineteenth century. But his voice was a lonely one. His influence was limited, and he met with great scorn. Not until the 1940s were his words heeded seriously. The Act of Liberation (1944) reads in part, "We liberate ourselves from the shame which has been brought upon the memory of ministers who in the past, openly fighting against the ideas contained in the aforementioned doctrinal decisions, served the churches before and after the Union of 1892 whose service enjoyed the rich blessing of the gospel".

13.9 Almost all of twentieth-century Christianity is under the power of the autonomous, self-reliant science of theology. Human thought has elevated itself above God's Word, and that Word has now become an embarrassment. It is now claimed that the only truth is scientific truth.

14. THE SYNOD OF UTRECHT 1905

14.1 The general synod of the Reformed Churches in the Netherlands, held at Utrecht in 1905, found on its agenda the objections against the teachings of Dr. Kuyper. A synodical declaration was adopted with which also Professor Lindeboom could agree. This declaration was not a doctrinal pronouncement, but it was an attempt to restore and keep the peace within the churches. One of the members of synod requested that the acts of synod show that he only agreed with this declaration because he considered it a basis for pacification. This declaration became known as the Pacification Declaration of 1905. (Shortly before this synod, Dr. Kuyper lost his election campaign and was forced to resign as prime minister of the Netherlands.)

Rather than condemning Kuyper's thoughts outright, synod was satisfied with a mild correction. "According to the confession of our churches, the seed of the covenant is to be considered regenerated and sanctified in Christ according to God's promises, until the opposite becomes clear in their lives and in the ideas they hold when they grow up. However, it is less accurate to say that baptism is administered to the children of believers on the ground of their presumed regeneration, because the ground for baptism is God's promise and ordinance."

This declaration is at best ambiguous. The Reformed Churches in 1905 did not reject outright those theological systems that elevated themselves above the Word of God. In later years, it became clear how disastrous this failure of the churches really was. In 1942, this Pacification Declaration was officially declared doctrine of the Reformed Churches of the Netherlands.

14.2 Synod Utrecht 1905 decided to delete the following words from Article 36 of the Belgic Confession: *all idolatry and false worship may be removed and prevented, the kingdom of Antichrist may be destroyed*. The paragraph from which these words were deleted describes the task of kings, princes, civil officers, and the civil government to safeguard and protect the ministry of the church. "Their task of restraining and sustaining is not limited to the public order but includes the protection of the Church and its ministry in order that all idolatry and false worship may be removed and prevented, the kingdom of Antichrist may be destroyed, the kingdom of Christ may come, the Word of the gospel may be preached everywhere, and God may be honoured and served by everyone, as He requires in His Word."

a.   Was the deletion of these words necessary? Utrecht 1905 answered in the affirmative because it considered that the contents of these words did not reflect the task of the government. However, the Reformed believers of the sixteenth century formulated the Belgic Confession over against the unscriptural practices of the Anabaptists. They distinguished between ecclesiastical and civil matters, between consistory and magistrate. They did not want to be counted with the despisers of authority and with the revolutionary Anabaptists. The unspiritual zealotry of the Anabaptist claimed to come from the Holy Spirit but was in reality an expression of raw power and violence against all idolaters. This zealotry was contrary to the Word of God in Zechariah 4:6, "Not by might nor by power, but by My Spirit. . . ." The reformers also opposed the doctrine of the church of Rome, which had made the church into an idol and demanded from the government total subjection to the church. Even today, the pope is very active in international politics because he claims to have the two swords: the sword of government and the sword of the Spirit. The reformers therefore opposed both zealotry and church politics; they were neither Anabaptist nor Roman Catholic.

b.   What, then, is the answer?

1.   Synod 1905 read the context of these words wrongly, as if they indicated the task of the government; if that were the case, then more should have been deleted. However, if we read these words in their correct context, we find that they refer to the purpose of the ministry of Christ's church in preaching the gospel. It is the task of the government to protect and safeguard this ministry. When the government fulfils its task, it uses its political means to enable the church to use the sword of the Holy Spirit (which is the Word of God) against all idolatry and false worship so that the kingdom of the antichrist may be destroyed.

2.   The writers of the original article thought of the international power and tyranny of the Roman Catholic Church when they spoke of the kingdom of the antichrist.

3.   A confession of faith must always be read in the light of God's Word. Read in their context and in the light of God's Word (which also stands above governments and gives them their unique task and office), it was not necessary to delete these words. Not all Reformed Churches have adopted this change in the Belgic Confession.

4.   Daniel loyally served the pagan kings of Persia, but together with his friends, he did not yield to the idolatry of the golden statue even though their lives were threatened. He disobeyed the royal decree not to pray to God despite the lions' den. (Remember: he did not know whether the Lord would rescue him.) In such situations, a firm and absolute "no" is required.

5.   Pagan governments also have been a blessing to the church. Promoted by the pharaoh, Joseph was able to maintain the

family of Jacob in Egypt. Only much later did Egypt become a house of bondage. Hiram helped Solomon with the building of the temple. Cyrus of Persia assisted Ezra, and King Artaxerxes provided Nehemiah with all the help necessary to rebuild the temple in Jerusalem. Paul, Silas, and the local congregation received the protection of the magistrate of Philippi. When attacked by the fanatical Jews, Paul was able to appeal to the emperor in Rome.

c.   Article 36 of the Belgic Confession does not contain a political programme of action. It is a confession that appeals to the government: you must not persecute the church of Christ. You must protect it because you do not need to fear rebellion from it. Instead, you may expect only good things from the church. One of the main parts of the public prayers in the church is the prayer for the government (1 Tim. 2:1ff).

d.   Christian politics is scriptural politics, different from neutral or liberal politics. In their political task, Christian governments cannot be neutral over against the sovereign Lord, the LORD God. But the task of Christian politics is more than merely protecting the preaching of the gospel and civil rights and freedoms of the church of Christ. We confess that it is the task of the government to use the sword (and this does not only refer to capital punishment) against political idolatry, for instance, of the state or of democracy. Neither the state nor democracy is a sovereign saviour of the people. It is the task of the government to guard against revolutionary takeovers by the spirits of this age, for instance, the spirit of lawlessness and immorality (homosexuality) and in public health (drugs and abortion). In this way the governments use their political responsibilities so that the kingdom of the antichrist may be destroyed.

e.   Prince William of Orange was one of the few sixteenth-century politicians who practised truly Christian politics in accordance with Romans 13:4: the government is "God's minister to you for good". For these reasons he strongly opposed the Dutch reformer Dathenus and the extremist consistory in Ghent in their attempts to persecute the quiet and orderly Roman Catholic citizens.

15. THE SYNOD OF ASSEN 1926

15.1 On Sunday, March 23, 1924, Dr. J.G. Geelkerken delivered a sermon on Lord's Day 3 of the Heidelberg Catechism to the congregation of Amsterdam South. Dr. Geelkerken accepted the historicity of Genesis 2 and 3, but he wished to allow for the possibility of an exegesis other than the traditionally literal one. He wondered out loud whether continued scientific investigation, as well as new information resulting from excavations in the Middle East, would not render a literal interpretation of these chapters untenable.

15.2 This rather sensational case was dealt with at the extraordinary Synod Assen 1926. Dr. Geelkerken was asked to declare that "the tree of the knowledge of good and evil, the speaking serpent, and the tree of life are, according to the obvious intent of the Scripture story of Genesis 2 and 3, to be understood in a real and literal sense; and that these were realities which were observable with the senses. Therefore, the opinion of Dr. Geelkerken, that one could question whether these facts were observable by the senses without contradicting the authority of Scripture as confessed in the Articles 4 and 5 of the Belgic Confession, must be rejected".

15.3 Dr. Geelkerken refused to sign this declaration and was suspended by synod. However, his suspension by synod was an interference with the responsibilities of the consistory of the local church of Amsterdam South. A synod has no authority to suspend office bearers. We must therefore say that Synod Assen 1926 allowed much of the benefits of the Second Secession of 1886 for the Reformed faith to slip away.

Dr. S. Greijdanus, professor at the theological college in Kampen, voted against this illegal exercise of discipline. He judged this action to be against the Church Order of Dort, which states that office bearers who do not heed the admonitions by the consistory, "shall be suspended from office by the judgement of their own consistory with the deacons and of the consistory with the deacons of the neighbouring church" (*Book of Praise*, p. 669, Art. 71 of the Church Order). Not the synod but the local consistory has the responsibility and the authority to suspend wayward office bearers. Dr. Greijdanus was one of the few who correctly diagnosed the symptoms of a new evil that threatened the church, that of the new church polity. The events of the Liberation of 1944 proved him correct.

15.4 Dr. Geelkerken and his supporters first established yet another Reformed denomination. Later this group joined with the Netherlands Reformed Church, the state church of the nineteenth century.

15.5 The church political decisions of Synod Assen 1926 are important ecclesiastical decisions. The issue was not so much the matter of freedom of exegesis. The critical point became the confession that the Word of God is the highest authority; God Himself explains what He says. The explanation of God's Word is not determined by human theology or scientific findings. Therefore Assen 1926 is an important moment in the struggle against the autonomous, scientific systems of thought that, by virtue of their own authority, started to unwrap the meaning of the Scripture stories, their contents and message, from the details (their wrappings). Such theological systems would make the congregation of Christ again dependent on the labours of the theological experts. Scripture explains itself. ". . . no prophecy of Scripture is of any private interpretation . . ." (2 Pet. 1:20).

Assen 1926 was a moment in the struggle to maintain the confession that Scripture is clear and understandable in and of itself. Calvin writes in his *Institutes* I:VII:2, "As to the question, How shall we be persuaded that (Scripture) came from God without recurring to a decree of the church? It is just the same as if it were asked, How shall we learn to distinguish light from darkness, white from black, sweet from bitter? Scripture bears upon the face of it as clear evidence of its truth, as white and black do of their colour, sweet and bitter of their taste." By listening to the Bible we learn to believe in the Bible. If you stand in the sun, you feel its warmth, and you see its light. The Synod of Dort, therefore, spoke of the clarity of the truth.

a. Surely when I use the expressions *the sun rises* or *the sun sets*, I am not guilty of backwardness and ignorance. Nobody would accuse me of ignoring the current state of scientific knowledge. It would be equally ridiculous when, as a result of excavations in the twenty-fifth or the twenty-sixth century, the conclusion would be drawn that twentieth-century man believed that the sun turned around the earth.

b. The Baal of evolutionistic unbelief haughtily rejects the teaching of the living God who does not speak according to the concepts of human science but who reveals the truth about His works. The history of creation and man reveals the enormous consequences of God's judgements and catastrophes because of man's fall into sin.
    Why are these facts ignored? Because the Bible has been reduced to a book for the soul and religion. The existence of the almighty Father, the Creator and Ruler of heaven and earth, is no longer considered relevant to our concrete, daily life here on earth.

c. The "waters under the earth" of Deuteronomy 5:8 are simply the fishing waters of Deuteronomy 4:18.

The decisions of Assen 1926, rejecting the views of Dr. Geelkerken, were rescinded by the Reformed Churches (Synodical) in 1967. They have no longer any doctrinal authority within these churches. This was a victory for modern theology, which attempts to demythologize the Bible. The tyranny of the unbelief of evolution in the sciences leads to abandoning the facts of the history of salvation and considers them to be at best teaching models. And who determines what these models might still teach us?

15.6 Scripture is a history book. The Christian faith rests on facts, otherwise "our preaching is in vain and your faith is also in vain" (1 Cor. 15:14). In his letters to Timothy, Paul makes special mention of Hymenaeus and Alexander (1 Tim. 1:20) and Philetus, whose "message will spread like cancer" (2 Tim. 2:17). These men preached that the resurrection had already taken place (in their own heart—Gnosticism), "and they overthrow the faith of some" (2 Tim. 2:18). Their talk about the deeds of God was no more than profane and vain babblings that will increase to more ungodliness (2 Tim. 2:16). Not only the miracles in Scripture but all that God has done and still will do is belittled and ignored. As a cancer, the new theology touches all knowledge of God, hiding the God who in His lovingkindness and grace seeks to save people from their sin and misery. Then man, touched by this cancer, can only laugh in derision at axes that float and asses that talk.

Today's modern theology denies the historical facts of God's work of salvation. Paul said, "Nevertheless the solid foundation of God stands, having this seal: "The Lord knows who are His," and, "Let everyone who names the name of Christ depart from iniquity" (2 Tim. 2:19). Peter wrote, "For we did not follow cunningly devised fables when we made known to you the power and coming of our Lord Jesus Christ, but were eyewitnesses of His majesty" (2 Pet. 1:16). When the facts of the history of salvation have been turned upside down, then also the norms by which believers must live will change. Peter spoke of the error of the wicked. (2 Pet. 3:17). The Apostle Jude puts it even stronger, "For certain men have crept in unnoticed, who long ago were marked out for this condemnation, ungodly men, who turn the grace of our God into licentiousness and deny the only LORD God and our Lord Jesus Christ" (Jude verse 4). In the past, homosexuality was considered unnatural (Rom. 1:26, 27), but today sexual mores have been revised, and homosexuality is now considered natural also by those who still dare to call themselves reformed.

In 1 John 4:1-6, the apostle draws a clear distinction between falsehood and truth, admonishing his readers to remain in God and in the truth. The Bible has been written for the church of all ages. And it is remarkable and comforting to note how relevant God's Word is for the struggle of Christ's church in each age.

This is the essence of Professor Lindeboom's defence of the clarity of Scripture, which is much greater than we think. God's Word is not out of reach for us; His Word is near you, in your mouth and in your heart (Rom. 10:8; Deut. 30:11). We can speak about it, we can meditate on it, we can study it: "He is not far from each one of us" (Acts 17:27).

16. REVIVAL

16.1 During the 1920s and 1930s, the Lord gave a glorious revival in the Reformed Churches in the Netherlands. A strong reformational movement developed back to the Word of God itself. This movement forms the background to a third secession, the Liberation of 1944, which cannot be understood without it.

16.2 Historically, this reformational movement found its roots in the renewed respect for the Reformed confessions of the Secession of 1834, the Secession of 1886, and the Calvinist *Réveil* of Kuyper and Bavinck during the final years of the nineteenth century. But this movement rejected the extrascriptural teachings of Kuyper, especially his ideas concerning the covenant of God and baptism. Following Professor Lindeboom's teachings, the scholasticism in Kuyper's works, which so badly hindered the preaching of the practical-prophetic living Word of the LORD God and made that Word into a set of theoretical, logical arguments was analyzed and exposed for what it was.

In his large body of works, Kuyper at times mixed the wisdom of God with the wisdom of men (1 Cor. 2:5, 7, 13), reducing God's Word to a (Reformed) system of thought; the confessions were reduced to a system of sterile, theoretical truths. We are reminded of the spirit that prevailed in the seventeenth and eighteenth centuries under the influence of rationalism. In the years following Kuyper's death (1920), spiritual backsliding and secularization crept into the church, and the worship of human reason that had started in previous centuries continued its irresistible invasion of the society of western Europe. The Reformed Churches had little in defence against all this.

16.3 Among the leaders of this reformational movement (ca. 1926) can be counted Dr. D.H.Th. Vollenhoven and his colleague Dr. H. Dooyeweerd; A. Janse, a schoolteacher in Biggekerke; and Dr. K. Schilder and Dr. S. Greijdanus, both professors at the theological college in Kampen.

16.4 Dr. D.H.Th. Vollenhoven and Dr. H. Dooyeweerd were the first ever to develop a philosophical system based on God's Word. This system is known as the school of Calvinist philosophy, or the Amsterdam philosophy.

a. Philosophy (love of wisdom) is the scholarly discipline that systematically examines God's creation. A Reformed philosopher asks questions such as, "What is man? What is knowledge? How does man acquire knowledge? What is society? What is history, language, economy?" He tries to find answers in the light of God's Word and works.

b. Most basic to the philosophy of Vollenhoven and Dooyeweerd is the statement that all scientific-theoretical thought and knowledge of man is preceded by nonscientific, practical, concrete understanding rooted in the Word of God which gives trustworthy, practical, living knowledge. The scientist and scholar, also, must listen to this Word, even before he starts with his scientific examination of God's works on this earth. Scholasticism and rationalism are dead systems of thought because they make the Word of God subject to man's reasoning instead of "bringing every thought into captivity to the obedience of Christ" (2 Cor. 10:5).

c.   This Calvinist philosophy rejected the claim of the Enlightenment that *scientific* means *without prejudice* and confessed that human reason is not sovereign. Man is not a reasonable-moral being, but a religious creature, created by God in His image and subject to his creator in order that he may have communion with Him. The bond with God is essential to man's very existence.

d.   Everyone, whether he believes or not, reasons on the basis of certain religious presuppositions, basic starting points that cannot be proven by intellectual reasoning. A Christian knows the great starting points for his life as well as for his scientific labours: Your Word is the Truth. "For with You is the fountain of life; in Your light we see light" (Ps. 36:9). This applies equally to all scientific and scholarly efforts.

e.   Vollenhoven and Dooyeweerd were among the few scholars who recognized the disastrous influence of the Greek-pagan thought of Plato and Aristotle on the thinking and life of Christianity in western Europe.

f.   This reformational philosophical system does not want to be static or closed. Its originators intended it to develop much further. They realized that true faith is very much alive and active. But unfortunately, the three basic motifs identified by this philosophy (creation - fall - salvation) have in fact replaced the confessions of the church. But in our scholarly endeavours, we are equally bound to and enriched by the Three Forms of Unity. These confessions do not need to be replaced by a number of Christian basic motifs. Although we recognize the value of the work of these philosophers for Christian scientific endeavours, there are serious objections against the manner in which this philosophy speaks about matters such as faith and church.

16.5 A. Janse (1890-1960) was principal of the school with the Bible (a Christian independent school) in the village of Biggekerke in the Dutch province of Zeeland. Janse was known especially for his reformational writings through which many (again) learned to read and understand the Word of God properly. He opened the eyes of ministers and other church members alike for the riches of that Word which speaks to us directly and concretely in our situation. Through his efforts, many rediscovered the concrete relevance of the covenant which the LORD God has made with us and which He maintains and remembers, both to our chastisement (the First World War, fought between Christian nations; the economic crisis of the 1930s; the rising catastrophe of fascism and national-socialism which was to overwhelm the nations in the Second World War) and to our good (the return of many to the concrete, relevant, living Word of the LORD God).

His writings include:
Van de Rechtvaardigen (Of the Righteous)
Leven in het Verbond (Living in the Covenant)
Heerlijkheid van de Psalmen (The Glory of the Psalms)
Het eigen Karakter der Christelijke School (The Unique Character of the Christian School)
Onderwijs en Opvoeding (Instruction and Education)
Unfortunately, none of these books has been translated into the English language.

16.6 Dr. K. Schilder (1890-1952) was a strong force toward reformation. He became professor at the theological college at Kampen, but already as a minister he warned against the exemplaric and moralistic preaching of his days. He opened the eyes and minds of the people for the riches of the history of God's works of salvation. History is the history of salvation, the history of the covenant—redemptive-historical preaching and teaching.

Already well before the terrible lie promoted by modernist theology in its rejection of the facts of God's Word (a theology that is really as old as the false teachings of the Gnosticism of the first century) became a matter of public debate, Dr. Schilder emphasized the reality of the historical facts of the Bible stories. "And it came to pass in those days. . ." (Luke 2:1). Enthusiastically he worked for a new rhymed version of the Psalms (to replace the version of 1773). Untiringly he fought against the rising influence of the German theologian Karl Barth, defending God's Word and the confessions of the church in his preaching, in public debates, in his writings (in particular his weekly columns in the *De Reformatie*, The Reformation), and in other scholarly labours. Relentlessly he exposed and opposed indifference and smugness in the Reformed Churches of his days.

Some of his works have been translated into the English language:
What is Heaven?
Christ and Culture
The Schilder Trilogy: *Christ in His Sufferings*, *Christ on Trial*, and *Christ Crucified*

16.7 Dr. S. Greijdanus (1871-1948) also contributed substantially to a better understanding of God's Word, especially in his Bible commentaries in the famous series *De Korte Verklaring* (The concise Bible commentary, in part available in English under the title *Bible Student's Commentary*). His struggle against the new church polity introduced by Synod Assen 1926 was of tremendous importance to the Liberation of 1944.

17. TOWARD ANOTHER SECESSION

17.1 As with each reformation, this Reformed revival movement met with resistance. First of all, Synod Amsterdam 1936 decided to establish a committee to evaluate in the light of Scripture and the confessions "opinions which deviate from the generally accepted teachings". Note that no names were attached to these deviating opinions. By phrasing the mandate of this committee in this vague manner, any teachings other than "generally accepted teachings" were immediately suspect.

These "generally accepted teachings" were by and large those of Dr. A. Kuyper. But it must be remembered that such a body of generally accepted teachings in themselves can never be considered a standard or norm. The Lord Jesus Himself was under suspicion because His preaching was contrary to the prevailing opinion. Luther also was accused of the same "heresy". The churches of the Reformation have never accepted the authority of traditions (generally accepted opinions and teachings)— *sola scriptura*!

This synod had no authority to order such an investigation. No church had made a request to do this nor were there any appeals from within the churches against anyone. Synod acted in a hierarchical manner, causing a great deal of misery in the churches. These synodical actions were the consequence of the wrong direction of Synod Assen 1926, which correctly condemned the teachings of Dr. Geelkerken but unlawfully deposed him from office.

17.2 The reports received by Synod Sneek 1939 clearly indicated that there was no ground for suspicion against the reformational movement. Since September 1939 saw the beginning of the horrors of the Second World War, many urged synod to postpone any further discussion of the alleged differences of opinion. But despite these requests, synod decided to continue its deliberations in closed, secret sessions. Because of the war situation, the meetings of synod were moved from the city of Sneek to the city of Utrecht in the centre of the country.

17.3 On Monday evening, June 8, 1942 (three years later!), synod made pronouncements concerning common grace, the covenant of grace and self-examination, the immortality of the soul, and the union of the two natures of Christ.

No one was accused or judged by name, but these pronouncements implied strong criticism of the reformational movement that confessed God's Word and maintained the confessions.

These matters were discussed without the request of the churches (1936), the discussion of these matters continued despite the churches (1940), and they were finalized without the churches (1942).

Synod did not deal with the doctrine of the pluriformity of the church, although this matter was part of the list of 1936. In principle, this doctrine had already been rejected as part of the agreements leading to the Union of 1892. At that time, the churches of 1834 and those of 1886 agreed that the Word of God and the confessions of the church demanded a break with the Dutch state church, hereby in effect, although not officially, rejecting the doctrine of the pluriformity of the church. In the meantime, Kuyper's view regarding this doctrine gained considerable support within the Reformed Churches. The weakness of Kuyper's view of the pluriformity of the church became clear after the Second World War when the Reformed Churches (Synodical) were unable to defend themselves against the temptations of false ecumenism.

In contrast, the reformational movement emphasized the importance of maintaining the doctrine of God's covenant and its consequences for all of life in the churches.

17.4 In particular, the decisions concerning the doctrine of the covenant caused a great deal of strife. The text of this pronouncement reads in part:

"a. On the Covenant of Grace

"1st. that the Covenant of grace is of such fundamental significance to the life of faith, that the preaching of God's Word as well as any other labour in the church must have its starting point in it, and that any presentation or practice that would strain the significance of God's Covenant should be avoided.

"2d. that the Lord, in the Covenant promise, undoubtedly promises to be the God not only of the believers but also of their descendants (Gen. 17:7); but His Word reveals that not all who are descendants of Israel belong to Israel (Rom. 9:6).

"3d. that therefore—in agreement with the statements of Synod Utrecht 1905 (Acts Art. 158)—according to the promise of God the seed of the Covenant must be regarded as regenerated and sanctified in Christ until, as they grow up, the contrary is evident from their life or doctrine; although synod correctly added that this does not in any way imply that every child is therefore truly regenerated."

17.5 The reasoning that led to these statements can be summarized as follows: indeed, the LORD says, "I am also the God of your children". However, the LORD does not mean that He is the God of each and every child, because He is only the God of those children who will be saved for eternity. Since we do not know which children will be saved, we must consider all of them regenerated. If later in life it becomes obvious that a child is not regenerated, then we have obviously been mistaken. The baptism administered on the basis of the child's presumed regeneration was evidently not a true or full baptism; it was no more than a baptism in appearance only.

The implications of this reasoning are far reaching. It suggests that we need to find out by means of self-examination whether we are predestined from eternity, and as a consequence, whether we share in the promises of the covenant. But this reasoning forces us to find certainty in our soul rather than in God's Word. The question now becomes whether baptism is a real baptism, whether it is a "full" baptism. These questions remove any comfort since baptism can be true only for those who have been justified from eternity. This leaves everyone wondering whether he belongs to that group.

17.6 The starting point for the reasoning of synod was the statement that God has a covenant only with those of whom He knows from eternity will be saved. But the Word of God does not contain such a theory.

a.   God established His covenant not only with Abraham, Isaac, and Jacob but also with Ishmael and Esau. The Israelites who died in the desert also belonged to that covenant without reservation or restriction. But they did not live in accordance with the covenant and did not believe in the LORD God who was really and truly their God. The Jews who crucified the Lord Jesus were also "sons of the covenant" (Acts 3:25), and Peter most earnestly and urgently called them to repentance.

b.   God's covenant promises, made to the parents and their children, are genuine promises. However, people might reject God's promises as well as God's grace which He gives in the blood and Spirit of Christ. It is even possible to insult the Spirit. Such a despiser of the covenant will be seriously punished precisely because God takes His promises most seriously (Heb. 10:29).

c.   These promises are not a mere theory; they concern the essence of our life and our being. "And I will establish My covenant between Me and you and your descendants after you in their generations, for an everlasting covenant, to be a God to you and your descendants after you" (Gen. 17:7); The Lord repeats this promise in the following verse: ". . . and I will be their God". Our baptism is an assurance that God indeed means what He says. Therefore God commands that baptism be administered to all children of believing parents without distinction. If one of them later turns his or her back on God and follows his or her own desires, then such a person breaks God's covenant and throws away the treasures that God has really given. Instead of enjoying its blessings, such a covenant breaker will suffer the curses of the covenant. That is the worst thing that could happen to anyone—to be cursed by the God of the covenant.

d.   Our understanding of God's Word is badly hindered by the theoretical theories of Kuyper and his followers about the covenant. These theories do not allow us to get to know our God and Father, leading as they do to the construction of a dual covenant (external and internal) and a dual baptism (full and not full). Kuyper and his followers saw a contradiction between Genesis 17:7 ("And I will establish My covenant between Me and you and your descendants after you . . .") and Romans 9:6 (". . . For they are not all Israel who are of Israel"). But Scripture never contradicts itself. The serious admonition not to throw away what we have been given by God Himself has been made powerless. After all, how can we lose what we did not have in the first place? God's Word clearly warns us not to receive God's grace in vain (2 Cor. 6:1).

e. God's Word urges us to self-examination, but that is not self-analysis or introspection to determine whether we are regenerated or whether we have the germ of the new life in us. Nowhere does Scripture speak like that. True self-examination is testing ourselves whether we fear the Lord seriously and whether we truly love our brothers and sisters as we have been commanded to. The certainty of our salvation is not found in the conclusions of introspection but in a continuous return to God's Word. "For (in the gospel) the righteousness of God is revealed from faith to faith; as it is written, "The just shall live by faith" (Rom. 1:17). It was Christ's Word that slowly but surely made the disciples into partakers of Him. Only through faith in Jesus would Nicodemus be reborn of water and the Spirit (John 3:5), and only in that way would he be able to enter the kingdom of God.

1. More than once have we warned against a scholastic and rationalistic approach to the Bible. Such an approach leads away from the living Word of God, resulting in opinions and theoretical constructs, replacing the living fellowship with the God of the covenant. Man cannot live by philosophies and theories of theologians. Their opinions and ideas will only lead to more differences of opinion. God's covenant is not a theoretical model; it is our lifeblood, the very basis of our existence.

2. Only when theology subjects itself in all humility to the Word of God will it be able to help the churches. But never can theology itself provide us with knowledge greater than the living, practical knowledge of Scripture. Knowing God (John 17:3) is not the same as being well versed in dogmatics.

3. Reliance on theoretical systems of thought creates careless and self-assured people. In the eyes of a scholastic Christian, the Bible is an untidy and unsystematic book. Even though a systematic theory might appear to provide a much clearer understanding and greater certainty, such understanding and certainty depends on human thought instead of on

the Word of God which alone is true and sure.

4.   The doctrinal pronouncements of Synod Sneek-Utrecht 1942 protected the generally accepted ideas and theories that were found in the church, and at the same time, these pronouncements raised suspicions about the men of the reformational movement, men who adhered to the old truths of Scripture and to the sure language of the confessions.

17.7 The peace within the churches was greatly disturbed by the following events:

a.   Synod, in its decisions of October 7, 1942, demanded that classes ensure that all candidates to the ministry adhere to the decisions of Synod Sneek-Utrecht 1942; that is, they were to teach that all children were to be considered regenerated until it became obvious that they were not. Thus this teaching was elevated to a confession to which candidates to the ministry were forced to subscribe. This doctrine of presumptive regeneration severely hindered a strong confession of God's Word and prevented a serious use of the Three Forms of Unity; in fact it became a form of disunity. No candidate with leanings toward the reformational movement was to be admitted to the pulpit.

1.   In 1905, the phrase *presume regeneration until the contrary becomes evident* had been included for the purpose of compromise. After 1942, this phrase received confessional status and authority.

2.   One of the synodical reports suggested that these decisions should be accepted as divine truths.

b.   Confusion increased as a result of an official *Clarification*, issued by synod on November 26, 1942. In defending the decisions of synod, this *Clarification* further demonstrated how human wisdom now exceeded God's wisdom.

c.   Synod continued to meet, contrary to Articles 30 and 49 of the Church Order. This action showed a hierarchical tendency, as if a synod had authority of its own. Ministers were ordered not to teach anything that was not in full agreement with the relevant doctrinal decisions. Many objected, including professors Schilder and Greijdanus.

d.   Attempts by synod to reach a compromise while maintaining all decisions failed. On December 13, 1943, Professor Schilder (who was at that time in hiding because of the German occupation of the Netherlands) advised synod by letter to let the decisions stand for the time being, but not to make them binding at the ecclesiastical examinations of candidates to the ministry. Professor Schilder suggested that after the war, matters could be discussed properly. This request to postpone the whole matter till after the war was

supported by many similar requests, but synod ignored them all.
Those who objected to the actions and decisions of synod were
warned to obey.

e.   By December 1943, synod appointed another committee to deal
      with all the problems. The mandate of this committee instructed it
      to travel around the country in an attempt to persuade all objecting
      consistories to comply with the synodical decisions. But the war
      situation (Holland was occupied by the German forces) made such
      travel impossible.

17.8 On March 23, 1944, Professor K. Schilder was suspended from
office on the basis of Articles 71 and 72 of the Church Order. These
articles deal with serious and gross sins on the part of office bearers. The
suspension of Dr. Greijdanus followed on August 1, 1944. Synod declared that these men were the cause of the schism since they had not
subjected themselves to the teachings and rulings of synod. In accordance
with Article 31 of the Church Order, Dr. Schilder advised his consistory
not to consider these decisions as settled and binding since they were in
conflict with the Word of God and with the Church Order. However,
synod made this article powerless by changing the little word *unless* into
until. This reading of Article 31 of the Church Order opened the door
even wider for hierarchy in the churches.

"CHURCH ORDER, Article 31. APPEALS

"If anyone complains that he has been wronged by the decision of
a minor assembly, he shall have the right to appeal to the major assembly; and what ever may be agreed upon by a majority vote shall be
considered settled and binding, **unless** it is proved to be in conflict with
the Word of God or with the Church Order."

17.9 For the third time, the Reformed Churches in the Netherlands fell
into the trap of hierarchy. Candidates to the ministry were refused admission to the ministry (Candidate H.J. Schilder) and ministers and elders
were suspended by synod. Whole congregations were excluded from the
federation of churches, an action that was not even included in the
official acts of synod! Indeed, this synod assigned "more authority to
itself and its ordinances than to the Word of God. . . . It persecuted
those who live holy lives according to the Word of God and who rebuke
the false church for its sins . . ." (Belgic Confession, Art. 29). These
illegal acts of discipline against the faithful office bearers brought shame
upon the name of the Lord by excluding those who are not excluded by
Christ Jesus.

In his struggle against Dr. Kuyper, Professor Lindeboom foresaw
this sad development. He wrote, "As the zealots in the New Testament
claimed to devote themselves to the law, but in the process deformed and
lost the law and the gospel, so will anyone who allows the science of

theology to go beyond the limits set by the revealed knowledge of God, and allows it to be normative to the congregations and her offices, lose both genuine scholarship as well as true theology, precisely because of the power of the gospel and God's judgement. Those who start with science and the thinking human being become servants of science, that is of human thought, in the same way as subjectivists become slaves of their emotions. Those servants (servants of scientific theology) will not fail to bring the congregation into servitude also. In this way the shepherd's staff can easily change into the whip of the driver. Therefore, guard the pledge which you have received!"

This was the situation in the Reformed Churches in the year 1944, the darkest year of the Second World War; it was a year full of despair caused by God's judgement over Europe.

But the victorious scholastic system of covenant theology did not recognize God's covenant wrath which shook the earth in the violence of a world war that centred on Europe. Its followers were caught in a human system of thought that they claimed to be divine truth. Indeed, the shepherd's staff did change into the driver's whip. "And the vinedressers took his servants, beat one, killed one, and stoned another" (Matt. 21:35). The name of the Lord was defiled by actions of discipline against those whom Christ the Lord did not discipline and by the gagging of mouths that He did not want to be gagged (See Act of Liberation or Return).

18. THE LIBERATION OF 1944

18.1 The war in Europe made it impossible for synod to continue. The publication of church magazines and newspapers was no longer possible. On the basis of Article 31 of the Church Order, a number of consistories and office bearers, followed by thousands of others, liberated themselves from the synodical decisions and pronouncements of 1942 and the illegal actions and discipline of the synod and other major (not higher) assemblies.

18.2 On Friday, August 11, 1944, the seceders met in The Hague, where Dr. K. Schilder presented the draft of the Act of Liberation or Return, which reads in part, "We, the undersigned, members (or office bearers) of the Reformed Church of, . . . having for some time already noticed the decay within the Reformed Churches in the Netherlands in the deformation or denial of the spiritual police, order, and discipline of the church as based on God's Word; as well as in the corruption of the doctrine on which according to the commandments of Christ in his Word the administration of the holy sacraments is based; as also in the now common misuse of ecclesiastical discipline; and as all of these, according to our Belgic Confession, Article 29, concern the marks of the true Church . . . we declare to have liberated ourselves not only from the synodical-hierarchical yoke, but also from the theological-scientific yoke which is not of Christ. . . .

"We liberate ourselves from the shame which has been brought upon the memory of ministers who in the past, openly fighting against the ideas contained in the aforementioned doctrinal decisions, served the churches before and after the Union of 1892, whose service enjoyed the rich blessing of the gospel; and we also return to the fellowship with the catholic Christian church and its offices, which neither adds to nor deletes from the adopted forms (of unity) of the churches which have always been gathered in this country."

18.3 The Liberation was in accordance with God's Word (Acts 5:29; 1 Cor. 7:23) and in agreement with the Belgic Confession, Articles 7 and 32, as well as with the Church Order, Article 31.

"I deny that those assemble in the name of Christ who, disregarding his command by which He forbids anything to be added to the Word of God or taken from it, determine everything at their own pleasure, who, not contented with the oracles of Scripture, that is, with the only rule of perfect wisdom, devise some novelty out of their own head (Deut. 4:2; Rev. 22:18)" (Calvin, *Institutes* IV:9:2).

18.4 After his suspension and dismissal, Professor Schilder liberated himself, and on August 20, 1944, he preached for the congregation of Bergsenhoek (near Rotterdam). His text was 1 Cor. 4:6-7, ". . . that you may learn in us (by our example) not to think beyond what is written, that none of you may be puffed up on behalf of one against the other."

a.   The Secession of 1834 was an act of separation according to the Belgic Confession, Article 28 "from those who do not belong to the Church."

b.   The Doleantie of 1886 rejected the synodical hierarchy of the royal regulations of 1816 because these regulations were totally unacceptable since Jesus Christ is to be acknowledged as Head and King of the church.

c.   The Liberation of 1944 was not an act of separation from those who do not belong to the church nor was it a rejection of royal regulations for the church. It was a liberation from unscriptural synodical decisions and from the illegal and ungodly synodical exercise of church discipline. It was a liberation in accordance with Article 31 of the Church Order in order to remain truly Church in accordance with the Belgic Confession, Articles 27-29.

d.   In each of these reformations, the key issues concerned the Kingship of Christ over His church, and the sole authority of His Word for the church.

18.5   Further Developments

a.   After the war, a provisional synod of the Reformed Churches (Liberated) was held in Enschede (1945). The name of these churches remained Reformed Churches but with the addition *maintaining Art. 31, C.O.* to prevent confusion by the postal services. In 1959, this addition was dropped.

b.   Synod Groningen 1946 of the Reformed Churches (Synodical) decided to rescind the Pacification Declaration of 1905 as being largely incorrect.

c.   In contrast with the decisions of 1834 and 1886, many courts of law decided in favour of the Reformed Churches (Liberated) because these churches acted correctly according to their own Church Order against the synodical rule. A federation of churches is a voluntary covenant between local churches of our Lord Jesus Christ. A federation of churches is certainly not a national church with local branches.

18.6   In the way of liberation, the LORD God maintained and continued His work of reformation, begun in the 1920s and 1930s. As the twentieth century draws to a close, it becomes increasingly clear that scientific thought and the theology of autonomous man gains prominence among many Christians, estranging more and more people from the Word of God.

18.7   The Reformed Churches (Synodical) made various attempts to undo the damage caused by the synodical pronouncements of 1942-1944, but these attempts did not really change the pronouncements. In 1959, they were removed but not withdrawn; however, the contents of these pronouncements were still not considered to be contrary to Scripture and confession.

a.   The Church Order of these churches was revised, legalizing and enshrining a hierarchical church government.

b.   In 1961, it was decided that only the Word of God and the confessions were binding in the churches. But the legality of previous decisions and acts of discipline was maintained, and the seceders were still considered responsible for the schism. There was no genuine desire for repentance and reconciliation.

c.   In 1967, these churches revoked the decisions concerning Dr. Geelkerken (1926). This resulted in freedom of doctrine, much to the concern of many members of these churches. These concerned members worried about the increasing influence of modernist theology in their churches, a theology that threatened to bury God's Word under the blanket of the new hermeneutics (method of explanation of Scripture).

18.8 The nineteenth- and twentieth-century struggle in Christ's church in the Netherlands shows how close the relationship is between Scripture and confession. The confession is and must be in full agreement with the continuing witness of the whole of Scripture. If this bond is destroyed by scholastic thought, then the confession loses its power; then it becomes a system of doctrine rather than an expression of the living faith of the believer. This, in turn, will lead to a crisis of faith in one's personal life.

Christ used three reformations to bring back many in humble submission to the living Word of God. This resulted in a renewed, cheerful profession of the faith as expressed by the church of all ages in her confessions.

19. THE ECUMENICAL MOVEMENT

19.1 The word *ecumenical* is derived from the Greek word *oikoumene*, meaning the whole (civilized) world (Luke 2:1). The objective of the ecumenical movement is the unity of all churches without distinction— one worldwide church.

19.2 The history of the ecumenical movement includes the following highlights:

a. The World Mission Conference at Edinburgh, 1910, generally considered the beginning of the ecumenical movement, was organized in response to the problems encountered in the mission fields, especially the question of whether the third-world churches should be westernized. However, such questions ignore the catholic-ecumenical nature of the sound and healing words of our Lord Jesus Christ (1 Tim. 6:3). In these questions we also detect the basic fault of the ecumenical movement, that is the rationalistic assumption that the gospel expresses the culture and thought patterns of western Europe and is essentially unsuitable for the third-world nations with different cultures and ways of thinking.

b. The leader of the World Conference for Practical Christianity (Life and Work), held in Stockholm, 1925, was Dr. Nathan Soderblom (1866-1931), whose slogan was, "Doctrine separates, service unites". In contrast, Reformed understanding of Scripture confesses that true faith unites to service.

c. World Conference on Faith and Order, Lausanne, 1927, resulted in attempts to remove the walls of separation between the protestant and the Roman Catholic churches since these churches supplement each other and make their own unique and pluriform contribution. However, this is a blatant denial of the great Reformation, which was a return to holy Scripture as a work of God's compassion.

d. At the World Mission Conference in Jerusalem, 1928, the question was raised whether the nonchristian (pagan) religions did contain elements of truth. The answer to this question should be that truth cannot be broken up in separate elements. Jesus said that Scripture cannot be broken (John 10:35). Further, the Word of God is of inestimably greater worth than the holy books of the world's religions. Since paradise, mankind has never been completely without the light of God's Word (John 1:1-5); but the old serpent has always tried to obscure and suppress that Word (Rom. 1:18), attempting to replace it with the lies of heathendom. The Gentiles were separated from Christ—they were far off. Only through the living faith in Jesus Christ can we come near. The Gentiles live without hope and without God in the world (Eph. 2:12, 13); their lands are the lands of Satan.

Nowhere did Paul find elements of truth that were Christian. At Athens he found a starting point in the words of the Greek poet Aratus. In fact, he turned the words of this Greek poet against the Greeks themselves: "Therefore, since we are the offspring of God, we ought not to think that the Divine Nature is like gold or silver or stone, something shaped by man's art and man's devising . . ." (Acts 17:28). The Greeks claimed that they were divine themselves, they were half-gods. Paul, however, proclaimed that we are by nature creatures created to serve God. Therefore God, overlooking the times of their guilty ignorance, declares to the people of today that they should repent (Acts 17:30). Paul changes a devilish element of truth (to be like God) into the serious and urgent gospel call to repentance because God has already determined the day of judgement and has already appointed the Great Judge.

e.   The World Mission Conference, held at Tambaran (near Madras), 1938, was strongly influenced by the dialectic notion of the truth developed by the German theologian Karl Barth. Therefore the conference searched for a synthesis between Western Christian thought and the great and holy ideas of the nonchristian thinkers from Asian countries.

19.3 These preparatory world conferences resulted in the founding of the World Council of Churches (W.C.C.) at Amsterdam in 1948. This founding conference was followed by meetings at Evanston (Chicago) 1954, New Delhi 1961 (where the Russian Orthodox Church joined the W.C.C.), Upsala 1968, and Bangkok 1973. The International Mission Council also joined the W.C.C. Headquarters were established in Geneva.

The basis of the W.C.C. has been formulated as follows: the World Council of Churches is a fellowship of churches that confess the Lord Jesus Christ as God the Saviour according to Scripture and therefore together seek to fulfil their common calling to the glory of the one God, Father, Son and, Holy Spirit.

Naturally, the W.C.C. leaves it up to the member churches to interpret this basis; for who would dare to elevate as divine truth his version of the truth over the thoughts and ideas of other churches?

19.4 At the same time and in the same city (Amsterdam, 1948), the International Council of Christian Churches (I.C.C.C.) was founded. This council functions as a kind of counter W.C.C. Its members are orthodox churches that want to adhere to the Bible, many coming from the United States. However, the I.C.C.C. is based on the view of the pluriformity of churches among its more fundamentalistic members, which include Baptist churches as well as the Dutch Christelijke Gereformeerde Kerken (in North America known as the Free Reformed Churches).

19.5 Evaluation of the Basis of the W.C.C.

a.   The W.C.C. uses the word *churches* in its basis, indicating that all churches throughout the world are equal, without making a distinction between true and false churches. Reformations and counter-reformations are ignored. In short, the W.C.C. denies the church-historical work of God in His blessings (reformation) as well as His curses (deformation).

b.   The basis contains the phrase *fellowship of churches*; note, it does not say fellowship in faith with Christ through his Spirit and Word and therefore also fellowship with each other. The scriptural term *fellowship* (Acts 2:42; 1 John 1:3, 4) is devalued to refer to an organizational unity only.

c.   The basis refers to *Lord* and *Saviour*. Do these terms refer to the redemptive-historical fact that Jesus Christ bought us with His blood, or do they refer to Christ as a lofty example to be followed by us on our personal (renaissance) road to self-actualization? Indeed, truth and lie come together!

d.   The W.C.C. speaks of *Jesus Christ as God*, certainly, but Arius also spoke of the divine Jesus, and so do many modernist theologians.

e.   The W.C.C. accepts *holy Scripture*, certainly, but does this phrase refer to the infallible Word of the living God, or, as Karl Barth teaches, to the book that can become the Word of God? Does this phrase refer to the view of many third-world Christians who consider Scripture merely as one of the means that God may or may not use to speak to us, or does it refer to the manner in which pagan mysticism of the East considers the Bible to be the book of the Western Christians, of equal status and value with the Eastern holy books?

19.6 The W.C.C. calls all churches to consider each other as equals and to respect each other's mission work. However, the protestant churches in

Greece are persecuted at the instigation of the patriarch of Athens and with the assistance of the government, although both church groups are members of the W.C.C. and therefore should not compete but complement each other. Since the truth is pluriform, and since it is not at all clear what in fact is truth, the distinction between truth and lie have disappeared.

Mission is no longer that which Paul did (antithesis between God and the serpent) but has now become a dialogue between Jew, Gentile, and Mohammedan because all religions may claim elements of truth.

Instead of reformations, people are encouraged to confess the sins of schism.

19.7 The Bangkok (1973) conference of the Commission on World Mission and Evangelism was a low point. This conference was prepared in style with the most advanced technology and had as its theme *Salvation Today*. It was, in fact, a dangerous call for a crusade against the scriptural mission effort.

a. Openly and without apology it was stated that the great error of the mission effort of the past was that followers of other religions were called pagan. (What an insult!) The word *pagan* means uncivilized. In fact, by using this word, we made these people into pagans. But we must meet these religions as of equal value and equal dignity with our own. By means of a dialogue between equals, it is now our task to depaganize those whom we paganized and to return to those religions their rightful dignity and value to the world.

b. The secretary-general of the W.C.C. suggested that the main purpose of mission lies in joining with the nonchristians against racial, political, and economic injustice in the world. In this worldwide struggle, the W.C.C. cooperates in brotherly fashion with communist revolutionaries and activist Buddhists.

c. This reminds us of Jesus' parable, "The kingdom of heaven is like a man who sowed good seed in his field. . . . How can (your field) have tares . . . (the tares of false ecumenicity)? An enemy has done this", an enemy, the devil (Matt. 13:24-30).

d. Paul was the first missionary in the history of the world. He forced his way into Satan's territory with the gospel that life is not senseless because Jesus rose from the dead. In Athens, the centre of the scholarly world and the basis for all the thought structures of the Western world, as well as in the imperial city of Rome, the centre of law and power, Paul proclaimed with great fervour the unity of all mankind, "And He has made from one blood every nation of men . . ." (Acts 17:26), and the unity of God's revelation since the creation, "so that they are without excuse" (Rom. 1:20).

e.   Therefore, ignorance is no excuse. Paul reproached the Athenians, "Your mighty philosophical systems result in desperate ignorance. You built an altar for the unknown God! But God is not to blame for this. You banished Him". Truth is always stifled. What a pretty business it would have been when rebellion, apostasy, and its resulting ignorance would be a lawful excuse to deny any guilt. After his conversion, Paul acknowledged that Stephen had been correct—you are always resisting the Holy Spirit (Acts 7:51; see also 2 Pet. 3:1-6).

f.   The faithful church must maintain over against the W.C.C. that Paul's missionary preaching brought no new gospel but rested in and built on all of Scripture, just as Jesus of Nazareth was not the founder of a new religion but continued and completed what God had already revealed to Moses.

g.   The W.C.C. considers the confessions of the churches to be no more than human theories: the theory of Athanasius over against that of Arius; the theory of Augustine over against that of Pelagius; the Remonstrant theory over against the Contra-remonstrant theory.

19.8 The church of Christ has three ecumenical creeds in which it confesses its undoubted, catholic Christian faith. This is the confession of the whole Christian church of all ages throughout the world (ecumenical means catholic).

The Three Forms of Unity are also truly ecumenical confessions. They are characterized as reformed because they are the fruits of the Reformation by means of which the LORD God brought His church back to His Word.

The confession of the Christian church as formulated in her symbols (creeds and confessions) is in agreement with the continued witness of all of Scripture. These symbols are not merely theological and theoretical documents to be explained with theological and theoretical arguments. They are very practical, prophetic articles of faith that do not need to be adjusted in emphasis from a sixteenth-century perspective to a twentieth-century position. As prophetic witness of all of the revelation of the LORD God, the confessions go far beyond the changing theological debates and arguments between contemporary theologians.

These confessions cannot and may not be replaced by or reduced to an ecumenical theology. The whole gospel must be preached to all heathen. That gospel is revealed in all of God's Word which the Holy Spirit teaches to the church of Christ and which that church professes in its six truly ecumenical (catholic, worldwide) confessions. Indeed, these confessions are of all-encompassing significance to the whole world.

The ecumenical movement, on the other hand, seeks a world church without the revealed and preserved teaching of holy Scripture and without discipline. In this movement, those who deny God allow those who adhere to the true gospel to sit next to them, provided that the latter also tolerate the first!

19.9   Further Decline

a.   Since the Bangkok Conference 1973, the W.C.C. has clearly continued on the road of decline and apostasy. In 1948, it spoke of the world church as an ecclesiastical matter, a church with a message for the world. Twenty-five years later, it spoke of a world church that must declare its solidarity with the world.

b.   The W.C.C. promotes unity not only among churches but also between the church and the world in order to exercise fellowship with all. In 1948, the word *ecumenical* referred to a geographical concept, signifying the church everywhere in the world. By 1973, this word came to mean *all of humanity*. The ecumenical theology (man's wisdom) teaches the brotherhood of all people and the fatherhood of God for all people, speaking of global brotherhood.

c.   At the Stockholm Conference 1925, greetings were sent to the socialist trade unions, "in the name of the Son of man, the carpenter of Nazareth." Already in those days the Marxist ideal of a new world appealed to many. Today the unity of service to the whole world is preached with reference to the kingdom of God and the kingdom of all humanity.

d.   The ecumenical movement wants the church to be of value for the world of today. The church, it is said, should not adopt an introvert attitude, turning its back on the world in concern for itself only; it must humbly acknowledge itself to be a segment of today's world. Since Bangkok 1973, the Marxist-Leninist ideal of a new world order has found a place on the agenda of the W.C.C. No longer does the world need the church; now the church needs the world in order to accomplish God's humanizing work. Notice how things are turned upside down, although the words have not changed much, the gospel of Scripture has been replaced by the gospel of socialism, supposedly to the benefit of all people.

e.   In 1948, the ecumenical task of the worldwide church was considered an ecclesiastical matter. Today the church has a global interest in the world—cosmic ecumenicity. Originally the church was concerned with the preaching of the Word, with mission, with repentance and conversion to God, with faith in Christ Jesus who shall return. The W.C.C. claims that the church at the end of the twentieth century must be concerned with service and action, with social reformation, if necessary, through revolution. Jesus was the great revolutionary, was He not? We encounter Him in our fellow man, and He will return in the socialist world revolution.

f.   It is not surprising that the W.C.C. supports various revolutionary liberation movements across the world and that it lauded the

Maoist cultural revolution in China. This support for revolution has increased ever since African and Asian churches have gained the majority within the W.C.C.

19.10 Rome and the W.C.C.

a.   In 1948, the pope refused to join the W.C.C. In 1969, Pope Paul VI visited Geneva, apparently in preparation for joining in order to take over the leadership of the W.C.C. The pope's opening words were, "I am Peter. . . ."

b.   Although all members were asked to swear allegiance to the decisions of the Council of Trent, the beginning of the Counter-Reformation, the first session of the Second Vatican Council, from October through December 1963, was intended to be the end of the Counter-Reformation. The Counter-Reformation was to be changed into an *aggiornamento*, a renewal. The second session, from September through December 1965, was characterized by a greatly increased spirit of ecumenicity, although all the doctrinal decisions of Trent, including those relating to the supreme authority of the papal chair (the authority of the pope), were fully maintained.

c.   Although not in deed, in fact the W.C.C. and the Roman Catholic Church are already one in their common but false religiosity. This religiosity satisfies the psychological need of twentieth-century man, living as he does in an age of the oppressive power of human thought, technique, and organization for worship, dedication, and reverence in an ecumenical liturgy (which might even include techniques such as sensitivity training) in which millions participate.

d.   Theologians, church rulers, hierarchs, church leaders, Anglican bishops, Eastern Orthodox patriarchs (under influence of the Kremlin and of Beijing) rule the twentieth-century church by means of their resolutions, messages, and political decisions.

e.   How far removed we are from God's Word, which speaks of the just, the meek, the merciful, the humble; of the sheep of the good Shepherd, walking in truth and salvation which is found in no one else but in the crucified Jesus (Acts 4:12).

19.11 The ecumenical ideology and theology are the bitter product of the apostate twentieth-century philosophy of autonomous man.

Third-world heathendom found itself reborn in apostate Western Christendom by means of scholasticism, mysticism, renaissance humanism, rationalism, enlightenment, and evolution of religion. In its arrogance, this ideology is now ready to reject the Christ sent of God as an old-fashioned and unnecessary idea. Syncretism (combining two opposing sets of beliefs) obscures and destroys the enmity between the seed of the woman and the seed of the serpent (Gen. 3:15). The facts of the history of redemption have been reduced to myths and are no longer essential since evil (for instance, the fall into sin) can be overcome by means of evolution.

Revolutionary Christendom is permeated with the spirit of the antichrist, against whom the Apostle John already struggled. It creates a new image for Christianity, without redemption and without the belief in the return of Jesus Christ.

Cain's generation conquers the world with the help of the all-powerful technology of Jabal, Jubal, and Tubal-Cain and the violence of Lamech.

The ecumenical crusade (God wills it!) is the fiercest and most dangerous attack yet of the power of darkness, of the beast and his prophet (Rev. 13). The ecumenical world church has buried the sword of the Spirit, no longer recognizing and acknowledging its power to life and its power to death. God's Word cannot be put in the closet; it never returns empty! "Professing to be wise, they became fools. . . . Therefore God also gave them up. . . . For the wrath of God is revealed from heaven against all ungodliness and unrighteousness of men who suppress the truth in unrighteousness" (Rom. 1:22-24).

19.12 Indian yoga has become especially popular. Yoga seems to be no more than a series of gymnastic exercises to promote a relaxed well-being of the body. However, these exercises cannot be considered without the background of the Gnostic-Hindu religion of India. India is the continent with the largest number of demon-possessed people. It is also the continent of the friendly, tolerant broadly ecumenical Hindu religion, which promises paradise to the weary Westerner, but a paradise where the serpent claims that there is no God but Brahma.

Eastern syncretist mysticism and yoga, together with the Western techniques of brainwashing, attempt to create a new race that is more divine than the present human race (New Age movement). Scripture answers with the mighty gospel of the risen Christ who dwells in us: "And if Christ is in you, the body is dead because of sin, but the Spirit is life because of righteousness. But if the Spirit of Him who raised Jesus from the dead dwells in you, He who raised Christ from the dead will also give life to your mortal bodies through His Spirit who dwells in you" (Rom. 8:10, 11). "If then you were raised with Christ, seek those things which are above, where Christ is, sitting at the right hand of God. Set your mind on things above, not on things on the earth. For you died, and your life is hidden with Christ in God. When Christ who is our life appears, then you also will appear with Him in glory" (Col. 3:1-4).

19.13 The only hope of the true believer is found in Christ's final prayer in which He prayed not for a unity between the Sanhedrin and His disciples nor for a unity between the disciples of the Apostle John and the antichrists but for the unity between "those who will believe in Me through their word; that they all may be one, as You, Father, are in Me, and I in You; that they also may be one in Us, that the world may believe that You sent Me" (John 17:20, 21).

Each reformation of Christ's church and each reformation of the personal life of the true believer is a result of God's mighty works in response to that high priestly prayer, in order that the covenant with the LORD God may be kept. The history of that covenant is the true kingpin of all history. Through the preaching of the gospel, God is in constant antithetical ("And I will put enmity between you and the woman . . ." Gen. 3:15) contact with the world, preparing for the day of the greatest of all reformations, the salvation of all who have their hope in Him, and the renewal of heaven and earth, when the Son of Man sits on the throne of His glory (Matt. 19:28).

> "He who testifies to these things says, 'Surely I am coming quickly'. Amen. Even so, come Lord Jesus! The grace of the Lord Jesus Christ be with you all. Amen" (Rev. 22:20, 21).

INDEX

SCHILDER'S STRUGGLE FOR THE UNITY OF THE CHURCH
by Rudolf Van Reest

Klaas Schilder (1890-1952), the author of the trilogy about the suffering of Christ, is remembered both for his courageous stand in opposition to Nazism, which led to his imprisonment three months after the Nazis overran the Netherlands in 1940, and for his role in the church struggle in the Netherlands, which culminated in 1944 with the suspension of scores of office-bearers and the formation of the liberated Reformed Churches. The connections between these two battles waged by Schilder are explored in this narrative account of Schilder's role in twentieth century church history. The original Dutch edition has been supplemented by the addition of two shorter writings of Schilder plus a short review of his impact of North American church life.

Rudolf van Reest wrote about Schilder in *Gedenkt Uw Voorgangeren* (published in 1952 — a memeorial volume on Schilder): He was a singular man in everything he did — a man with a tremendous style, an enormous range of knowledge, a giant among the leading minds of his day. But at the same time he was a man of the strictest simplicity, the deepest piety, burning with love for God and for his neighbor, with an unshakable faith in the authority of God's Word over everything, and a faithful confessor of the Reformed Confessions.

ESSAYS IN REFORMED DOCTRINE by Dr. J. FABER

A collection of seventeen articles, speeches, and lectures which are of fundamental importance to all who are reformed.

N.H. Gootjes in *Clarion* of May 25, 1990: . . . those who love the church of Christ will benefit from this book.

R.J. Rushdoony in *Chalcedon Report* of July 1990: The Reformed tradition of careful, conscientious scholarship is here clearly in evidence. . . It is refreshing too that he calls attention to sometimes neglected aspects of Calvin's thinking, such as Calvin's statement that man as God's creation, "is a balanced work of art." It is a pleasure to know through his writings so fine a man as Dr. Faber.

Cecil Tuininga in *Christian Renewal* of Aug. 20, 1990: This book is easy reading as far as the English goes. It can, I judge, be read by all with great profit. . . I found the first chapter on "The Significance of Dogmatology for the Training of the Ministry" excellent. The six essays on the Church I found very informative and worth-while. . . What makes this book so valuable is that Dr. Faber deals with all the aspects of the Reformed faith from a strictly biblical and confessional viewpoint.

THE COVENANTAL GOSPEL by Dr. C. VAN DER WAAL

What Significance does the Old Testament have for the church of the new covenant? What is the difference between the old and new covenants? What is the relationship between the two? Some have said that the new covenant has a different structure than the old; others maintain that this is a matter of "more" and "less." But what do these terms mean?

These and many more questions are pertinent for every Bible reader. What about the gifts of speaking in tongues and healing of the sick that are mentioned in the New Testament? Are these gifts also given to the church of today? Should today's Bible reader strive to speak in tongues? Or are these special gifts specific to the early church?

Dr. C. Van der Waal answers these and similar questions in this book, in a style that is directed at non-theologians as well as scholars. He examines the structures and typifying elements of both Biblical and social covenants, and proceeds to study commonly accepted distinctions such as "covenant of works" versus "covenant of grace" and "law" versus "gospel." The Author then describes in detail the relationship between the old and new covenants, followed by an analysis of the special but passing nature of the apostolic era and the permanent "more" of the new covenant. A most timely book for today.